KAREN STABINER

SIMON & SCHUSTER

NEW YORK LONDON

TORONTO SYDNEY

TOKYO SINGAPORE

INVENTING DESIRE

INSIDE CHIAT/DAY

THE HOTTEST SHOP,

THE COOLEST PLAYERS,

THE BIG BUSINESS

OF ADVERTISING

SIMON & SCHUSTER

Simon & Schuster Building

Rockefeller Center

1230 Avenue of the Americas

New York, New York 10020

SIMON & SCHUSTER and colophon are registered trademarks
of Simon & Schuster Inc.
Designed by Pei Loi Koay
Manufactured in the United States of America

1   3   5   7   9   10   8   6   4   2

Library of Congress Cataloging-in-Publication Data

Stabiner, Karen.
Inventing desire : inside Chiat/Day : the hottest shop, the
coolest players, the big business of advertising / Karen Stabiner.
p.   cm.
Includes index.
1.   Chiat–Day, Inc.   2.   Advertising agencies—United States.
3.   Advertising—United States.   I. Title.
HF6181.C49S73   1993
338.7'616591'0973—dc20   93–16263
CIP

ISBN: 0-671-72346-4

For Sarah, who loves words,

and for Larry.

ACKNOWLEDGMENTS

There are two ways to find out how a business works: Ask lots of people and piece together their observations, or stand in the middle of it and watch what happens. I prefer the second approach, but it requires a cooperative subject, someone who is willing to tolerate the prolonged intrusion. I'm still not sure why Jay Chiat said yes to a stranger who wanted complete access to his agency for a year, but I thank him for it—and for honoring the commitment even on those days when he wished I would disappear and take this book with me.

Lee Clow, who was prouder of the agency than he was protective of his own image, was always willing to talk. Bob Wolf was equally ready to explain and analyze, no matter how busy he was.

Bob Kuperman stepped into the presidency of Chiat/Day's Venice office and found out that he had inherited a full-time shadow. I thank him for accepting his fate graciously. Jane Newman was always straightforward about what was, for the New York office, a turbulent year. I admire her tenacity.

I also want to thank Tom Patty, Dick Sittig, Bob Grossman, Bonnie Baruch, Rob White, Laurie Coots, Sharon Stanley, Simon Bax and Jennifer Golub for the hours they spent rehashing their lives with me. Dozens of other employees—including Hank Antosz, Richard O'Neill, Amy Miyano, Elaine Hinton, Dave Butler and Mas Yamashita—made sure I knew and understood what was going on. Carol Madonna, Margherite Vetrano, Louise Hoven, Donna Nadler, Jigisha Patel, Dede Dalton and Julia Leach got me everything I needed, from interview appointments to meeting schedules.

Chiat/Day's clients took the time to discuss their business with me. I am particularly grateful to Nissan's Tom Mignanelli, Bob Thomas, Ron Hannum and John Rinek; Home Savings of America's Richard Deihl, Charles Reed and George Winston; Nutrasweet's Nick Rosa and Cameron Hall; Energizer's John Sweetwood; Sparklett's Dave

Neufer; Toshiba's Tom Martin; and Foster Farms' Tom Orr.

I thank Sue Clamage and Freddie Odlum for turning the resulting boxes of tapes into piles of transcripts.

Jim Silberman, my first editor, was a supportive, dependable presence during the research and early writing. Chiat/Day was ever-changing; Jim was always there. This is his book, too.

When Alice Mayhew took on the book at Simon & Schuster, she made me feel that it had been hers from the start. I am grateful for her fierce interest, and a happy beneficiary of her insightful and elegant editing.

Her associate, Eric Steel, managed to fool me into thinking he had no other books on his schedule. I also want to thank Simon & Schuster's Carolyn Reidy for her responsiveness, as well as Emily Remes, Victoria Meyer, Annette Swanberg, Marcia Peterson, and Frank and Eve Metz.

My agent, Kathy Robbins, is the best advocate a writer could ask for. Hers is an expansive excellence: I thank her for her business acumen—and for her good and generous heart.

Elizabeth Mackey and the rest of The Robbins Office staff make doing business more pleasant than it has a right to be.

For three years, my friends kept asking how it was going. For their affectionate endurance I thank Judy Gingold, Harry Shearer, Marcie Rothman, Lucy Stille, David Shaw, Ruth Reichl, Michael Singer, Carolyn See, Ginger Curwen, Jack Nessel, David Freeman, Patty Williams, Kenny Turan, David Paletz and Howard Rubin. I thank Martha Bonilla for making it possible for me to keep up with Chiat/Day's schedule.

My husband, Larry Dietz, is a wonderful editor. I am hardly the first writer to have figured that out, but I am the luckiest. Sarah Ivria Dietz drew pictures for my office walls, shared her paper clips, and laughed at the page about the bicycle. I thank her for all that, as though her simple existence were not cause enough for gratitude. She is my joy.

Karen Stabiner
Santa Monica, California
February 1993

Ridley Scott had to make the car fly before noon. Any later and the sun would make even whimpering about the heat seem like too much of an exertion. He put fifty people to work before dawn, but by midmorning they moved slowly, as though pushing through the shimmering, 104-degree air required an extra effort.

Scott had brought them all to the edge of California's Mojave Desert, to a corner of a vast, parched flatland rimmed by the Sierra Nevada to the west, and the Argus and Slate mountains to the north and east. There were no clouds, no birds, not even power lines to break the boiled sky. No distractions. Just the August sun—hot enough to steal spit off a person's tongue, to bleach the skin that tightened around his fingernails, to make his scalp constrict.

The employees of the Inyokern Airport, locals who knew how to take care of themselves, spent their morning coffee break sitting on folding chairs in the shade, chuckling at the antics of their guests. But Scott's crew was made up of city kids, most of them from Los Angeles or London. All they knew was that they were miserable, and they were in a hurry.

They passed lip balm among themselves as though it were precious contraband, swilled mineral water by the liter—and whenever possible, scurried over to the makeshift tent, a sheet of fabric on four poles, where they could fool themselves into believing it was five degrees cooler. They dressed in terror of the sun: one slight young man covered himself with a wide-brimmed hat, oversized sunglasses, a long-sleeved shirt, long Bermudas, knee socks, and hiking boots. He rubbed sunblock on his hands compulsively and wore a damp handkerchief against the back of his neck. Only the foolish, or the particularly hardy, worked without a shirt and hat.

At the far end of the runway, cool, impossibly composed and sleek, sat the smug object of all this attention: a $32,000 1990 Platinum Mist Nissan 300ZX Turbo, purring under the polishing rag, accompanied by three identical stand-ins, just in case the mere mortals who attended her had any trouble defying gravity.

No one could make a car fly. But the way to make a car look like it was flying was to launch it on a wooden ramp at fifty miles an hour. It was a split-second proposition: the front wheels hit a "kicker," a horizontal two-by-four at the end of the ramp, which dislodged an L-shaped bracket that held the ramp in place. Instantly—and, crucially, before the rear wheels reached the edge—the surface of the ramp dropped six inches. The front wheels left solid ground higher than the rear wheels did, providing the illusion of flight.

Scott calculated that the car's nose would shoot straight up into the air. To capture that brief moment, a camera was being bolted into a wooden floor and sandbagged into place, at the bottom of a five-foot-deep hole, fifteen feet past the end of the ramp.

Stunt driver Hubie Kearns, Jr., had first seen a kicker jump in Spain back in the 1970s, but this was going to be a tougher jump than he was used to. It was a brand-new ramp, longer and lower than any he'd ever tried; it wouldn't throw the car as far into the air as a short, steep "pop" ramp would. And it was narrow. He had only a foot of clearance on either side.

There couldn't be a single blemish on the front of the car—so instead of a standard kicker pole, a higher one, as easy to hit as a fence, there was this little six-inch-high kicker, which was supposed to achieve the same effect without dinging the car, assuming Kearns aimed right. Even if he did, he had to worry about ripping the low-slung spoiler off the car. Nobody had told him about that spoiler, which sat only nine inches off the ground. He showed up for work today to find out that he had three inches of grace.

He donned his crash helmet and shin guards and lazily drove the Z down the deserted airport runway, far past the end of the ramp.

Scott and a handful of assistants scurried from the camera in the hole
to a video monitor mounted a safe distance from the runway, and back
again, making minuscule adjustments in the angle of the shot, reassuring themselves one last time that the camera was firmly in place.
There couldn't be any wobble. They needed more than just a perfect
flight. They needed a flawless cinematic record of the event.

Finally, just after lunch, they were ready. The fabric cap Scott
wore, its rectangular neck flaps a rather pathetic defense for his milky
skin, was stained with sweat. He took his place in front of the video
monitor, surrounded by a dozen others, and waited to see what would
happen.

The county paramedic's truck pulled up near the camera. A voice
came over a bullhorn: "People, if anything goes wrong, Bob and one
of the firemen are designated to run to the car. *Nobody else go near
it.*"

Then the voice called, "Roll cameras." In the bleached distance
the Z started to move and, still 100 yards away from the ramp, hit its
jump speed of 51 miles per hour. It roared down the ramp, sailed into
space, and hit the dirt, about thirty-five feet behind the camera, with
a bone-shaking thud. There was a burst of applause, followed by
bleak silence. The video footage showed the car rise into the air—and
then, as Kearns had feared, a chunk of fiberglass fell off the front end
and floated to earth, as the car passed out of the frame.

Instantly, everyone had a theory. The piece fell off upon impact
with the kicker. The piece was loose and fell off by itself. Perhaps the
car got lower to the ground as it sped up, and the kicker would have
to be lowered even further than it already was. After five minutes of
debate, the kicker was removed completely. Scott would have to
settle for a smoother takeoff—a car sailing through the air rather than
a car leaping into it—and hope the effect was dramatic enough.

The first car was temporarily out of commission, having lost its
front bumper when it landed. Two men feverishly dusted off a second
car, and Kearns drove it out to the starting point.

If this attempt didn't work—and who knew what would happen,
with no bar at all?—there was going to be trouble. The first two cars
had been earmarked for this effort; no one expected them to come
back alive. But the third and fourth cars were not supposed to leave

13

the ground. They were here for other maneuvers, for flat-out speed work, and had to be returned in perfect condition. Any damage to them was going to cost money that wasn't in the budget.

Scott busied himself with the next jump. All he could do was try to make this one work, since he was not exactly in a position to demand another chance. That decision belonged to Richard O'Neill, vice-president and director of production for Chiat/Day inc. Advertising—the man in charge of making sure that Scott came home with what he was supposed to get, at the price it was supposed to cost. The agency had spent most of that year, 1989, devising a new "Fantasy" campaign for Nissan's 1990 model line. The 300ZX Turbo shoot alone was a $1.17 million endeavor, which would yield the campaign's flagship sixty-second commercial, as well as a thirty-second version. A surprise over-budget expenditure or a video image that was anything less than thrilling—either way there would be an unhappy client.

O'Neill watched the preparations for the second jump and began to worry. He eyed the two remaining Z-cars covetously.

"What do I have to do to jump the third car?" he asked his assistant.

"Buy the car," said the kid. "It's a parts car."

Who would pay the $32,000? Maybe O'Neill could scrounge parts from the third car and replace them later. It would be time-consuming, but it would be cheaper. He sent the kid off to find out if he could cannibalize the third Z, and elbowed his way to the director's side at the monitor.

The jump appeared to be flawless—even if the car's brakes failed in midair, forcing Kearns to steer it into a ditch to stop, and reducing the pool of available free cars by half. But it didn't look quite right on the monitor. The car shot into space at less of an angle, and skewed just a bit to the right. A horizontal float, and a crooked one at that, was hardly the triumphant image Scott was looking for.

"Does it look like it's landing, not taking off?" asked one man.

"Should they raise the ramp?" asked another.

In a frenzy, a dozen men raced over to a pile of lumber next to the ramp and started sawing planks into shorter lengths. Then they lined up on either side of the ramp and, in a single motion, lifted up the high end and shoved the planks underneath, to make it steeper. Meanwhile, the men from the car preparation company hurriedly attached a new bumper to the first car and dabbed on a little touch-up paint.

Kearns climbed in and tried again. This time, the arc was perfect. Scott managed a controlled little half-grin. O'Neill, who could now stop running numbers in his head, curved his arm over his head to mimic the flight and beamed. Together they watched the monitor. The camera caught the car in midflight, without a hint of its imminent descent. It soared overhead as though it could go on forever.

Scott and O'Neill had two weeks to edit down about 22,000 feet of film into the 90 feet that fit into a 60-second commercial. An impatient hierarchy waited: the people at Nissan Motor Corporation in U.S.A. wanted to see what they had got for their money. The executives on the Nissan account at Chiat/Day were not about to let them see a single frame until creative director Bob Kuperman saw and approved the work. Ridley Scott didn't want Kuperman to see it until he was satisfied.

Kuperman was supposed to look at the rough cut at Scott's Hollywood offices on Friday, September 15. He had a date to take the client (always referred to in the monolithic singular, no matter how many people were involved) out for a pep-talk dinner with Scott that evening, and enthusiasm would come more easily if he'd actually seen something.

But Kuperman was delayed, so he headed straight for dinner—while Scott, who was also running late, tried to finish up before he joined his employer.

The rough cut of "Turbo Z Dreamer" wasn't done yet because Scott, a perfectionist about sound, had been working day and night for three months on the sound mix for his feature film, the police thriller *Black Rain,* which was scheduled to open in one week. He'd had to wedge the commercial in when he had the time—and on Friday he didn't get started until 4:30 P.M. Two hours later he was still piecing together the effects, shadowed by two fretful emissaries from Chiat/Day, producer O'Neill and art director Mike Mazza. They took a furtive break in the parking lot to mutter about how quickly time flew and how slowly the sound mixer worked, and then slunk back into the chilly mixing room.

Scott took his place at the back of the room, at a counter littered with items that entertained his other senses while the ears and eyes worked: a huge thermos, three tins of various teas, a few celery sticks and orange segments on a limp paper doily, and a white Styrofoam cup full of fruit peels and cigarette wrappings. The sound mixer sat in front of him at a computer keyboard, trying desperately to keep pace with, and accurately interpret, the director's suggestions.

Scott knew exactly what he wanted. He was used to bending the physical world to his will, to manipulating perception—his feature films, including *Alien* and *Blade Runner*, were full of mutant creatures and futuristic machines. His most famous commercial, the Apple Computer "1984" spot he directed for Chiat/Day, hinged on a single sound, the heroine's victorious cry as she hurled a hammer at the televised face of oppressive uniformity.

The surreal soundtrack for "Turbo Z Dreamer" was playing, quite specifically, in Scott's brain. He described it in a low voice, as though he were communing with his own muse. The "slashing sound, like gnashing steel," toward the end of the commercial wasn't substantial enough. Each slash had to have "an explosive beginning," but not as explosive as the final boom when the car took off, which he likened to a sonic boom. He wanted lots of "metallic sound." And then, as the car took flight, he had to have "a more crystalline sound. So it comes up to a warble. Almost a white sound."

An hour later Scott was still explaining and refining. He looked at his watch, grimaced, and mimed raising a drink to his lips. O'Neill decided to leave "to hold hands a little" with Kuperman and the client. Scott would follow when he could.

Since the client expected to see the spot on Monday, Kuperman would have to look at it on Saturday morning, an arrangement that frustrated the director, who couldn't be there. Even though this commercial was destined for television sets of varying sophistication and quality, Scott wanted it shown to Kuperman under laboratory conditions—the best video system, with the best sound. He pleaded with art director Mazza to make sure the set-up was right. "You can get your hands on it, can't you? Just crank it up."

* * *

On Saturday morning, Kuperman met O'Neill and Mazza at Chiat/Day's main office in Venice, the oceanside Los Angeles neighborhood created at the turn of the century to mimic its Italian namesake, complete with a network of canals and rows of arched buildings. Chiat/Day occupied a compound two blocks from the beach: a warehouse, production building and two adjacent conference rooms, dubbed the Treehouse and the Boathouse.

The Boathouse was usually used for client meetings, and had astonished its share of first-time visitors. Architect Frank Gehry had covered the walls with corrugated paper in an industrial tan. A curved couch in the same material grew out of a wall at the back of the room, facing a couple of corrugated-paper easy chairs that strangers almost always asked permission to sit on. A fat white fish made out of a Formicalike substance called Colorcore sat above the couch, and light from the bulb in its stomach shone between its scales.

The conference table was granite, long and thin. Above it hung a light fixture shaped like a canoe, and next to the canoe hung two crossed logs. The story was that Gehry installed the logs and then decided they looked like they were floating on the water. If they were on the water, surely a boat would be, too.

A twenty-seven-inch color television monitor hung above one end of the conference table, and an identical model was cut into the wall at the other end. Bob Kuperman, a short, bearded, impeccably groomed man who affected the inch-long ponytail currently in vogue among West Coast ad men, took a seat near the wall monitor and waited to be impressed. In his white polo shirt, navy linen Bermuda shorts, slouch hat and bare feet slipped into casual shoes, he was the epitome of offhanded cool. Kuperman was a clotheshorse, whose vast, snappy wardrobe both distracted people from the issue of his height and proved that the one-time art director still knew how to put together a great look. Clothes were his personal compensation and his professional sandwich board.

In silence, the three men watched a rough cut of the sixty-second commercial. In it, a thirty-five-year-old man recounted his recurring dream, behind sleek images of a Turbo Z being trailed by a series of sinister vehicles.

"So I'm havin' this dream—I'm in a Turbo Z . . . and these guys are after me," said the voice, as a motorcyclist took off after the hero's Z.

"But they can't catch me." They cyclist shook his arm menacingly, screamed in frustration, and gave up the chase.

"So they get a car . . . But they can't catch me." A black, slope-nosed car pursued the Z, but couldn't keep up the pace.

"So they get a plane." A jet fighter inched just above the Z.

"Just as they're about to catch me . . . The twin turbos kick in." After quick successive shots of the accelerator, shift and tachometer, the Z jumped ahead, out of the jet's range.

The original script had a punch line: "I guess I better return those library books." If that line didn't work well, there was an alternative: "I guess I shouldn't have torn that tag off my mattress." This was signature Chiat/Day copy, deadpan clever, based on the assumption that the consumer was intelligent enough to get a sly joke. It had been added in response to a specific request from Nissan for an element of humor.

But Scott cut the line out. He had a different idea for the ending. The script called for a final shot of the Z flying over the camera in slow motion, with no sound but the desert wind. Once out of frame, the engine sounds kicked in again. Scott filmed an additional shot that he felt would reinforce the notion of the Z's great power and speed: He had the jet run the same path as the Z had, at only twelve feet off the ground. He wanted to see the jet playing catch-up, and losing, at the end.

Kuperman, who hadn't seen any of the work on the spot since the original hand-drawn storyboards, watched without comment or expression.

"So," he said, noncommittally. "You guys are happy with this?"

Mazza, who had inherited the project from the art director who designed it, winced. A high-strung man who liked to describe himself as having the nerves of a Chihuahua, Mazza had often found himself caught between the egos of the copywriter and director on this project—and he immediately worried that he he hadn't exerted enough discipline on the shoot. O'Neill was more secure about his status—he had ten years' seniority on Kuperman, and had worked on big shoots before, from Apple Computer's "1984" to the Nike "I Love L.A." commercial—but even he felt defensive.

Kuperman did that to people. His composed exterior was deceptive, a willful effort on his part to impose calm from the outside in, as though he hoped that serenity might seep from the natural fibers down into his very being. He was, by nature, a firecracker, the kind of guy who barged into a creative team's cubicle and uttered a challenging "*So?*" His native tongue was sarcasm, his instinct, to force people to defend their work. That was how he kept them on their toes. Any question coming from him sounded like an accusation. O'Neill and Mazza started babbling excuses: The sound needed work, the color wasn't right, and the voiceover wasn't the guy they intended to use.

In the midst of their explanations, Kuperman started to laugh.

"It's fabulous," he said. "It's absolutely fabulous."

They watched the spot a second time.

"Great," said Kuperman. " 'And now, accepting the award . . .' "

Kuperman was delighted by what he'd seen and heard. Work like this made existing clients proud and potential new clients interested. It was as much an advertisement for the agency as it was for the car. He forced himself to discuss which images would survive in the thirty-second version, and whether the lost last line about the library books was a significant casualty. But his mind kept wandering back to what he'd seen. Like a kid with a Tinkertoy, he wanted to dismantle the spot and see how all the moving parts worked.

He loved the cyclist's yell, as the Z shot out of his reach.

"What *is* this?' he asked. "Swahili?"

"Swahili backwards?" suggested Mazza.

"No," said O'Neill, authoritatively. "It's Sudanese. Forwards."

To congratulate themselves, they watched the spot a third time. Kuperman shook the art director's hand.

"Guess we kicked some ass, didn't we?" he said. "Boy, am I happy with this. It's Super Bowl material."

"It'll blow them out in Poughkeepsie," said O'Neill.

The finished commercial had a steely chill to it, a bluish, smoky cast. Even the sun's rays had an icy, unforgiving glint. The film image bore no resemblance to the tanned landscape of the Mojave.

It had no more to do with the desert than the commercial had to do with getting people to buy the 300ZX Turbo. Only five thousand people would make that purchase in any given year, representing less than 1 percent of Nissan's total customer base. But this spot was aimed at the 79.5 million people who would watch the Super Bowl XXIV on Sunday, January 28, 1990—a universe that included not only the owners of expensive Japanese sports cars but people who were philosophically opposed to owning foreign cars, as well as people who hoped merely to own a Sentra, Nissan's bottom-of-the-line model.

No matter. This commercial was supposed to make people long for a Nissan, regardless of which model the customer could afford. It was about yearning, part of an image campaign devised to promote Nissan as the carmaker for the enthused driver. It was supposed to build the brand—to create a personality for Nissan as though it were a human being, not a corporate entity, and then promote that personality to the public. Each of the six spots in the 1990 Fantasy campaign had to do more than sell a specific model. "Turbo Z Dreamer," along with commercials for the normally aspirated Z, the 240SX Maxima sedan, Pathfinder sport utility vehicle, and Nissan truck, had to increase purchase intention. That is, they had to make people equate wanting a new car with wanting a Nissan.

When Nissan moved its $165 million national account from Campbell-Mithun-Esty to Chiat/Day in 1987, it was the largest single piece of advertising business ever to change hands in the United States. Chiat/Day had worked for a year just to get invited to the pitch, setting up carefully orchestrated chance encounters with Nissan executives, based on research about what clubs they belonged to, what charities they favored, and where they might show up for a round of golf. The pitch itself cost the agency $1 million in speculative creative work, as well as three months of intensive effort. Meals appeared in the Venice office so that people wouldn't have to leave to eat. Toward the end of the siege, when people were working twenty hours a day, even personal hygiene was an intrusion, so a hairdresser was hired to come in and cut the pitch team's hair.

The investment paid off. Winning Nissan doubled the size of Chiat/Day's Los Angeles home office and, even more important, promoted the agency from the ranks of the hip boutiques into the more rarefied realm of the major established agencies. Chiat/Day was no longer a band of brash guerrillas who snuck into a stagnant business and blew up its image, only to take to the hills again at the first sign of trouble. Now it was a major agency with a maverick point of view. Nissan bestowed respectability on an agency known for its creative bravado. It helped build the Chiat/Day brand.

It was Chiat/Day's task to repay the favor, and elevate Nissan from its position as an also-ran behind Toyota and Honda. The goal was to make Nissan an "aspirational" choice—the car people wanted to buy, not the one they had to settle for. The agency had to find a way to invent desire.

ay Chiat was tired. Late one night, in the autumn of 1989, he paged through a stack of appointment calendars and came to a daunting, if not surprising, realization. Over the past ten years, he had never slept in the same bed for more than three weeks in a row—except once, when he was on vacation.

He had boarded planes the way other men got into their cars for a half-hour morning commute, shuttling endlessly between his agency offices, his clients, and his prospective clients. For twenty-two years, ever since the day he and Guy Day took their kids to a Dodger baseball game and decided, over hot dogs, to merge their two small advertising agencies, Chiat had been on the run. He told people that he was on a quest for what he called "ads with a jolt," ones that broke through the bored defenses most people put up when confronted by traditional commercial messages, but that was only the literal veneer of the truth. He was propelled by an odd disdain for any objective he managed to attain, as though his ability to accomplish it diminished the inherent value of the achievement. At any point in the quest, what Chiat was after was that which he did not yet have.

His singular obsession built and sustained Chiat/Day, which was one of the reasons he was constantly on the move. He had to churn things up to keep people from becoming complacent. Since 1980, when he opened the New York office, he'd been based on the East Coast, but he was never anywhere long enough to call it home. Chiat preached the power of constructive chaos, and nobody disrupted things as well as he did. He was quality's keeper.

At fifty-eight, he was concerned with more than just the next campaign, or even the next new business coup. Winning the Nissan account had forced him to redefine success. The agency could, and would, continue to chase big accounts, but those would be redundant victories. Chiat wanted something more. He was gambling on an ambitious expansion program, into new cities, new countries, new ancillary services. He would reinvent Chiat/Day for the coming decade—make it not just an advertising agency, but a full-service firm that offered its clients everything from package design to public relations. It was as though Nissan marked the end of the advertising agency and provided a foundation upon which Chiat could become a global marketing presence.

The key was to grow without diluting the work for which the agency had become famous. People still spoke with awe of Doyle Dane Bernbach, founded in 1949, whose whimsical, elegant work in the late 1950s and early 1960s—most notably for Volkswagen ("Think small"), Avis ("We try harder"), Ohrbach's department store and Levy's Bakery ("You don't have to be Jewish to love Levy's real Jewish rye")—revolutionized an industry mired in dull, repetitive ads. For ten years, Doyle Dane Bernbach was the best. Chiat/Day's award-winning creative streak had already lasted twice as long, with memorable work for Honda automobiles, Apple Computer, Nike, and NYNEX, the company that printed the New York Yellow Pages. But Chiat was not about to settle for extending an existing record.

He had begun to tell people of his new goal: to pass the agency on, its spirit and direction intact, to the next generation. No one had ever done that before. Even the vaunted Doyle Dane had gone into a tailspin once Bill Bernbach, the creative spark of the agency, handed responsibility over to younger men.

This was uncharted territory, which was part of its appeal. Chiat had always taken delight in, and drawn energy from, dancing at the obstinate edge of his business.

*   *   *

He had been raised not just to work hard but to embrace hard work as his religion, and to believe that its eventual reward would surely be success. His father, Sam, never had the luxury of making a career choice, not with a son and daughter to raise in the years after the Depression. He had drive. All he lacked, Jay thought, was a great opportunity.

He had never stopped looking for it. Sam Chiat started out as a small stockholder in a Bronx laundry, for which he also drove the delivery truck. When the laundry went out of business, he moved the family to Neptune, New Jersey, and opened his own dry-cleaning establishment. That went belly up, so he moved into food service. He and his wife Min opened a drive-in restaurant next to a miniature golf course and driving range, drove a food van to construction sites, and when they got too old for that kind of active enterprise, managed a coffeeshop in a summer resort in Connecticut. He employed his son at every stop along the way—delivering laundry, brushing cuffs, working as a short-order cook.

Sam Chiat retired when he was seventy. He and his wife moved to Florida, where he took a job at a Miami souvenir shop—a job he reluctantly quit after he was mugged on his way home from work. One day Jay found him avidly reading the newspaper. He walked over to see what his seventy-two-year-old father found so interesting. It was the "business opportunities" section of the classified ads.

Jay Chiat graduated from Rutgers University in 1953 with an out-sized hunger for a job, any job, and not a clue as to what he wanted to do. He also had a wife and baby daughter, which meant that any soul-searching he might have done had to be postponed. Like his dad, he had to make a living.

He worked at the trade magazine *Editor and Publisher*, and then as an NBC tour guide, until the Air Force invited him to fulfill his ROTC obligation. Lieutenant Chiat was sent to Scott Air Force Base in Belleville, Illinois, where he faced the unenviable possibilities of being sent to Korea, although the war was already over, or to a base in Greenland. When a captain in the Officers' Club Bar asked him what he did, Chiat remembered all those NBC tours and responded that he was in broadcasting. Two weeks later he was assigned to Mather Air Force Base in Sacramento, California, as the information officer.

He got out of the service in 1956, at twenty-five, another baby on the way, and took a job as a technical recruiter in the aerospace industry. The company sent him to Southern California to work with the advertising agency that handled its $1 million recruitment program, and, thanks to a contact from his Air Force days, he snared his first real job in advertising, as a copywriter for the newly formed Leland Oliver Company.

It was there that he met the man who taught him about aspirations. Chiat wrote ads for a company that made fiberglass fishing rods and employed, as its spokesman, John Dieckman, the world champion at fly-fishing. Chiat was charmed by the man. He was the personification of excellence. It didn't matter that his specialty was a narrow one; what counted was that he owned the category.

Chiat had never stopped to consider that there might be rewards for hard work beyond a growing steady paycheck. Now he reconsidered his future, and wondered, "What is it that I could do, that maybe could get me up there, doing it as well as it could be done or close to it?"

Advertising might be the answer. At that time, Southern California was the wild frontier; all the famous, established agencies were based in New York or Chicago. There was little competition, there were great expense account lunches, which appealed to a copywriter not yet in a position to spend his own money on fancy meals, and he enjoyed the work. When his employer informed him that a new man was coming in as vice-president, and that Chiat would have to vacate his office to make room for the executive, he quit. He borrowed $4,000 against his insurance, opened his own agency without any clients, and set out to become the best.

Thirty years later he ran an agency with $1.2 billion in billings. His first marriage had broken up, and he had married and divorced a second time. His partnership with Guy Day dissolved when Day, satisfied with what they had made and uninterested in further growth, sold his share of the agency to Chiat and departed to write a novel. His biggest clients—Honda automobiles, Nike, Apple Computer, Pizza Hut—had come and gone. What endured was Jay Chiat's relationship with his agency and its potential. He took great pride in the fact that Chiat/Day had always been profitable, without ever resorting to partners' paycuts or conservative forecasts that were easy to beat. Chiat had always preferred an aggressive agenda and vigilant management, and his approach had paid off.

In the two and a half years since Chiat/Day won the Nissan account, the agency had opened offices in Toronto and London, in addition to its existing offices in Venice, New York and San Francisco, and had acquired five North American subsidiaries, offering clients a range of services that included direct mail, corporate design, business-to-business advertising and public relations. The acquisition of Australia's Mojo agency, that country's second largest and a freewheeling creative complement to Chiat/Day, had just been completed. It represented the beginnings of an international communications network.

Other agencies had gotten big, toward the end of the 1980s, by becoming part of something bigger. Many of the publicly owned giants of American advertising were lucky to survive an international merger with their founders' initials intact, let alone their vision. Doyle Dane Bernbach and Needham Harper Worldwide became DDB Needham Worldwide Inc., owned by the holding company Omnicom, which also owned BBDO. Saatchi & Saatchi Company bought Backer & Spielvogel and Ted Bates Worldwide. In 1987 the London-based WPP Group, headed by Martin Sorrell, succeeded in a hostile takeover of the JWT Group, which owned J. Walter Thompson, for $566 million—and a year later paid $864 million for the Ogilvy Group and its Ogilvy & Mather agency, as part of a buying spree that included fifteen other companies.

Not all the mergers were happy ones. The Saatchis began building their empire in 1986, and two years later, faced with an unwieldy conglomerate whose earnings were below expectations, had to import the first non-family member to take charge of the business. When the WPP Group moved to take over the Ogilvy Group, agency founder David Ogilvy referred to Sorrell as "an odious little jerk," although he had reconsidered by the time the lucrative deal was completed.

Chiat watched the circus of spiraling price tags (and their constant companion, debt) from the sidelines. He had always insisted on being the acquirer, never the acquired, and had kept his agency private to protect it from marauders. He figured that going public was the quickest way to lose control to anonymous stockholders to whom the agency's product was of only incidental interest, strangers who might be tempted by fast cash from a takeover bid. He prized his independence: the agency's flag was a pirate's skull-and-crossbones; Chiat/Day regarded the big corporate agencies as the bureaucratized, slow-moving navy.

Still, he was not immune to the financial machinations of the 1980s, particularly since the agency worked for Drexel Burnham Lambert, birthplace of the junk bond. The trick would be to see if there was a way both to protect his privacy and to cash in on Chiat/Day's assets. In 1984, Chiat had bestowed equity in the company on about two dozen valued employees, who were invited to purchase stock at 20 cents per share, as a reward and an incentive to build the agency. In 1988, Chiat/Day engineered an internal leveraged buyout, using $42 million in bank loans and $11 million in junk bonds to buy back employee stock at $6.78 per share, almost thirty-five times its original purchase price. Each stockholder got $2.86 per share in cash, while the remaining $3.92 became part of the agency's $20 million junior debt—a tantalizing investment in the future, redeemable at the next recapitalization, which was scheduled for 1992.

Chiat's largesse made a half dozen people millionaires. He also remembered loyalists who did not have equity. He personally handed out $25,000 checks to employees who had been with the company for more than five years, and $100,000 checks to those who had worked for him for a decade.

He had realized his father's dream of success, on a level that neither of them could have imagined. The other dream—of being the best in his field—was a more elusive one. Being the best implied arriving at a plateau, from which one could see the competition far below. But Chiat had been raised to be a scrambler. He might be the best at his brand of advertising, but he was moving too fast to appreciate the view.

On this night, though, he was weary—and uneasy. The question, for a man who seemed to equate rest with death, was what his role in the beckoning future would be. Chiat chafed at the notion of continuing to manage what already existed, but he was hardly ready to retire: everything about him conveyed an insouciant disregard for the passage of time. Aside from an incipient paunch and a thinning mane of silvery-white hair, which he wore combed straight back from a broad forehead, Chiat had managed to hold advancing age at bay. He was a robust man, a one-time runner who still tried to shoehorn the occasional five-mile jog into his tight schedule, a man who had no time for ailments and was impatient with the physical frailties of others. The good suits only came out of the closet for client meetings. His standard wardrobe ran to billowing silk or cotton shirts, pleated pants and designer eyeglasses. When he was in Venice he tooled around town in a bright yellow Nissan 300ZX.

He was drawn to the long chance. Chiat had always behaved as though the horizon were drawn in pencil, as though he could simply pick up an eraser, rub out reality, and redraw it a few feet further out. Europe needed prospecting—London was to be the stepping-off point for a network of offices on the Continent—and the new subsidiary businesses needed to be developed. They would invigorate him.

Besides, there was the delicate issue of mortality. If Chiat wanted his agency to outlive him, he had to plan for succession—which meant that he had to accept his own eventual obsolescence. A handful of people were in place to run the agency, but so far he had not formally surrendered control to them. He'd tried, over the summer, to find satisfaction away from the agency and let his executives out from under his shadow, but the six-month sabbatical he'd planned evaporated after six weeks because he missed working. The list he'd drawn up of things he wanted to do languished somewhere, ignored.

As long as Chiat was involved in managing the business, his was the emphatic last word. If endurance was really the issue, he had to step aside and let the others take over. He was caught between two vanities—between a desire to be irreplaceable and a yearning to be immortal.

It was time for a change, both for his sake and for the sake of the agency. He was not a rash man; he'd had a plan in mind since spring. If everything worked out right over the next couple of months, he was going to walk away at the end of the year.

CHAPTER 3

A *Chiat/Day Christmas party* had to have many of the attributes of a Chiat/Day advertisement: stylish, a little outrageous, great production values, memorable in a surprising kind of way. Money was not much of an object.

The 1989 Los Angeles party invitation read, "This year we're going to celebrate Christmas a bit more traditionally. With a really big goose." The agency had rented the world's largest clear-span aluminum dome, the Long Beach home of Howard Hughes's legendary wooden airplane, the *Spruce Goose*. It loomed in the middle of the drafty room, parked over a reflecting pool, the Chiat/Day/Mojo name projected, for tonight, in lights on its ample side. Not a practical vehicle, but one whose only voyage—a sixty-second trip, seventy feet off the ground, right over the spot where it lay in state—was etched forever in the public mind. An appropriate enough venue for people who lived to get the message across.

Everything about the party was big, an unconscious nod to how quickly the agency had grown, and promised to grow in the coming year. The *Spruce Goose* was 219 feet long and 320 feet from wingtip to wingtip. Even with such a hefty centerpiece, the room stretched out forever, in blank defiance of any attempted intimacy. A half dozen employees of a local party-decorating company had been in the hall since six in the morning, trying to make the arena festive for the 550 expected guests. They installed a giant lighted arch made up of four hundred balloons, three mammoth snowflakes, some eight-foot-tall Santa Clauses, five twenty-foot-tall candy canes around a cluster of small tables, and lighted balloon columns on either side of the bandstand.

The food was lavish, but that would have been true at any gathering of more than four people from the agency. In the Chiat/Day vernacular, food meant love. Internal agency meetings meant breakfast, or muffins and fruit in the late morning, lunch, or cookies and fruit in the afternoon, and dinners. The Venice office spent $1,000 a month on pizza alone, and its public kitchen was always littered with leftovers from mealtime buffets. Client meetings meant even more and better food, the menu chosen to cater to particular client tastes. It was as though someone had proven a direct physiological link between a full stomach and a happy mind.

In a room this size, it was important that no one have to go out of his way to eat. There were six full bars in the hall, as well as an international coffee bar which offered a concoction of coffee, cream, chocolate, cinnamon sugar, and orange peel, spiked with any one of a half dozen liqueurs. Long draped tables satisfied the agency's love for Mexican food, for pizza, for chocolate. To add a note of sophistication, there were three pastas in Italian flag sauces, white Alfredo, red marinara, and green pesto; whole hams and turkeys; mini-Wellingtons, both chicken and beef. And there was seafood, 3,500 fresh crustaceans and mollusks, oysters, clams and crab legs, prawns so big that they would become the shorthand ("Those shrimp. They were the size of *baseballs*.") by which people approvingly recalled this party.

The evening ended up costing the agency about $60,000; the Christmas season would run almost double that, since the smaller offices in New York, San Francisco, Toronto and London all had their own parties. There had never been a formal budget for this night, never a financial ceiling. Quite the opposite—Chiat had been known to complain if the party didn't look grand enough. The mandate was always to beat last year's celebration, to come up with something that would make this the best Christmas party ever. Create a memory to eclipse the ones that preceded it.

For the Christmas party was the single night of the year when everyone who worked for Chiat/Day was encouraged to indulge themselves. All other agency parties fell into two well-defined categories:

internal agency events, which, to encourage camaraderie, were limited to employees only; and industry functions, which were minefields of competitors who wanted your job, or clients who might take umbrage at the random snide comment.

It was also a chance to get dressed up, in a business where people on the creative side were suspect if they wore anything more elegant than an inside-joke T-shirt (except for Kuperman, for whom dressing well was a vocation), and account management types had to keep to white shirts and dress-for-success suits.

Everyone overcompensated. Women skittered across the darkened parking lot like bright, frantic butterflies, their chilled shoulders twitching, their ankles buckling uncertainly as spike heels hit the pavement at the wrong angle. The dominant fashion, this year, ran to short dresses in hot colors, full skirts and big bows; lots of shiny, noisy taffeta (or more subdued silk, depending on a woman's place on the wage scale) and long kid gloves. Men wore wedge-shaped tuxedos and slicked back their hair. They lined up to have their photographs taken in front of a mottled mauve backdrop—with spouses, with dates, or, if they'd come alone, with pals from their department.

Lee Clow didn't wear a tuxedo; the tuxedo wore him. The forty-seven-year-old president and chief creative officer of Chiat/Day, a man to whom formal attire meant long pants and socks, was thrust into an unnaturally stiff posture by this sarcophagus of cotton, silk and wool. Even his long, mournful face, usually easy to coax into a grin, was fixed in a less elastic, woeful expression. Normally he loped around the office, body bent forward at the waist, head eagerly up, the stance of a man on the happy make for a good idea. He only wore clothes that stayed out of his way—T-shirts, the occasional pliable cotton dress shirt with permanent wrinkles where he rolled up the sleeves, khaki shorts or, if it was really chilly, vintage bluejeans. Even shoelaces were an irritating distraction. He almost always wore shoes he could slip on.

As the agency's chief creative officer, he had come to symbolize its renegade aesthetic, and as an art director he appreciated the impact he had. His clothes communicated not just an irreverence for fashion, which might be misconstrued as adolescent rebellion, but a total disregard for it. Clow's wardrobe let the client know that he was too busy working on how the ads looked to waste one minute on his own appearance. He always looked as though he had just stepped out of the shower—or, more likely, given his love of surfing, the ocean—spanking fresh and ready to go. He would have thought the same thoughts dressed in a suit, but the impact would have been weaker. In shorts, even his knees were exposed to inspiration.

But this pleated shirtfront fairly pushed his shoulders back and his chest out. He held his chin up as though to keep his graying blond beard from getting snagged in his red bow tie. His beach-thonged shuffle was replaced by a purposeful stride. The day-to-day Clow was a man who couldn't sit still in his office for more than thirty minutes at a time, preferring instead to roam the creative department looking at everyone's work. The formal Clow looked uncharacteristically like a statesman.

He was decidedly not in his element. Lee Clow didn't like tuxedos—or late parties, or forty-five-minute drives to get there. He preferred to spend his evenings at home with his wife Eileen, have an early dinner, play with his two middle-aged shepherd mutts, and watch some television. If he couldn't be there, he'd just as soon be at work. Pizzas in the editing room after a long day were party enough for him, though he did mourn the demise of the Bubba Weinie party, an annual gastronomical travesty perpetrated by Bubba, who used to work in the mailroom and made his own sauce for dunking cocktail franks.

Clow traveled the ten minutes between home and office, a satisfied man. He had been married to the same woman for twenty-one years, and to the same agency for almost seventeen; he had an instinct for the appropriate choice, and, once made, a fierce devotion to it. Clow wouldn't even go out to lunch with competitors who wanted to lure him away. It wasn't fair, since he had no intention of ever leaving.

The agency was his family—from Chiat, whose approval meant so much, to the young copywriters and art directors who were Clow's children, his reverential acolytes. Lesser known creatives might have worked on campaigns with Clow, or come up with ideas, but time had cleared away the clutter of other names. He had become creative director of Chiat/Day in 1977, and had been its guiding force ever since. In the mythic history of the advertising industry, Lee Clow was one with some of the most memorable television commercials ever made. Clow *was* Apple Computer's "1984" commercial, and the 1984 Nike "I Love L.A." spot with Randy Newman; he dug into his own surfer history for the California Cooler campaign, and set loose the Energizer Bunny, who romped through parodies of more traditional commercials.

He didn't quite see it that way—he compared himself to the guy who used to be on *The Ed Sullivan Show,* spinning plates on sticks, scrambling back and forth to make sure none of them hit the ground. He didn't draw or paint, he wasn't a director, and he didn't take photographs or shoot footage. Other people had those skills. What Clow had was an unerring eye for how a client's ad ought to look, and the instinct to know who, among the people he worked with, could best deliver that look. Clow agreed with the architect Mies van der Rohe: God was in the details—in this case, of daily work. The trappings, from the fancy parties to the titles to the name on the door, meant nothing to him.

He could have had everything, had he wanted it. He could have run the agency. Nine months earlier, in the spring of 1989, Jay Chiat had sprung a homework assignment on five of his top executives— Clow, Venice office president Bob Wolf, chief financial officer Pete de Vaux, San Francisco office president Fred Goldberg, and CPA David Weiner, the only outside member of the board, whose New Jersey accounting firm handled both the agency and Chiat's personal finances. He wanted each one of them to write what he called a "term paper" describing the agency's future—where it ought to go and how it ought to get there.

Chiat had been talking about backing off for the past couple of years, but he hadn't meant it, not as far as Clow was concerned. He was still right in the middle of of things, the chairman and CEO of both the worldwide operation and North America. But this assignment signaled a change. It meant he was looking for the man to take over.

Clow wrote a paper that stressed the things he'd always cared about so passionately. He wanted to make sure that the agency continued to be creative-driven. That meant taking small accounts that didn't make much money but allowed for groundbreaking work, and staying away from conservative clients, no matter how big they were. A cautious client would demand compromise, and if there was enough money at stake, the agency might try to go along rather than lose the revenue. Growth for growth's sake threatened the standards he and Chiat had worked so hard to uphold. The profit wasn't worth the potential loss.

He knew exactly what the agency ought to look like in the nineties—bigger, carefully so, and always better—but he didn't want to take it there. He didn't see himself as Chiat's successor. Clow liked to work in person, in Venice. He had once decreed that he'd only work on new business if it was in a city that was a non-stop flight from Los Angeles, but he would have preferred never to leave home at all. He didn't like the surprise of a new city, even New York, where he knew dozens of people. Left to his own devices, he sat alone in his hotel room after work; one of the women in Venice always informed the New York office of his pending arrival, so that someone would be sure to invite him out to dinner. He hated doing business on the telephone, since it robbed him of all the visual clues to a person's feelings. Clow wanted people to come to him. He was hardly the one to assume control of four offices in two countries.

Besides, there were personal considerations. An inveterate tinkerer, a perfectionist who had been known to rework storyboards the night before a pitch, Clow had never taken all the vacation time due him. There was always something to be done at the agency. But lately he'd felt the need to get away. His wife, Eileen, was thirteen years his senior. He couldn't keep putting off their time together.

What he wanted was a position that would enable him to protect the agency's greatest asset, the quality of its creative work, and give him a semblance of a personal life. He would be the creative conscience of the entire agency, the one, he said, "who would keep the creative directors from being minimized as we get big." Let Bob Wolf, the Los Angeles office president, preside over North America.

The past demanded that Chiat offer the job to Clow first, though he understood full well how awkward the fit was. Clow was his heart's choice, the man who embodied the spirit of Chiat/Day. They had worked together for over sixteen years, in a business where staccato résumés, three jobs in as many years, were the norm. Chiat had come to believe that Clow was something more than a great art director. The younger man had an instinctive understanding of clients' marketing problems. His work over the years had exemplified what Chiat called "breakthrough creative"—ads that were always grounded in an appropriate strategy, as well as being entertaining to look at.

Theirs was an affectionate, tolerant symbiosis: they both believed that Chiat had goaded Clow to do better work than he'd thought himself capable of, and that Clow had modulated Chiat's mercurial temperament, had soothed the agency's spirit when his combustible boss was in a less than nurturing mood. They saw themselves as brothers, though one longtime creative thought of them more as husband and wife: Chiat out making a good living for his family, the absent distracted father, and Clow the good mother, who kept the brood together.

Chiat felt obliged to offer Clow the job of chairman and CEO of the North American operation, titles Chiat had held for six years. Chiat would remain chairman and CEO worldwide. He could concentrate on Europe, knowing that Clow was looking after the agency they'd effectively built together.

It was the obvious succession. But Clow turned the job down, and Chiat, for once, did not press him.

Three other men—Chiat's two chief financial advisers, and Bob Wolf himself—agreed that Wolf, who had joined the agency in 1983 and engineered its biggest account wins in the years since, was the man for the job. Wolf presented his ideas to his boss not in writing, like the others, but in person, which was at once a more intimate and more secure means of communication. For Wolf had grand ideas, in terms of growth and acquisitions, that he was not yet prepared to share. He wanted Chiat to see this as a package deal: Make Wolf the CEO, and Wolf, in turn, would make the agency grow.

"We could be billing over a billion dollars in three or four years," he said. It was an ambitious vision, a doubling of what was then a $600 million operation, but Wolf could see that Chiat was tempted by it. He knew his boss to be a gambler, having once accompanied Chiat to a high-stakes poker game. If Clow was obsessed with maintaining the agency's creative reputation, Chiat was alternately protective and impatient, eager to see if he could parlay it into something more. Wolf was the kind of man who could help him try.

As for his personal objectives, Wolf was very clear. This was a young man's business. He believed the axiom that if you haven't made it to the top, or near the top—if you can't *see* the top—by the time you're forty, maybe even thirty-five, you're not going to get there. Wolf, forty-seven, had been able to see the top since he became general manager of Wells Rich Greene West in 1979. When he became president of Chiat/Day's New York office in 1983, he assumed that was where he was headed—to the top. He was, he believed, the next in line.

"My goal," he told Chiat, "is to run North America."

His only competition was Lee Clow, who had already confided in Wolf that he didn't want the job, and Fred Goldberg, president of the tiny San Francisco office, who believed that wholesale expansion would spell the end of the agency Chiat had invented. Goldberg preached maintenance, not a philosophy that had much appeal to an entrepreneur like Chiat. Once Clow said no to the promotion, Wolf was the logical choice.

History endorsed the notion. Wolf had assumed control of the three-year-old New York office in 1983, stopped its financial hemorrhaging, and in three heady years turned $15 million in billings into $108 million. When Chiat asked him to take over the floundering Venice office in 1986, he did so, even though he had no desire to transplant his family to California, and guided that office through four years of explosive growth. In 1986, Venice billings were $141 million. Now they were $422 million.

Wolf succeeded at the agency despite himself, since he embodied everything the Chiat/Day lifer was taught to be skeptical of. He had spent his career in packaged goods, the one category regarded by most people in the agency with outright disdain because of its generally boring advertising—first as a brand manager for Lever Brothers on Wisk and other products, and then on the agency side, as an account executive on Procter & Gamble. Wolf was a "suit" who defined reality in terms of billings, not the more amorphous, aesthetic goals that made Clow such an endearing figure.

As Los Angeles office president, Wolf had already resigned Grandee's, a small fast-food chicken account, reasoning that if Chiat/Day pitched Kentucky Fried Chicken and had to resign Grandee's to avoid a conflict, the small chain could sue the agency—or worse, sue Kentucky Fried Chicken for inducing Chiat/Day to resign, which caused Grandee's irreparable harm. Wolf's intention always had been to go after the big clients, and he wasn't going to let the possibility of a conflict get in the way. The couple of million dollars a year in billings from a small account just weren't worth it.

Even more unsettling, he wasn't particularly interested in being pals with his co-workers. Wolf didn't instinctively embrace the Chiat/Day tenets of egalitarianism and access. Longtime employees worried that Wolf was guided by his ego, by a desire to make himself famous as the man who turned the boutique into a worldwide presence. All he talked about was how he was going to "grow the business," a favorite industry idiom that implied the possibility of unimpeded progress.

Still, he had earned some grudging respect, even if vestigial suspicions clung to it, and, more importantly, he had Chiat's admiration. Chiat liked to point out that he and Clow had no real training in how to handle or approach a client. They'd just done ads all their lives, and for the rest depended on hunches. He confessed that he was easily bored by the management side of his business. He had gotten this far in spite of his short attention span, but he could not get any further without help. Wolf had a master's degree in marketing from Adelphi University, and he knew how a brand manager thought. He could break into the lucrative new categories that would expand the agency's realm of influence—and, although no one would publicly entertain the possibility of failure, he would be a convenient scapegoat, the carpetbagger, if the plan went awry.

Chiat had his misgivings, even after hearing what Wolf had to say—he joked that Wolf always needed an extra minute to translate his ideas into the Chiat/Day dialect, while Clow instinctively understood what the agency should and shouldn't do—but Clow reassured Chiat that Wolf was the sensible choice. Clow wasn't walking away. The two men would run the agency as partners.

"I can be one part of you," said Clow, "but I can't be the other part, and Wolf can be one part, but he definitely can't be the passion and the vision." They seemed a perfect complement.

Just weeks later, at an April 28, 1989, meeting, Chiat informed the members of the World Board that he was going to take a six-month sabbatical, starting on June 15. He was going to learn how to cook and speak Italian. He was going to ski for a month, lose ten pounds, take an art history class, learn to scuba dive, and take a performance driving class. He wanted to become bored enough to figure out what he wanted to do with the rest of his life.

Chiat laid out his plans for an orderly transfer of power. Clow would retain the title of president and chief creative officer of the worldwide operation. The job he turned down, North American chairman and CEO, would go to Bob Wolf, the Los Angeles office president and CEO. Wolf's job went to the man he selected, creative director Bob Kuperman. Kuperman's position went to his hand-picked successor, copywriter and nine-year agency veteran Steve Rabosky. They would assume their new responsibilities now, but none of this would be official until January 1990. Chiat wanted to be satisfied that the experiment was working before he announced it publicly. They were to refer to Wolf as "acting CEO," and to say nothing at all about Chiat's sabbatical. For public consumption, he was on vacation.

He launched them with a warning. In addition to getting used to life without Chiat, they were going to have to address the conflicting issues of growth and recession, of how to achieve the former while the latter ate away at the agency's coffers. He anticipated an economic nosedive. "The nineties are going to really be a bummer, I think," he said. "Business is really going to go into the toilet. Let's get in shape. Let's get down to the people we need. Let's hunker down and get ready for it before it happens."

But Chiat had a reputation for gloomy predictions; it was almost as though he could stave off disappointment by making his anticipation of it public. Despite his prognosis of rough times for the new regime, Wolf was thrilled. He'd gotten promotions before and always thought, privately, "Maybe I'm not going to be up to this," or, "Maybe this is biting off more than I can chew." For the first time, he felt totally in control. He was capable. He could handle the job. This was the natural order of things.

Having the Christmas party at the *Spruce Goose* was Wolf's idea, and it fitted him just fine. He was Clow's opposite—everyone who worked with them joked that Clow was the right brain and Wolf the left, Clow the emotional artist and Wolf the cool strategist. But it was more than that. Wolf genuinely seemed to enjoy being a citizen of the world. He shared Chiat's penchant for drop-of-a-hat travel, in part because of the adrenaline, in part because he firmly believed in his own ability to affect events.

He knew, from his tenure as Venice office president, that people distrusted him, that epithets even less flattering than "suit"—like "the bean counter"—had been uttered behind his back. People simply did not understand. They listened to him spout numbers and called it greed, and they wondered if his detachment would increase the level of office politics in an office that pretended there were no politics. Wolf wasn't one of them, nor did he seem to care about becoming one of them, and he knew that was considered traitorous behavior.

He was used to the doubters by now. His successes were his armor. He would prevail, the first man to run the creative-driven agency who was not himself a creative, the first who had not been bred by Chiat/Day.

Wolf wandered into the hall, a dark silk scarf flung casually around the neck of his tux, his manner advertising his delight. He was an imposing man, tall, broad-shouldered and barrel-chested. He loved well-tailored clothes and wore them in a manner that suggested he always paid attention to how he looked. Wolf had a heavy jaw and deepset eyes, which reinforced the impression that he was hard to reach; to make eye contact it was first necessary to convince the rest of his face to yield. The only unruly thing about him was his hair, a rebellious thatch of salt-and-pepper that refused to agree on a direction.

Clow always arrived at parties early, often to a half-empty room, so that he could leave early without seeming asocial. Wolf waited until the room had filled and sorted itself out, until the chatter was at a respectably urgent pitch and he could move easily from one brief conversation to the next. He was here to have a good time. As soon as the agency's in-house band, the Ad Punks, took the stage at ten, Wolf and his wife hit the dance floor. They stayed until eleven and then made the long drive home. The next day Wolf began a two-week vacation. When he set foot in the office again, he would be the new CEO.

The only one who missed the party was Chiat. He was never a dependable guest—it was always a matter of what city he was in on party night—but this year he had said he was going to come to Venice. Then, at the last minute, he changed his mind, pleading jet lag for the first time in anyone's memory.

The press release that formalized the management changes went out two days later, on December 15, 1989. It did not make Lee Clow happy, but he saw it too late to do anything more than register his reaction. Clow had assumed that any unease he had felt during the preceding six-month trial period was the natural consequence of a major management shift. He and Wolf had to work out the kinks in their new relationship. But the release caught him completely by surprise. It seemed as though he was the only one who was still thinking in terms of a partnership. He had felt uncertain, over the summer, and chalked it up to the transition, and to his own changing role. Now he felt vulnerable.

"WOLF TO ASSUME CHAIRMANSHIP OF CHIAT/DAY/MOJO IN NORTH AMERICA," was the headline.

SECOND GENERATION OF SENIOR MANAGEMENT POSITIONED
TO LEAD AGENCY IN THE '90S
Bob Wolf, 47, president and chief executive officer of Chiat/Day/ Mojo Los Angeles, has been named chairman and chief executive officer of Chiat/Day/Mojo North America as part of a major reorganization of senior management unveiled today by Chiat/Day/Mojo Worldwide chairman and chief executive officer Jay Chiat. The announced moves have been made to secure the leadership of the $1.3 billion international agency as it enters its third decade.

Wolf, who replaces Chiat as chairman of the agency in North America, has been serving informally in this capacity for several months while Chiat devoted his time and energies to international expansion and creative issues. Wolf will have responsibility for the agency's offices in Los Angeles, San Francisco, New York and Toronto.

The announcement of Kuperman's and Rabosky's promotions was followed by a quote from Chiat.

"Bob Wolf has done an extraordinary job during his seven-year tenure at the agency," commented Chiat. "During his four years as

*President of the New York office, billings grew from $15 to $150
million. Now, the Los Angeles office, under his stewardship, has
become the largest agency on the West Coast without losing its
creative edge."*

Then Wolf got his turn to speak.

*"Chiat/Day emerged as the hottest and most successful agency of
the 1980s as a result of our creativity. I believe we are extremely
well-positioned for even greater growth in the 1990's because along
with our unique brand of creative come the resources to handle the
biggest clients who believe breakthrough work can set them apart
from their competition."*

Clow was relegated to a brief respectful quote about Kuperman,
toward the end of the release.

This was not what Clow had envisioned. The release didn't talk
about Wolf in the context of the worldwide operation. It certainly
didn't make him sound like Clow's partner, even though technically
Clow held the senior position. It sounded as if Wolf had inherited the
earth, Chiat had retired, and Clow had become the *éminence grise* of
the agency, some grizzled, kindly consultant who dropped in from
time to time. It sounded as though he and Chiat had kicked themselves upstairs.

Clow had always believed in the Chiat/Day management credo:
Leadership, which was what he felt he provided, should be visible.
Management, which was Wolf's job, should be invisible. Clow intended to judge Wolf's performance by how little people felt his
presence, but the press release as much as guaranteed that his profile
would be too high for Clow's liking. Wolf's momentum, coupled with
his ease in the public arena, his inclination to be quoted, could
quickly make it seem—to the agency, to clients, to the industry—
that Wolf had taken over.

For the first time, Clow wished he had asked for a new title, or at
least discussed his view of the future with Wolf. Until now, the two
men had managed a functional alliance, Clow coasting on seniority
and Wolf preoccupied with the Venice office's severe management
deficit. Clow had assumed that they would continue to compensate for
each other, because that was what he believed ought to happen, but
now he regretted that he hadn't been more assertive about his expectations.

He told Chiat, "This is going to be confusing. This is not what you and I talked about. At least it's not stated clearly enough, because I always thought that if Wolf stepped up to be the CEO of the agency, you would match me up as COO—so the paramount vision of the agency was still represented by the highest office."

"No no," said Chiat, reassuringly, "everyone will understand. Because you're the president of all of Chiat/Day's holdings and he's only chairman of the North American Chiat/Day."

"Jay, I don't think so," said Clow. "This has to be a very confusing signal to people, because Wolf wants to be the guy anyway. This is going to make everyone believe that Wolf is now in charge."

"No no no," said Chiat. "I thought a lot about this. It's very clear." If he seemed unresponsive to Clow's concerns, it was partly naivete—*he* had always known how essential Clow was—and partly defensiveness, in case he was about to be proven wrong. He couldn't imagine that labels would matter so much; but if they did, he had just dealt Clow a serious political blow.

On Monday morning, December 18, stories ran in *The New York Times*, *The Wall Street Journal* and the *Los Angeles Times*. *The Wall Street Journal* reported that Chiat was "giving up day-to-day operating control" of the agency to Wolf. Clow was nothing more than a sartorial aside: "Mr. Wolf, a native New Yorker, still wears conservative dark suits to the Chiat/Day office in Venice Beach," said the *Journal*, "where attire runs more to shorts and sandals and where creative chief Lee Clow keeps a surfboard."

The New York Times and *Los Angeles Times* ignored Clow completely. "An 'Outsider' Takes Over Chiat Unit," reported *The New York Times*. "In a significant reorganization that caps its decade of growth from a small California shop to a billion-dollar international power, Chiat/Day/Mojo on Friday named Bob Wolf its North American chairman and chief executive," the story began. Wolf was interviewed on his agenda, which included going after clients in the $50 to $100 million range, arresting the rash of client defections that had hobbled the agency in the 1980s, and adding new client services like direct mail and public relations.

The *Los Angeles Times* reported that "Jay Chiat, the ad man who co-founded the largest and most successful agency in Los Angeles, began to relinquish the reins of his fast-growing advertising empire on

Friday." It implied that Bob Wolf was the answer to the as-yet-unasked question of who would eventually replace Chiat as chairman of worldwide operations. "Some advertising executives say Jay Chiat may be laying the groundwork for his retirement," the story continued, even though Chiat and Wolf went on to deny the rumor.

Clow got a call from his eighty-three-year-old mother.

"Okay now," she confronted him. "What's Jay going to do now that he's quit? And did you lose your job?"

Clow wrote Chiat a note. "I told you it was going to confuse people," he complained. "My mom thinks I'm out of a job." He warned Chiat, "This is not the right signal."

Two days later, *Advertising Age* polished off what was left of Clow's partnership concept: "Bob Wolf, president and ceo of Chiat/Day/Mojo, L.A., has been given the reins of the $1.3-billion agency's North American operations." The piece mentioned that "overall creative direction" was still the province of president and chief creative officer Clow, but then reported that he would be responsible only for L.A., San Francisco, and the Australian/Pacific Group, while Tom McElligott, whom Clow had hired in October, would look after the offices in New York, Toronto and London.

McElligott, a legendary copywriter who had started—and then walked away from—his own agency, was quite a coup for Chiat/Day, and Clow originally had loved the idea that McElligott would be flying around, putting out fires, saving him from that kind of manic travel. But in the context of the announcement about Wolf, it was all too easy to assume that McElligott's ascendancy was linked to a lessening of Clow's role.

The stories all sounded frustratingly the same. Men like Clow have an unusual relationship to words. Within their universe, within the ads they create, they control language. They believe in its absolute power, and in their ability to discipline it for their purposes. The appropriate adjective could motivate a businessman with a family to buy a Maxima; the wrong words would go by him. Each ad was a painstaking lesson in communication—words were chosen, researched, discarded, recombined in a way that made a creative proud, a consumer responsive, and, so, a client satisfied.

It was a proprietary alliance. Words were like willing little workers who marched into the room and waited, obedient, until creativity beckoned them up onto the desk. The news story that failed to pay homage to all the players in this drama seemed a betrayal to Clow. Other practitioners of the printed word had chosen to depict reality in a way he found inaccurate, using a tool that normally did his bidding.

Clow wasn't the type to parade around telling people that he'd been offered Wolf's job first and turned it down, so dark theories abounded. Some assumed that he had been passed over, while others figured that he had stepped aside in deference to the more forceful Wolf. Was Wolf's new position a sign that money, not work, was now the agency's primary motivation? Did hiring McElligott mean that Clow was going to step back? The members of the creative department nursed the vague hope that Clow would continue to be a strong presence, a hope that didn't hold up well against the chilly fear that he wouldn't.

By the time Chiat arrived in Venice, a week after the announcement, the anxiety was palpable. Even though there had been a six-month audition period to get everyone used to the pending change, the official announcement of the new cast had made people apprehensive. Chiat summed up morale at his biggest office. "Everybody's paranoid," he said.

The following week *Advertising Age* named Chiat/Day the Agency of the Decade, which would have been more of a thrill had many not greeted the news as a funeral announcement marking the end of an era.

CHAPTER 4

An *advertising agency* was always hungry, always looking for ways to grow and to compensate for the inevitable loss of existing sources of nourishment. There was no such thing as a stable account, and anyone who thought he was working on one was, by his very complacency, contributing to its impermanence. Every account, whether $3 million or $150 million, was either an active flirtation or a soured romance. Chiat liked to say that the moment you signed a contract with a new client was the moment you started to lose that client.

Agencies made their money by charging a commission, usually around 15 percent, on the work they did for clients, but that income was as unpredictable as the process it subsidized. The problem was that an agency lacked a quantifiable product. Its assets were the dreams and inspirations of human beings who took their mental inventory with them when they changed jobs—which they did with unnerving alacrity, lured by the promise of more money, more visibility or the opportunity to work on a particular account. The notion of what an ad should be was equally elusive: there were no design specifications for a piece of advertising, no reassuring blueprints to which the agency could refer a skeptical client. For all the talk of brand position and strategy—of deciding where a brand ought to stand, relative to the competition, and then determining how to communicate that position to the consumer—advertising depended as much on intuition as on research.

More and more goods these days were parity products, essentially the same as what the competition had to offer, which meant that the foundation of an ad was often nothing more than an imaginary distinction. An Energizer battery ran a tape recorder the same way a Duracell battery did, and a Nissan Stanza's specifications sounded remarkably like those of the Toyota Camry or Honda Accord. It was incumbent upon the advertising agency to skew the consumer's perception, to communicate an advantage that was based on style, not content.

If the agency devised a great campaign, which delighted the client and got the public shopping, there were still plenty of things, all of them beyond the agency's control, that could go infuriatingly wrong. Critics of advertising might like to believe that ads make people buy things, that commercial messages commandeer the collective brain and make that hand reach for that wallet, but ads are mere co-conspirators. Shelf positioning makes the grocery shopper reach for one brand of detergent over another, and a display rack near a cash register is a proven temptation. If the client fails to keep up his end of the bargain—if there isn't enough product in the stores, or if Nissan ships sedans to a rural dealer who wants four-wheel-drive Pathfinders—then all the advertising in the world won't make a difference.

But clients do not like to cast blame on themselves, and advertising, while it may not be the only thing that prods customers, is certainly the most high profile of sales tools. Ads are supposed to enhance image and move inventory, and if they don't it is easy for a client to find an agency that will swear it has a better answer.

Perpetual motion—of people, of accounts, of alliances and enemies within an account—is a given in advertising. Rampant anxiety is the underlying theme, however deft people are at covering it over with wit and self-congratulation.

This is true at all agencies, to some degree. But the venerable giants, like Chicago's Leo Burnett U.S.A. and New York's J. Walter Thompson, had worked hard to offset the vagaries of their business. They had done what was necessary to achieve order. Some devised immortal, if predictable, campaigns, like Leo Burnett's Pillsbury Doughboy, that as much as guaranteed an ongoing association with the client. Other agencies forged strong bonds between their account management executives and the client, grounded in everything from ski weekends to expensive evenings on the restaurant circuit.

Chiat/Day had refused to take out any such insurance. On the contrary, Chiat seemed to take perverse pleasure in selling contentiousness as a virtue. His reverence for good creative work was legendary, and carried the implication that any client or account executive who did not embrace it was a coward. Although the agency was structured like any agency—creatives to come up with the ads, an account management staff to shuttle between the agency and the client, researchers to hunt for validation from consumers and a media department to buy time or space for the ads—the similarities ended with the skeleton. In its early days Chiat/Day was just Chiat and a handful of employees, and job distinctions were almost nonexistent. People did whatever needed to be done. It was only when the agency started to grow that a structure emerged and account management became a distinct discipline. The newcomers were regarded as a necessary evil, and their status improved very slowly. Even now, Chiat/Day's account management people held a more servile position than their diplomat counterparts at other agencies: they were to take what Chiat and Clow deemed great advertising and figure out how to convince the client to buy it. Anyone who caved in and abandoned a wonderful ad clearly was not cut out for Chiat/Day.

Chiat's researchers were the first in the United States to practice the British discipline of account planning, which rejected traditional quantitative research on completed campaigns, in favor of qualitative research done throughout the creative process. Chiat/Day used focus group research, talking to small, prescreened groups for hours at a time about everything from the product itself to proposed executions, and if the results refined the agency's strategic efforts, they also gave Chiat/Day more ammunition for sparring with clients.

Chiat had what he figured was the perfect three-pronged weapon with which to wage his crusade: the best creative in the business, an account staff that considered sycophancy toward the client a terminal disease, and a research team to footnote any position the agency took. Ongoing campaigns and intimate client relationships were not what he had to sell. He worshipped flux and dismissed the kind of work that bought dependable relationships, the jingles and songs, as the product of tired minds.

Chiat/Day's work was memorable not because it was repetitious or insistent but because it rattled consumers—and often clients—who thought they knew what to expect from commercials. The "1984" commercial for Apple Computer was almost killed by the client the day before it went into production, and the week before it was supposed to air on the Super Bowl, Chiat/Day was instructed to sell off the time. Chiat/Day managed to sell one minute. The only reason the commercial did run was because the agency couldn't find a buyer for the remaining sixty seconds. It won four major advertising awards that year: the Cannes Gold, the Grand Effie, the Belding Sweepstakes, and the Clio.

The print campaign that introduced Honda automobiles to the United States was more sedate, just a full page of copy and a photograph of the car, under the headline, "The Honda Car," but it identified Honda so succinctly as a company that made something besides motorcycles that for years people talked about the car as though its proper name were Hondacar. And the agency's work for Nike during the 1984 Olympics was a triumph of arresting creative and savvy media buying: Chiat/Day bought walls on downtown buildings and painted huge portraits of famous athletes, and that, in combination with the Randy Newman "I Love L.A." commercial, convinced people that Nike was the official shoe of the Olympics—a painful connection for Converse, the company that had paid for the right to make that claim.

None of those accounts hung around to savor the victories—Honda left in 1974, and Apple and Nike in 1986, an exceedingly bleak year. Honda complained that the agency wasn't growing as fast as the car company was, and that account management was weak. Nike didn't like all the attention Chiat/Day was getting in the press, and Apple succumbed to personality problems. The gist of the message, each time, was the same: Strong creative work was enough to lure a client to the agency, but not sufficient to keep him. It did not compensate for perceived weaknesses in the way the agency was run.

Nissan's executive vice-president for operations Tom Mignanelli had recently observed that Chiat/Day had a tendency to get into trouble in the third year of its relationship to a client, a comment that was etched on every Nissan staffer's brain, since this was the third year of that association. The agency sped through the normal account life cycle at warp speed, and along the way earned a reputation for being brilliant but arrogant.

It was a smart-ass shop, and its Venice headquarters was now in the hands of a man who inspired similar epithets, even from those who liked him. Bob Kuperman, his ponytail shorn, came to work the first week in January 1990, sat in his cubicle in the creative department and felt like an alien. For the first time in his professional life, for the first time in twenty-five of his forty-seven years, his name was not on the roster of creative department employees. He was corporate. He joked that he could say whatever he wanted now, be as frank as he liked, and no one would get upset—because no one would listen, now that he was only the office president. Four years before he'd turned down the same job at DDB Needham's Los Angeles office, fearing that it would take him too far from the work. He was about to get the chance to find out if he'd been right, and how much he'd mind the separation.

The difference, this time, was that he perceived a need. DDB Needham had been so big that the office president was pretty much a figurehead, a comfortable position, no doubt, but to Kuperman an empty honor. Chiat/Day, on the other hand, was in an oddly precarious state—healthy but stretched a little thin.

Kuperman had done his homework: only 85 people, of the 350 in the Venice office, had been around for more than two years. Too many newcomers, hired too quickly to meet the instant demands of the Nissan account, none of them indoctrinated in the ways of Chiat/Day. If the agency embarked on an aggressive growth program without tending to Chiat's idiosyncratic garden, bigness could become its guiding principle. Although he'd only been there for three years himself, Kuperman believed he could restore the office's soul without forsaking growth. What made him appeal to Wolf was that he talked about agency culture without Clow's elusive dreaminess. He might venerate the small account, but he loved a big win as much as Wolf did.

He was an unlikely savior, the one man who had elicited an even more negative reaction when he joined the agency than had Bob Wolf. When Kuperman was hired in late 1987 to replace Clow as creative director, some creatives left immediately. Others hung around and complained. Who was this guy, to have the audacity to think he could replace Lee Clow? Kuperman was not from Chiat/Day; therefore, he could not be of Chiat/Day, no matter how hard he tried. Kuperman felt as though he had bought a furnished house and been told, in no uncertain terms, that he could not move the furniture. It was where it was supposed to be.

His combative nature was probably the only thing that had kept him alive. First he had served notice on Clow: Lee would have to stop meddling and let him do what he was supposed to do, which was run the creative department. Then he had bullied his way into cubicles where he wasn't welcome and basically demanded cooperation. Bit by bit, he had won the others' wary approval, if not the lavish affection they displayed toward Clow.

What no one yet understood was that Kuperman considered himself an insider, because he had been down this road before. Kuperman had seen a hot creative shop give in to ambition and lose its way when he had been too young to do anything about it. Chiat/Day was his chance to rewrite history.

Kuperman had been—and it was the seminal fact of his professional life, the credit that informed everything he did—a wunderkind at Doyle Dane Bernbach in New York in its heydey in the 1960s. In 1963, his third year studying painting at the Pratt Institute, he had faced the fact that fine art was not going to make him a decent living, so he had taken a job cutting mattes at a mediocre advertising agency. Three weeks later, a call came from DDB—and Kuperman, not realizing what a plum he'd been offered, said he was going to take the weekend to think it over.

One of his co-workers, who had spent too many nights dreaming of just such a move, screamed at him, "Take it, you idiot. Take it." Kuperman accepted the job with as much grace as a callow, ambitious young man could muster.

"I'll take it," he told his new employer, "but I'll only stay in the bullpen six months. If I'm not out of there within six months, I'm gone."

Two months later he was out of the bullpen, and at twenty-six he was the youngest vice-president in the agency's history, one of the art directors who worked on the agency's legendary Volkswagen advertising, under its creator, Helmut Krone. In 1971 he left DDB to become creative director at Della Femina Travisano, where he created the Meow Mix campaign for Ralston-Purina; and if his later creative work was not as memorable, if he became an administrative, rather than an active, creative director, it didn't matter. At DDB in New York, Bob Kuperman had lived through advertising history. He kept an 8×10 black and white portrait of Bill Bernbach in his cubicle, along with the poster from the 1979 opening of the Cooper-Hewitt Museum's "20 Years of Volkswagen Advertising" exhibit, to remind people of where he had been.

But Doyle Dane had faltered when Bernbach handed the creative department over to younger men. Kuperman felt that the agency had gone after clients it had no business pursuing, like the mammoth Procter & Gamble, which awarded the agency seven of its brands in the 1970s. The work had suffered. When Chiat offered Kuperman the creative director's job in 1987, it seemed like a chance to start over.

The office presidency was even more than that. It was an opportunity to pay off a debt of gratitude to Chiat, and to the memory of Bernbach. Kuperman faced the year with two goals in mind, knowing that neither was possible without the other: he had to get himself, and his office, under control. In both cases, it was a matter of paring away the excess, the self-destructive emotionalism, without losing the inspiration and energy. If he reined himself in—if he led by example—then maybe he could bring all the disparate elements of the office into harmony, and diminish the backbiting, the general confusion about who was doing what to, or for, whom.

On the first Tuesday morning in January, Kuperman took what had been Bob Wolf's seat at the head of a long conference table in the Treehouse, a high-ceilinged room, stark white and bare concrete, that was tucked just behind the Boathouse. Two dozen faces stared back at him expectantly, too many of them young, newer than he was, new to their positions, or all three. Kuperman was in just the position Chiat liked for his talented people—mildly out of his depth and totally under the gun.

He turned to Tom Patty, executive vice-president and the Nissan national account director, a thirteen-year agency veteran—reliable, linear Tom Patty, a man whose waking moments were so consumed by the Nissan account that he complained, "I try to say, 'I love you,' to my wife and it comes out, 'I love you Nissan.'" He was as close as the advertising industry got to reliability, a trait that might sometimes bore his co-workers but was marvelously reassuring to the client. Patty had just assumed responsibility for Nissan's regional dealer business as well, a $150 million piece of business that the agency had acquired in 1988, a year after winning the national account. Three quarters of the office's billings rested on his white-shirted shoulders.

Kuperman asked him to give his report first.

"Not ready," said Patty, without looking up from the papers in front of him.

"Arrest him!" screamed Kuperman, and threw his reading glasses across the table at Patty.

Patty, who was used to histrionics from Chiat and Clow, ignored the outburst and kept reading.

One by one, the department heads gave their reports. Mitsubishi Electronics, at fifteen years the agency's oldest client, had suffered a 20 percent drop in sales of television sets over the past year, but had no plans for new television or print ads. The $21.5 million Home Savings of America account needed a new lending commercial for the spring, but the agency and client could not agree on the proper strategy. Foster Farms Poultry, Inc., a $4 million account, had just rejected a slate of radio ads. Dep, a $6 million account that included Dep hair-care products, Porcelana skin cream, and Topol smoker's toothpaste, was contemptuous of the agency's latest efforts. The extremely popular Energizer battery commercials, which featured a battery-powered Bunny tromping through parodies of other commercials, were a hit with consumers, who were beginning to identify the brand with the attribute of being long-lasting—but that $25 million account had just run out of media dollars, which meant that the Bunny might well disappear between April and September.

So far, what Kuperman heard was a familiar litany of roadblocks: not enough money, disagreements on strategy, not enough money, clients who wouldn't listen to what was clearly reason, not enough money.

Patty's report didn't improve his mood. Nissan's sales for December were "lousy—34,000 units" in a month when the company had projected sales of 52,000, primarily because an incentive program that had meant cash back for the dealer had ended on November 30, and with it dealer momentum.

Kuperman didn't care whose fault it was, whether the dealers should have worked harder or Nissan should have set a more realistic sales goal. Chiat/Day enjoyed an unusual, reassuringly close relationship to Tom Mignanelli, who had joined the company in 1987, just after the account review got under way. Choosing a new advertising agency had been one of his first executive decisions, a chance to set the tone for his administration, so he had a personal stake in the association. He had been a faithful ally during the agency's disastrous first year on the account, when its "Engineers" campaign, featuring actors portraying Nissan engineers in a documentary-style commercial, was ridiculed by advertising critics. The agency was not about to squander Mignanelli's investment. It was up to Patty to make sure that the client did not blame the agency for the poor showing.

The cavernous Venice warehouse that housed Chiat/Day resembled a kid's clubhouse: raw wood cubicles with five-foot walls and no doors, the halls full of more corrugated furniture and slouchy couches, as well as outsized items from Chiat's extensive modern art collection, like the pair of eight-foot tall metal horses who grazed at opposite ends of the building. There were no private offices. Chiat believed that hierarchial design encouraged stagnation in those who had the big corner offices and intimidation in those who didn't. His cubicle was the same size as everyone else's.

What would have been the central corridor in a traditional office was a wide swath of pavement, called Main Street, that ran the length of the building. It was anchored at one end by the Fish—a large meeting room that resembled a beheaded, gutted fish, with wooden interior ribs and metal scales wrapping the outer walls—and at the other end by a row of potted ficus trees, which Clow had smuggled into the building before the last windows were installed, to give what he considered a bleak landscape a homier, neighborhood look. A digital read-out by artist Jenny Holzer, entitled *UNEX*, presided over Main Street. It was mounted over the rear door that lead back to the computer room, its message changing every two minutes, temporarily paralyzing people with statements like, "Slipping into madness is good for the sake of comparison."

The three small conference rooms along Main Street were dubbed Huey, Dewey, and Louie. The conference rooms on the creative department's cross street were Huntley and Brinkley, and another pair, back by the finance and administrative cubicles, were Laurel and Hardy. Across Main Street on the other side was 3 Mile Island, so named because it overlooked the toxic waste dump that had been discovered on the intended site of the agency's new home. All the meeting rooms had windows cut into them. Chiat's attitude was that employees were paranoid anyhow. Might as well let them stand outside, read lips and find out what other people were saying about them.

The lofty 25-foot-high ceilings gave the illusion of being inside a big bubble; the ceiling appeared to crown in the center, over Main Street, even though it was perfectly flat. It was as though the warehouse was its own little planet, floating inside the larger universe, separate and safe from it.

Whenever there was an excuse—and a proper excuse was that too much time had passed without one—there was a party on Main Street. Sometimes it was just to bring people up to date on new hires, promotions and account activity, a "tree meeting," so called because speakers addressed the crowd while standing on the rim of the three-foot pot that housed the largest of Clow's trees. But any special event merited its own celebration, which was why Kuperman walked out of his cubicle on January 15 and into his own surprise birthday party.

Everyone milled around a table full of cupcakes with Day-Glo frosting and, for the health-conscious Kuperman, a low-fat, low-sugar apple cake. The idea behind any party was communication—get everyone from the receptionists on up into a space and see who talked to whom—but intimidating little knots tended to form. When Wolf, Clow and Kuperman huddled together, talking in low voices, no one broke in.

The others knew too well what they were discussing. Only five days earlier, Wolf, Clow and Chiat had been in New York as part of an all-agency attempt to prevent Reebok management from putting the $40 million account into review. Since coming to the New York office in 1987, Reebok had slipped from its position as market leader, on an $8 million advertising budget, to being second to Nike in performance shoes and losing share to L.A. Gear on the fashion side, at a cost of $40 million in annual advertising. Chiat/Day's two campaigns so far—the fashion-oriented "Reebok Lets U.B.U.," which was pulled early, and the "Physics Behind the Physique" performance commercials—had met with stinging criticism from the press.

Spending five times as much for weaker results was not acceptable. Reebok company president Frank O'Connell had been on the brink of announcing a review when Clow distracted him with the promise of an intramural review. New York, Venice and San Francisco had spent almost three months preparing new creative, as though each one was pitching the account.

Now, sunk in an adrenaline deficit, the men who had mounted the attack had nothing to do but worry, second-guess themselves, and try to rouse each other out of their anxiety. Waiting was the worst part of this business. Wolf, Clow and Kuperman replayed the presentation. They tried to convince themselves that every compliment had been genuine, every criticism inconsequential, and wondered whether a five-day wait was good news or bad.

The following week, Nissan provided an unwanted but urgent distraction from Reebok. Nissan and CBS had been getting letters protesting the upcoming broadcast of "Turbo Z Dreamer," because press coverage of the Fantasy campaign commercial had made it sound as if it glorified speeding. At first both the auto manufacturer and Chiat/Day stonewalled the issue, assuming the protest would fade. But then Brian O'Neill, president of the Insurance Institute for Highway Safety, an industry-supported research organization based in Arlington, Virginia, held a press conference, showed a videotape of "Turbo Z Dreamer," and demanded that it not run during the Super Bowl.

It required a response. Tom Patty was in the midst of a regional marketing meeting at Nissan's Carson, California, headquarters, on Saturday, January 20—a week and a day before the Super Bowl— when Bob Thomas, vice-president and general manager of the carmaker's Nissan division, turned to him and said, offhandedly, "I think I want you guys to develop a scenario whereby there are some words that precede the commercial."

That request—"some words" being a gentle euphemism for a solution—begat four days of craziness. Patty, who had to leave town the next day on regional business, bequeathed the crisis to Kuperman. Early Monday morning, as Nissan issued a public statement insisting that the criticisms of the commercial were not valid, Kuperman met with Lee Clow and Dick Sittig, the new creative group head on Nissan. "I think," Kuperman said, "we want to take a look at running a disclaimer before the spot."

He could offer no guidance—conversations with the client over the weekend had agitated, not enlightened, him. Nobody at Nissan knew what to do, only that the agency ought to do something. Kuperman felt bound to accommodate them, but he couldn't figure out how. "Brain squalls," he complained. "Not brainstorms. Just brain squalls."

Sittig was prepared to be cooperative until he heard about the client's suggestion to run a text message that stressed safety. The thirty-one-year-old copywriter, considered his generation's whiz kid, thought to himself, "I'm going to leave the agency. I'm out of here. I *hate* this."

"It'll be completely hypocritical," he complained to Kuperman and Clow. "You'd have to run a Volvo ad for it to make any sense."

There was another idea—point out that the commercial was a fantasy. He hated that one even more. "I don't want to say, 'Sit back and enjoy . . . and keep in mind, it's only a commercial. And it's really neat.' "

Clow was the only one who seemed not to mind the drill. He shared Sittig's irritation, and groused about watchdogs who acted as if people needed to be saved from themselves, but he was more intrigued by the puzzle at hand than he was put out. Clow had dealt with too many odd and irrational requests to get rattled by another one. He'd perfected the art of the finite outburst for really impossible situations; more often he responded with bemused diligence. He liked working in compressed time. People often did their best work on a tight deadline because they couldn't overthink the ideas.

"We only want to do this," he said, in an attempt to calm Sittig, "if we can add to the cool factor."

Sittig would not be placated. He stewed for hours. He thought about all the reasons that people died in auto accidents. Alcohol. Not wearing seat belts. He'd never heard of advertising causing a car crash. Advertising just didn't have that kind of impact. Which led him to the thought: "If advertising was that powerful, then people would believe there's talking fruit in their underwear." Everyone knew the fruit characters in Fruit of the Loom underwear commercials weren't real. Everyone would know the Turbo Z dream wasn't real, either. If he could write a disclaimer that gave people credit for being intelligent, and made the critics look stupid, maybe this wouldn't be such a bad assignment.

By the end of the day Sittig had his disclaimer written, and Richard O'Neill was making up an instant video version to show the client. There was white text against a plain black background:

> *A message from the Nissan Motor Corporation:*
> *Do you believe raisins can dance?*
> *Do you believe beer bottles really play football?*
> *Do you believe there's dancing fruit in your underwear?*
> *If you answered yes,*
> *Maybe you shouldn't watch this next commercial.*

Sittig and Clow also came up with a second, more straightforward effort, though nobody at the agency liked it as much. It read:

> *Americans love cars and the experience of driving. They've even been known to dream about their cars. They dream of windy roads and falling leaves. They dream of city lights reflecting in the shine of their paint. They dream of the wind in their hair and the sun in their eyes. . . . and then some people's dreams are weirder than others.*

The agency sent both versions down to Bob Thomas and Tom Mignanelli on Tuesday, with the strong recommendation that they not run anything at all. As Nissan debated, Chiat/Day submitted both proposals to CBS for clearance. The network refused the disclaimer about the dancing raisins because it was demeaning to other advertisers and accepted the second version. Now the agency had a statement it liked and couldn't run, and one it disliked and could run.

Luckily, by the end of the day Nissan had decided to stand fast and run the spot by itself.

It was a short-lived victory. The sixty-second version of "Turbo Z

Dreamer" ran in the second quarter of the Super Bowl, at a cost of $1.4 million for the time, and never ran again. The thirty-second version was never aired. Follow-up research showed that the spot had the highest recall rating of all the Super Bowl commercials, but Nissan had to abandon it. Despite its public stance in support of free speech and a consumer's ability to discriminate between an advertising fantasy and real life, Nissan could hardly risk continuing to run the ad. All it would take was one grisly accident involving a Turbo Z, and Nissan would become a villain, the company that had encouraged drivers to go too fast.

The agency had behaved just as Chiat wanted it to. The creatives had responded to the client and kept their integrity. Some agencies might see honor and maturity in compromise, but as far as Chiat was concerned they were selling retreat in a fancy package. He wanted his people to behave like adults, but that didn't mean he wanted them to cave in. They were members of an exclusive club, who were supposed to obey an elevated set of rules.

He made them feel set apart from their peers through a combination of indulgence and deprivation. The perks, beyond the oft-repeated reminder that anyone who got to work at Chiat/Day was lucky enough, included the parties and a routinized schedule of gifts: employee anniversary flowers, Christmas and Valentine's Day presents, and an endless run of commemorative T-shirts.

What Chiat withheld was effusive praise—and money. In the early years he had paid his people less than the prevailing rate because he couldn't afford anything more. Now he paid them less because it was part of Chiat/Day's reverse cachet. A senior creative who earned $100,000 at Chiat/Day could, and sometimes did, defect for double that sum from a big New York–based agency. The ones who stayed wore their salaries as a badge of honor, proof that they cared more about the quality of the work than about their compensation.

In the industry's currency, with its stereotype of the burned-out executive who had sold his soul for cash, it was an oddly reassuring incongruity. People still made very good money, and the gap between what they did and could make was a psychological buffer. The joke around town was that the agency's name was Chiat Day and Night, because of the often excessive hours employees put in. But somehow the pay scale, the democratic office space, the constant exposure top executives faced, made it special. This wasn't a job. It was a calling.

Kuperman saw himself—not Clow, who was too much the creative partisan, nor Wolf, who was more concerned with strategy than with morale—as the new club leader. He had inherited Wolf's 320 Club, a watchdog committee made up of a dozen agency lifers and named for the agency's Hampton Drive address. At his first meeting he sat impatiently through the requisite discussion of how to hire and train new people so that they embraced the Chiat/Day way. What he really wanted to talk about was the event that would define his administration, the Agency of the Decade party, celebrating the *Advertising Age* award.

The question was one of tone. Wolf's administration had been characterized by elegant black-tie affairs like the *Spruce Goose* Christmas party. But there had been some grumbling that it lacked warmth, that it wasn't the kind of party that inspired a sense of belonging. Kuperman wanted a party at the warehouse, something loud, raucous, full of memories: old photos, reels of old commercials, a guest list heavy on alumni. He wanted to see people in vintage Chiat/Day T-shirts.

He did not want spouses. "I was thinking of spouses," he said, "but if you have spouses, then you don't get the melding."

He wanted people to feel part of a family again. "What's the general morale?" he asked the people in the room. "Up? Down? Confused?"

"Busy," said Patty.

"The unhappy ones are quitting, which I think is better," said the woman who ran the print production department. "If it's personal or if it's attitude, it's better if they move on."

"There was a post-holiday letdown," said Hank Antosz, the senior vice-president who handled media buying on the Nissan account. "People took time off, found things to complain about. But now they're busy. . . ."

"Once you start working weekends again," said Patty, with a wry smile, "the morale just cranks right up."

CHAPTER 5

The rumors began the last week in January, when *The Wall Street Journal* reported that Reebok planned to divide its United States operation into two units, one for fashion and one for performance, each with its own advertising. Reebok president Frank O'Connell would oversee the lifestyle unit. The performance division would come under senior general manager Stephen Race, a vocal critic of Chiat/Day's work.

There was bad news every day. People who worked at Reebok told people at Chiat/Day that the intramural experiment had failed, although no one had officially informed the agency. They said that a review was a given, that Reebok was already talking to other agencies, that Race was badmouthing Chiat/Day. *Adweek* predicted a review for the performance division, and reported that at least two other agencies had been contacted.

Chiat/Day called Reebok every time a new story surfaced, and each time the agency got the same reassuring denials. Still, the rumors continued. It looked like Chiat/Day would be lucky to keep the fashion business.

Frank O'Connell set up a breakfast for Wednesday, January 31, with Chiat and New York office president Jane Newman. He chatted amiably about the new work he'd just seen—and then stunned them with the news that he did, in fact, want a review for the entire account, to be held in early April. Chiat/Day was cordially invited to participate.

It would be a costly gamble, with almost one fourth of New York's total billings, about $40 million, as the prize. It would require two and a half months of intensive work, at a cost of at least $100,000 for a new round of speculative creative, for the chance to continue with an erratic client who might swap administrations six months down the line and begin the process all over again, a client who had just turned down the best work that New York, Venice and San Francisco had to offer.

Chiat thought about all the effort that had gone into the internal review, and about what it would do to morale to ask those people to try again. Without hesitation, he resigned Reebok.

Bob Wolf was furious. The most upsetting thing wasn't the loss of income. Sure, some people would lose their jobs, but that was a given in this business: win an account, staff up; lose an account, staff down. What really distressed him about losing Reebok was that it fueled Chiat/Day's reputation for not being able to hold on to accounts.

That, in turn, hurt the agency's chances for new business, and got in the way of Wolf's plan to add a "big-time very credible client" every year. The agency had won Nissan national in 1987 and the regional dealer account in 1988, and American Express Gold Card and New York Life in 1989. He'd already endured one $30 million frustration in 1990: Continental Airlines had inquired surreptitiously as to whether Chiat/Day would accept an invitation to pitch; the airline didn't want to be embarrassed by a rejection, but Wolf got the strong sense that the agency was being offered the inside track. He wanted an airline desperately—but Qantas, which Mojo handled in Australia and Chiat/Day serviced through its San Francisco office, vetoed the idea. Having to turn down the Continental invitation gnawed at Wolf for weeks. Now, with Reebok, he wondered how many potential clients would think better of making the call at all.

The Reebok resignation occurred just as the first signs of client budget cuts began to appear throughout the industry, suggesting that Chiat's dire predictions of the previous summer were imminent. Less than two months before, *Advertising Age* had anticipated a 6 to 10 percent increase in ad spending in 1990. Now the magazine predicted as little as 3 percent increase in the automotive category, with cuts to come in beer and computers.

A recession held two dangers for the advertising industry: an increase in account mobility, and a decrease in spending. Anxious clients would look at dwindling profits and decide to shop around for a new agency that would improve sales, or they would cut their advertising budgets to plump up the overall financial picture and placate worried stockholders. It was testimony to the nature of the business that clients could simultaneously find advertising essential and dispensable.

Clow joked that Chiat was to blame for having made his forecast too often, too loudly, until everyone had started to believe him. All he got was nervous laughter in return.

During Wolf's six-month trial run as CEO, the agency had come precariously close to losing Home Savings because of a high attrition rate among account executives. Wolf began his official administration determined to stop the erosion. Although Home was smaller than Reebok, he believed it was essential to Chiat/Day's future. Reebok had a reputation as a tumultuous, personality-driven corporation that had met its match in Chiat/Day. Home Savings was one of the few institutions to have escaped the savings and loan scandal unscathed, thanks to the conservative investment and loan practices endorsed by its founder, Richard Deihl. If Chiat/Day was mature enough to satisfy the needs of a respected company like Home Savings, then surely it could be trusted with an airline or a soda pop. Wolf called the account his "Rolls-Royce." Everyone who worked on Home was on notice to make the client happy.

The new management supervisor on the account was Bonnie Baruch, whom Wolf had been pursuing ever since he arrived in Los Angeles. Baruch had spent three years at J. Walter Thompson's Los Angeles office, and before that, eight years at a small agency where she was eventually made a partner. She was married to media director Hank Antosz, who had been at the agency since 1978, and had spurned Wolf's advances in the past because Chiat/Day seemed, from everything her husband told her, a "boys' club," where the top executives reinforced their exclusivity with after-hours baseball and basketball. This year she caved in, for a number of reasons: the New York office had a powerful woman president, Jane Newman; the notion of rescuing a faltering account appealed to her; and most important, Wolf promised her the chance to work on new business.

Baruch's first responsibility, however, was to stabilize Home Savings. She had a formidable array of tools at her disposal, not the least a voracious appetite for research. At J. Walter Thompson she had worked on the Vons account and become the reigning expert on grocery chains. Now, just three months into her new job, she sounded as if she had been studying savings patterns and trends in home loans for years. Even more important, given the tension between agency and client, she had a style. Ingratiating smiles, supportive glances, the kind word at just the right moment—Baruch used them all to convince both sides that she had their best interests at heart.

The creatives had been trying vainly to come up with an acceptable execution for the spring lending commercial for weeks. The problem boiled down to a lingering disagreement over strategy: Chiat/Day felt it was time to leave the savings and loan scandal behind, claim the high ground, and talk about what Home Savings did well; but the client, painfully aware of every day's negative headlines, felt that Home still had to set itself apart. The agency wanted to produce a series of low-key little dramas about the comforting allure of dependability—the dog who always got out of the way of the lawn mower, the little girl hypnotically swinging back and forth, images that symbolized the bedrock financial services of Home Savings—but the client had turned it down and begged for something more provocative.

On February 1, Home senior vice-president George Winston showed up at the agency for a creative work session. Chiat/Day believed in bringing in the client at the developmental stage, late enough so that he wouldn't fall in love with a bad idea, but early enough to make him a participant, not just an observer. It was important for the client to feel he had a proprietary interest in the work. A middle manager who was involved in the process could be a valued ally when it was time to sell the advertising to his boss.

Winston was a pleasant, prematurely white-haired man, but methodical and hard to budge. He always seemed on the lookout, as though he expected the agency to try to slip something past him. The presentation to Deihl and Home's first vice-president of marketing, Chuck Reed, was only three days away, and it was Winston's job to make sure the agency had work that would satisfy them.

But Clow was tired of what he called Home's "chest-beating bullshit," and had neither the interest nor the energy to generate more ideas based on a strategy he was eager to discard. He had only one new idea to show. The rest were tinkered revisions of existing executions.

Dave Butler, the droll, forty-six-year-old copywriter on the account, had run the Nissan national account until this year, when he was moved over to help stabilize Home and his old job given to Dick Sittig, whom Butler had once turned down for a job. This was something of a demotion in terms both of national visibility and budget, but Butler and his art director partner, Mas Yamashita, had been in the business too long to let their egos get in the way. They took the work given them and did what they could. At this point, the only people they competed with were themselves; every assignment was an internal test.

Butler raised his half-glasses to his nose and recited the spot Reed preferred, called "Us versus Them," which contrasted Home's conservative investment philosophy with savings and loans that put their money into windmill farms or shaky foreign governments.

> *While some savings institutions were investing in pork bellies . . .*
> *. . . Home Savings invested in Tom and Sharon Morrisey.*
> *While others invested in junk bonds . . .*
> *. . . we invested in the Carruthers.*
> *When banks put their money in foreign countries . . .*
> *. . . we put our faith in Pam Gilbert.*
> *As America's largest . . .*
> *Home Savings makes home loans for one, simple reason . . .*
> *we know a good investment when we see one.*

Winston listened, eyes closed, hands clasped, prayerlike, in front of his face. He asked to have it read again.

"I think in this one I'm longing, and Chuck will pound the table, for more specificity," said Winston. He worried that it was too tongue-in-cheek, that the viewer wouldn't understand how risky pork bellies and dictators were.

Jeffrey Blish, the senior account planner on Home for five years, piped up: *"They know."* It was his job to know that they knew. He spent most of his time conducting focus groups to find out how consumers felt about the savings and loan industry.

Winston was unconvinced. "This is the conversation we always have," he complained, "about explicit versus implicit." He asked for a third reading.

"I continue to long for the things you tell me I don't have to long for," he said. In addition to the line, "More people trust us than anyone else," he wanted the script to mention the 563,000 new accounts Home got last year. Why couldn't he have both?

"Because you can't afford more than thirty seconds," snapped creative director Steve Rabosky, a dour disciple of Clow's. "Tell us to buy sixties and we'll put it all in."

Winston tried again. Calling the company "America's number one" took less time to say than "563,000 new accounts." Wasn't there room for America's number one?

Rabosky jumped. "It's like being the head of Hell's Angels," he said. "Number one of a group everybody's suspicious of? And number one doesn't mean much anymore. It sounds like an advertising slogan."

Butler read the scripts for the lawn mower series, but Winston rejected them. He loved the one new idea, an animated Fat Cat banker character who would appear in contrast to Home's solid management, but he knew it would never win approval.

"Those are wonderful commercials," he said, wistfully. "But are they in keeping with us as an institution?"

It was a rhetorical question. Cartoons were not the answer, and everyone in the room knew it.

Rabosky suggested that the lawn mower series had a lot of dignity. Winston fended him off. The "smallness of the visual" bothered him.

"I think," said Winston, raising his voice ever so slightly, "that a good TV commercial has to have an element of drama."

At that Rabosky forgot his manners.

"I can show you two hours of commercials that are brilliant communications and don't have an element of drama," he snarled.

"Will I stay awake?" Winston shot back.

Baruch quickly stepped in and gently chided Winston. The lawn mower series might not be what he wanted to see, but it had tested well with the consumer. Apologetically, Winston backed off a bit.

"There is a notion and a goodness and a purity to it," he allowed, "if no drama. . . ."

"Three out of four ain't bad," said Butler.

The rest of the meeting was taken up with the question of what Winston was, and wasn't, prepared to sell to Reed in advance of Tuesday's session.

Winston said he would recommend "Us versus Them," and explain that the lawn mower series had found solid support among consumers, but Baruch pressed him. She pretended to be Chuck Reed, and said, in a bellowing voice, " 'But are you excited?' "

"I'm going to give him back his standard answer," said Winston, coolly. "It doesn't matter if I'm excited, as long as you're excited."

The tenor of the meeting had shifted subtly. Simply by holding his ground, by withholding enthusiasm, Winston had taken control. Butler and his partner resigned themselves to another weekend marathon, in the hope of coming up with an alternate execution before the meeting, and Baruch, when she was sure Winston was safely out of earshot, expressed her disappointment.

"The frustrating thing is how much time is spent selling the advertising," she said. "Doing great advertising is not it. You have to *sell* it."

The hated word for an advertising agency's relationship to its clients, uttered at Chiat/Day only as an insult, was "vendor." Good clients treated the agency like a partner, bad ones, like a vendor. Being a vendor meant delivering the service that the client wanted to buy—and although Chiat/Day's client list allowed more latitude than most, there were days, on every account, when people felt choked.

The Venice office was hardly hurting for revenues, but Bob Kuperman's ambition demanded a new business win. Wolf could talk about his North American expansion strategy as much as he liked. Kuperman was more a street fighter; he just wanted to go out and bag an account.

He grabbed a half dozen people, including Baruch and account planning director Rob White, a thin, taciturn Scot with a background in mathematics who was one of Kuperman's favorites, a dependable foil for his emotional excess. They crowded into Huey for a fast indoctrination. There was no point to waiting for an invitation to a review. Kuperman preferred guerrilla tactics: Why not make a list of vulnerable clients and try to stage a raid on other agencies?

"We get a list of good creative agencies and see who they've got," said Kuperman. He ticked off the cities they should look at besides Los Angeles—San Francisco, Dallas, Seattle, Phoenix. Then he started laughing.

"Some poor little guy in Phoenix sitting there under the big shadow of Chiat/Day coming down," he said, his face reddening, "screaming, 'I'm going to get that little fucker!' Dum-de-dum-dum. . . ."

The traditional way to grow would have been to acquire new brands from existing clients, but Kuperman had little patience for such a methodical approach. He put the others in the room on notice. The Agency of the Decade wanted new categories, not new brands. He wanted an airline or a fast-food account, and he was prepared to live with the fact that fast-food advertising could be deadly dull. He wanted to exploit Baruch's grocery contacts. He liked the idea of stealing Sprint from J. Walter Thompson's San Francisco office.

Fragrances were an attractive, high-profile category, but Chiat/Day wasn't quite ready for fragrances. The agency had sent Clow to talk to Cher about her namesake fragrance, and Kuperman still marveled at the mismatch—sending a man who cared nothing for appearance to talk to a woman whose appearance was of paramount importance.

Someone suggested going after Kellogg's.

"What if they give us a cereal?" asked Rob White. "Want Ralston-Purina to be pissed?" Ralston-Purina owned Eveready, which was Venice's second-largest client, as well as a lucrative network of potential clients, including cereals, just waiting to be pried from their existing agencies.

It was a reasonable question, and Kuperman knew the answer. He would never do anything that might result in a conflict with a valued client. But business reality was not at issue here. He wanted his team to walk out of the room inspired and impressed by his determination, even if it required him to stretch the truth. "Unless *they* give us a goddamn fucking cereal," said Kuperman of the company that had given Chiat/Day the opportunity to create its most popular campaign, the Energizer Bunny, "tough shit."

hiat's trip to Los Angeles for the Agency of the Decade party should have been a triumphant jaunt. Instead, it was a bittersweet lesson in humility. He arrived in Venice on Friday afternoon, February 2, two days before he'd resigned the Reebok account, barely two hours before the party was to begin. He would have one evening to revel in the past and a weekend to catch his breath before he addressed the consequences of losing a $40 million account.

The party started at five thirty sharp, an early call in deference to employees who were torn between the desire to party and the need to get home, since Kuperman had prevailed and no spouses or dates were invited. The lights in the warehouse went down, the food stations and bar opened up, and everyone migrated onto Main Street, like a pack of college kids heading for the local bar after exams.

People were in adamantly high spirits, defying the bad news of a single week to intrude on the celebration of an entire decade. Most of the newer, young employees wore the bright white commemorative T-shirts that had arrived that afternoon, with "Agency of the Decade" on the front and "(This is the last official Chiat/Day T-shirt)" on the back, since the name change to Chiat/Day/Mojo had become official on August 7, 1989. The shirts only came in one size, Large (in this image-conscious business, few people were larger than Large), so smaller employees customized them with belts, knots, or extra shirts underneath. It was the creative challenge the agency had always faced, in microcosm: How to be unique when you were working with the same tools everybody else had.

The veterans didn't have to concern themselves with style. They proudly wore history on their backs—faded, shapeless T-shirts from an earlier era. There was Chiat's rallying cry, "Good Enough Is Not Enough." There was "Life's a Pitch and Then You Die," "I Survived a Year with Nissan," and "I Survived 1982," when the entire industry was hurt by a recession. These people had lived the decade. That was what singled them out.

Clow planted himself near the Fish, where a TV monitor was playing a reel of Chiat/Day commercials. There was a fresh gash running from the outer corner of his eye, under his cheekbone to his mouth, and he wore a note pinned to his shirt, which read, "It happened at lunch. I'm okay. Don't ask." Clow had been at the building site for his new home, twenty miles down the coast on the Palos Verdes peninsula, when a carpenter dropped a piece of wood that hit him in the face. He gave the same answer to everyone who disobeyed the note and inquired. "I had a tough client meeting, but I sold the ad."

Chiat entered quietly and lingered near the bar that had been set up outside the Fish, a subdued figure in the midst of all the back-slapping congratulations. In the watery light that emanated from the TV set he looked like a ghostly apparition, his white hair and pale complexion tinted an unhealthy blue. A few old friends approached him, but for the most part Chiat could move through this crowd unmolested, as though he were invisible.

There were employees who didn't really know him, people who had been in kindergarten when he started Chiat/Day, and there were employees who knew him but pretended not to. Being an advertising legend had its drawbacks—some people were so terrified of saying the wrong thing to him that they said nothing at all, leaving him to wonder if he ought to pin a note to his shirt suggesting an appropriate topic for conversation, something like, "The situation in Poland." But the joking covered an uncomfortable truth: Chiat had stopped being part of Venice daily life when he left to open the New York office, and now he was a visitor no matter which office he was at. It might be a triumph of managerial planning, but the victory had its sour side.

*　　*　　*

At seven the lights came up and Chiat strode from the bar to the back of the room, where the microphones and speakers were set up for the Ad Punks. As he walked, he changed: he lifted his chin, squared his shoulders, and became the pugnacious rogue who had managed, often in a single, provocative act, both to enthrall his fans and outrage his detractors. Let *anyone* say this wasn't the best agency around and they'd have him to reckon with. The sea of people parted to make a path for him, and a crescendo of hooting, whistles and applause followed him to the bandstand.

He gazed out at the crowd. "It's been mind-boggling, this last year," he began. "Surreal. I got a call from my mother after we were named Agency of the Decade and she said, 'Does this mean you'll get the Honda account back?' "

It was his patented derogatory style. His humorous delivery was meant as praise; it was as close as he usually got to a compliment. The angry version, if he felt he had been let down, could be crippling. No one was exempt. In fact, the closer he was to someone, the likelier he was to express the full range of his feelings. Strangers got subtle modulations of sarcasm, or the occasional hostile outburst. Those nearest to him had been insulted, belittled and dismissed—and then adored and indulged. What bound them to him was that he admitted his mistakes. He was capable of the abject apology, and the contrite gesture, even if he didn't alter his behavior.

He was as harsh on himself as he was on everybody else, which was the one thing that saved him from seeming a dictator. And his demands carried with them the assumption that his people were capable of excellence, a nice bit of recognition from a man whose favorite line was, "Always disappointed, never surprised."

He had fenced in his life with such slogans, the copywriter's equivalent of a life philosophy, spoken in a dialect that this crowd understood and appreciated. His cocky challenge, since the beginning, had been, "How big can we get before we get bad?"—a perfect example of how he pushed and flattered people at the same time. The question suggested the ever present threat of mediocrity; but there was a shared, smug, insider's belief that the answer was, "As big as we feel like." An agency that was in danger of going bad wouldn't be smart enough to ask the question.

"I know how little I've done this decade, so I'm really proud of you." He paused for a long moment. There were baby faces in this crowd, people who were no further from puberty than Chiat was from the traditional retirement age of sixty-five. There were men in the room who were running his business. He had guided the agency through the decade for which it had been honored. He would not guide it through the nineties.

When he began to speak again the edge in his voice was gone, rounded off like a stone worn by the water. "I was such an articulate devil in 1970," he said. "I'll see you in 2000. We'll have a bigger party. Take care."

Kuperman wouldn't let Chiat walk away. This was not the moment for self-effacement. He exhorted his people. "Jay says he hasn't done anything in a decade," Kuperman said. "He *has*. He's changed the industry." Then he announced the latest honor: Chiat had just been named the Leader of the Decade by the Western States Advertising Association of America (WSAAA), yet another inflated title for a man who had already been Leader of the Year, in 1978.

Everyone clapped and hollered. The Jenny Holzer sign flashed: *"Exceptional people deserve special concessions."*

On the Monday after the party, Clow occupied himself with a planning session for his annual creative conference, a spiritual pow-wow for all the agency creatives, complete with guest speakers, custom-designed souvenirs, and games. Wolf met with the North America office presidents—Jane Newman, Fred Goldberg, Kuperman, and Chuck Phillips from Toronto—to figure out what to do about Reebok.

Wolf was matter-of-fact about what he saw as a rather simple business proposition. Fifty percent of the agency's income went to salaries, 30 percent to overhead, and 20 percent, ideally, to profit. He couldn't cut overhead—"the building doesn't shrink"—and he didn't want to cut profit. People had to go.

To maintain appearances, there would be no firings. Instead, the agency would fire by attrition—and if some staffers were encouraged to resign because they had been switched to small accounts or could not manage to get their work produced, so much the better. Wolf wanted to lose thirty people. If that wasn't enough of a cut, he was prepared to consider salary and hiring freezes, as well as a temporary end to spot bonuses, which were payments of as much as $5,000 to individuals who had done a singularly good job. He was going to lengthen the amount of time between salary reviews for people making between $75,000 and $100,000 from a year to eighteen months.

Lest anyone feel squeamish, he reminded them that personnel cuts now were a defense against larger cutbacks later. "If you don't deal with the people side of it, you will fast go out of business," he said. "There are tough decisions you have to make. It's basically very callous sometimes, or it seems that way, but all you're really doing is protecting more jobs. You're saying, 'Okay, I have to do some minor surgery to protect the rest of the body.' "

Chiat had a tendency to agonize that increased in inverse proportion to the need for it. The better his life was, the more inclined he was to poke at it, to worry it until he raised a psychological welt. A billion-dollar award-laden agency, handed to what he believed were capable hands, was enough good fortune to make him very agitated.

But he had taken a vow of silence when he gave over control of the North American operation. He was not going to interfere with Wolf, regardless of how he might feel about what his new CEO was doing, which meant that he needed to find new repositories for his prodigious supply of energy. In the days after the agency party he went trolling for trouble. He met with chief financial officer Pete de Vaux, Clow, and CPA David Weiner to discuss ways to weather a tight economy, and he reminded them that this, as he had predicted, was "hunkering time." He wanted a concerted new business effort, he wanted $250,000 to come out of travel and entertainment costs, and for the record he wanted them to know that he had no trouble at all with the notion of firing people.

De Vaux suggested one expenditure, which Chiat approved: taking $12 million from the agency's cash reserves to pay off $8 million of the agency's bank debt and buy back $4 million in equity held by outside investors. As long as Chiat/Day was running lean, they could afford to chip away at the debt.

Chiat reviewed the year's best creative work with Clow and found it lacking, as he always did, but the exercise seemed to invigorate him. The next morning he hauled the people responsible for producing that work into an eight o'clock meeting, to let them know that he was not so far removed from the agency that he didn't recognize the waste and irresponsibility that was being tolerated in the name of great work.

He read out Clow, Kuperman, production vice-president Richard O'Neill and his second in command, Elaine Hinton, and no matter what explanation they had, he had another complaint. The creatives were spending too much on star directors. The creatives were doing shoddy work, which cost more money to second-guess once shooting started. The creatives were too intimidated by the star directors to stick up for what was right. And nobody was addressing the issue of how to cut production costs.

Everyone but Kuperman was prepared to let Chiat rant until he ran out of steam, posing only the slightest objections, but the new office president seemed to relish sparring with his boss. Chiat suggested that they should discover cheap talent and nurture it, and he wanted to put together reels of spots produced for under $200,000. Kuperman shot back, "Got thirty seconds?"

Chiat persisted. He had another idea. Maybe they could set up an in-house film editor to save the money the agency had to spend on post-production houses.

Kuperman couldn't contain his sarcasm. "Maybe," he said, with an insulted drawl, "we can lead the way back to quality with strong concepts and well-executed ideas."

He had what he considered to be inspiring news. As of today, Clow was going back to work as an art director, as Dick Sittig's partner on the Nissan account. The car company had demanded Clow's more active participation—80 percent of his time, spelled out in a revised contract with the client—and since Sittig was without a partner, Clow was the obvious choice. It satisfied Clow's need to define a role for himself, and offset Nissan's concerns about Sittig, the young upstart.

But Chiat wasn't about to let the meeting end happily, particularly if the news made Clow look like a savior and let everyone else think they were off the hook.

"The work speaks for itself," he said. "That's all that counts, and it isn't good enough. I don't want to hear excuses. Fix it." He walked out the door.

*   *   *

Two weeks after the Reebok resignation Clow sat alone in 3 Mile Island and watched a rough, silent videotape of two men standing on a bridge, one wearing Reeboks, one wearing Nikes. They had Bungee cords tied to their ankles. Together, they jumped off the bridge and sailed into space, the cords billowing above them, until gravity prevailed and the lines jerked taut. The man in Reeboks dangled from the end of the cord, over rushing waters. The Nikes swung, empty. Clearly, Reeboks fit better. Just as clearly, though the viewer saw nothing but the swinging shoes, the Nike owner had plunged into the water, a victim of the wrong choice in performance footwear.

He watched several takes of each shot, removed the tape from the VCR and slammed it on the table.

"I'm going to take this tape and put it on [Reebok CEO Paul] Fireman's desk and say, 'You fucking find an agency that can do a better job than this, you ought to hire them.' "

The "Bungee Jumper" spot had been approved before the Reebok account went into review, and now that Clow had the footage, he was enraged anew. Either the same minds who had found the agency lacking would condemn a great commercial, or they'd run it, and reap the benefits of an association they'd abandoned.

He ran outside to grab Chiat, who watched the tape impassively. After all these years, Clow could still give, and then lose, his heart to what he thought was great work. Chiat was the one who brought the process back down to earth.

"It's not a clear enough product I.D.," he said. "In order to make this the spot it's supposed to be, you need equal product shots. Or take Nike out and do a generic." He anticipated legal problems with any shot that lasted long enough for the viewer to recognize the Nike logo; no one had actually ever fallen out of a pair of Nikes.

Then he broke off, laughing. "Why," he asked, "am I caring about Reebok?" He had called Fireman a couple of times to offer a gentlemanly farewell, and had missed him. Eventually they'd connect and that, Chiat had managed to convince himself, would be that.

He wandered out of 3 Mile Island, back to his cubicle, which was decorated with a collection of photographs—favorite print ads, a posed shot of a trench-coated Chiat leaning on a Checker cab, a sepia-toned high school graduation photo of a dreamy-eyed Chiat, an assortment of baby snapshots, and a scribbled drawing inside a heart inscribed "To Zadie," the Yiddish word for Grandfather. Chiat had three grown children, and each of his two daughters had a child of her own. Eighteen-month-old Hannah and her mother, Elyse, were coming over for a visit this afternoon, and Chiat had a gift for his granddaughter, a big pink plush Energizer Bunny.

When they arrived, he sat in his office chair bewitched, abruptly transformed into a supplicant by the presence of a child who, for the moment, had no interest in him. He waited for her to turn to him, but she was too busy being distracted by Chiat's assistant, Carol Madonna, by flowers on the desk, by the passing scene.

Chiat pulled the Bunny out of its plastic bag and held it out to her. No reaction.

"Tell me when you're going to sleep," he said, ruefully, "and I'll come over."

He waited a beat.

"Don't you watch your TV commercials?"

She ignored him.

"Should I put this plastic bag over my head?"

Before he left, Chiat felt compelled to inform Kuperman of his conversation with Clow and the agency's financial officers, so that he would be prepared if the cutbacks reached all the way to the Venice office. So far, only New York faced raise and hiring freezes, as well as layoffs, but that might not be enough. Chiat felt that it would be wise to begin what amounted to an economic education program, to let employees know that management expected at least two years of account shrinkage. Reebok wasn't the issue. Client cutbacks were the real problem. The entire industry was being squeezed, and agencies that failed to take prudent measures now would face wholesale layoffs in the future. People needed to understand that freezes meant jobs saved. They ought to be grateful for smart, preventive fiscal management, not depressed by its short-term consequences.

Kuperman resisted the idea vigorously. He would tell the department heads, but no one else, in the interest of maintaining morale.

"Your morale booster, kid, is that you still have your job," replied Chiat. "It's like protecting kindergarten kids from the real world."

"It's a question of timing," said Kuperman. "You can't do it after losing a $40 million account. Maybe a month from now."

"But you come into advertising, that's how it is."

Kuperman hesitated, and then spoke in a low voice. "There's some feeling here that, Why should we suffer? L.A. didn't lose Reebok."

At that Chiat exploded. *"What about when L.A. lost Apple?"*

"A lot of these people weren't here then. They didn't know about it. They just know that they work hard and do good work. They don't like what they hear about raise freezes."

Chiat was furious; it was as though his children were spitting and clawing at each other in front of his eyes. How could one office turn against another, when each was painstakingly cloned from the experiment that had been the original Chiat/Day?

"That's a bullshit childish way to look at it," he shot back. "It's not just the L.A. office. It's Chiat/Day. That's what we have to teach, because obviously it's not being learned. We'll have to have mind-adjusting sessions."

The next morning, February 15, everything changed—or rather, nothing changed except for the renewed possibility that it might. Clow ran down the hall, ebullient, full of energy, having just learned that Reebok U.S. Division President Frank O'Connell was out. He would be replaced by John H. Duerden, who handled the international divisions and had hired Chiat/Day's London office in December 1989 to handle the $20 million international account—which covered everything but Great Britain and the United States. Duerden, who would now oversee the business worldwide, might be just the friend the agency was looking for, the man who could choose to reestablish the relationship.

Clow, who still clung to the belief that great work could overcome all odds, was determined to get the Bungee spot on a plane to Boston for a Friday meeting with Fireman. Chiat wanted to be as optimistic, but his field of vision was littered with all the things that might go wrong. He lingered near his cubicle, having missed one call from Fireman, not wanting to miss another. If Chiat was wandering the building, as he liked to do, his assistant's only recourse was to walk over toward Main Street, shouting: "Jay. *Jay!*" He didn't want Fireman to be a casualty of the paging system, so he hung around and mused about Duerden.

"I don't know if we're back in the running," he said. "It could be too embarrassing for them to bite that particular bullet."

He leaned against his cubicle wall and stared out into space. "We'd love to continue," he sighed.

Wolf did what he could, from his side. He flew to Boston to have a breakfast meeting with Duerden and made a speech about the agency's enduring dedication to the account.

"Look, we have been loyal soldiers for three years, trying to make this thing work," he said. "We think you can be great for Reebok. You've been terrific on the international side. We liked working with you there. We're giving you great work now—everybody loves what we've been doing. Not just the stuff that's been produced, but the stuff that's in development." He implied that O'Connell's departure meant there was little internal support at Reebok for the review. Without asking explicitly—which would have made him vulnerable to rejection—he wondered aloud if there weren't some way to make the review disappear so that Chiat/Day could get back to business.

He even suggested a face-saving scenario: Duerden could say that the June back-to-school campaign deadline was fast approaching, so Reebok had decided to postpone the review until that work was completed; then all he had to do was never bring it up again.

Having made his case, Wolf listened. The new head of Reebok admitted that the review was a vestige of the previous administration, but he worried that canceling it would undercut Race. He was worried about the review getting in the way of back-to-school work, but it did seem to have a life of its own.

Wolf committed as much of the conversation as he could to memory, so that he could go back to the agency with an analysis of the odds. His hunch was that Duerden wanted to go through with the review, have Chiat/Day participate, and then choose to remain with the agency. He had promised Wolf a "level playing field." Next to canceling the review altogether, that was probably the most encouragement he could offer. Wolf was prepared to recommend that Chiat/Day re-pitch the account.

Chiat/Day's new home was going up across the street from the warehouse in haughty defiance of the economy, a $16 million investment in commercial real estate at a time when empty new office buildings were offering two years' free rent. Chiat had commissioned a Frank Gehry design amplifying the elements he had introduced in the warehouse, with a copper-covered Treehouse wing joined to a white Boathouse wing by a mammoth pair of binoculars designed by Claes Oldenburg and Coosje Van Bruggen. The project had so far taken seven years, delayed by the question of who had dumped toxic waste on the site and who would remove it, but construction had finally begun on May 1, 1989.

Originally, the agency had planned to move into all three floors of the new building, but the staffing up for Nissan regional had made that move impossible. There were too many people to fit into the new building; the agency would have to keep the warehouse as well.

Wolf and Kuperman wanted to lease space in the new building to a tenant and settle for two floors, or maybe a floor and a half, but Chiat refused to acquiesce. He assumed that a piece of new business, with more revenues and a demand for even more bodies, would spare him that compromise. He was not about to share a work of art with some stranger shopping for floorspace.

At 6:30 A.M. on February 23, a little band gingerly climbed down a wooden ladder into the thirty-foot-deep pit. The construction crew was ready to pour the new building's concrete foundation, but before they did so Chiat/Day intended to bury a time capsule, to be opened in one hundred years. A dozen people from the agency, including Clow, Kuperman, creative director Steve Rabosky, and account planning director Rob White, as well as a still photographer, all in hard hats, picked their way across the pit to the place where concrete machines waited, running and ready.

They had plastic glasses and a bottle of champagne. The time capsule, a neon pink piece of PVC pipe with caps at both ends, sealed with pipefitter's glue by one of the construction site plumbers, was already wedged into the foundation grid. White had assembled the contents, which included three videotapes—a sample reel of Chiat/Day commercials, a focus group discussing lifestyle and a tape of Chiat/Day employees—as well as instructions on how to build a VCR, which might well be obsolete in a century. White packed in souvenir T-shirts, print ads, information about media trends, "since satellite TV should be hysterically funny in a hundred years," and goods from the vending machines. There were Energizer batteries, a Nissan model car, a Home Savings passbook and samples of pro bono work on pediatric AIDS.

One of the workers told the group that they had a five-minute window.

"But I've got a ten-minute speech," said Kuperman.

They opened the champagne. Clow and Kuperman clicked glasses, the others held theirs aloft, and then they threaded their way over to a construction table next to the time capsule. Kuperman faced a dozen familiar faces and the same number of amused, impatient construction workers.

"Thanks," he said. "I hope we're all *here* a hundred years from now, and Chiat/Day's still the most creative agency around."

"One hundred years from now," added Clow, "all advertising will be through ESP, just telepathic suggestions right into your brain. Whoever has the best machines wins."

Then they moved back out of the way and the workers started to cover over the capsule. At the last moment, someone wondered if the archaeologist who discovered the treasure would be able to open the capsule—only to be reassured that the city had instructions on file.

*   *   *

Wolf was in a position to buy Chiat's way into the new building, if he could get his new business strategy off the ground. Chiat/Day had always had good luck pitching entrepreneurial clients looking to break through to a larger audience, and was fairly successful at insinuating its way into a pitch if someone at the agency had a contact at the prospective client. But Chiat/Day was no good at seducing unhappy clients whose distress hadn't yet congealed into the notion of review, or at getting what Wolf called the "water on stone" accounts, the ones that weren't going anywhere at the moment, but might someday. Long-term personal relationships were hardly the agency's strong suit.

Wolf despaired that too many clients still thought the agency was full of dope-smoking dart throwers. The only way to grow the business was to reposition the agency, and to do that he needed help. On Thursday, March 1, *The New York Times* carried the announcement that Don Peppers would be joining Chiat/Day as head of worldwide new business development. After a year's negotiation, Wolf had hired himself a rainmaker—a man who had distinguished himself, during those protracted discussions, by bringing in $107 million in new business to his employer, the Lintas agency in New York.

Chiat/Day had never before felt the need to hawk its wares, but Wolf insisted there was nothing unusual about the hiring, nor about the other outsiders, such as Tom McElligott, who had recently joined the agency. They did not indicate that Chiat/Day was changing, only that it was growing, and required top talent.

"If you look at our growth, which was explosive during the past decade," he told the *Times*, "we've basically done it with the same group that was here in 1983. We recognized that if we were to achieve more growth in the '90s, we needed to supplement that management team."

The only problem was that members of that management team, including executive vice-president Tom Patty, knew nothing about Peppers's hire until they opened their morning newspapers. Being informed was a right at Chiat/Day, one that Wolf seemed to have forgotten. People were almost as upset about not being told as they were with the implications of the *Times* reference to Peppers's "hundreds of thousands of dollars" salary at his previous employer.

*   *   *

The advertising industry was often accused of creating an artificial demand for material goods, of seducing the innocent citizen into yearning for something he did not need or could not afford. The truth was more complicated than that—and depending on one's point of view, either an essential part of a healthy economy or proof of an even more insidious plot to manipulate the collective psyche.

Lee Clow liked to say that any advertisement was a piece of communication. It was not an omnipotent, hypnotic force that somehow overpowered the populace. Its success depended on what was an oddly intimate conversation, given the public arena, between business and the consumer. On one side was the agency, with its focus groups, telephone tracking studies, demographic and psychographic research, creative teams and media experts, all instruments to bend public loyalty toward the client's brand. On the other side was the target customer. Chiat/Day's job was first to identify the type of person who might be interested in a particular product, and then to learn the idiomatic dialect he spoke.

Clow had been preoccupied with figuring out what he called the "point of view of the Nissan brand" since he began working on the account. He relished the mental exercise. Japanese cars had started out as a reliable, economic alternative to American cars. Then the manufacturers began to stress quality as well, adding amenities to what had been basic transportation. Where were they headed? Clow had always believed that the future for Japanese cars was an upscale one. He envisioned Nissan's line as substitutes for pricier European models: the Maxima instead of a mid-range BMW, the Z instead of a Porsche, the Pathfinder instead of a Range Rover. He wanted to position Nissan as the car that made a statement about its owner's intelligence. The consumer should be proud to say, "I'm too smart to spend an extra $15,000 for a hood ornament."

The popularity of Nissan's Infiniti and Toyota's Lexus, two new Japanese luxury lines, was strong evidence that Clow was nudging the company in the right direction. The enduring question was, how best to popularize Nissan's complete model line. Clow liked the Fantasy campaign, particularly "Turbo Z Dreamer," because it defined Nissan as a company that loved cars and made them for people who loved to drive.

Nissan had requested a special meeting in early March, a general review of all the creative work Chiat/Day had generated over the past three years, and in preparation Clow and Patty stayed up late the night before, discussing their vision of the company. The next day they spent a pleasant enough two hours with a group of Nissan officials watching reel after reel of television commercials in a darkened conference room.

But when the lights came up, Bob Thomas surprised Clow with a complaint. Thomas didn't feel that the agency staff listened to the people at Nissan. They were always trying to placate the executives, rather than attending to their needs.

"That's not fair," Clow blurted out, stunned that his best intentions should be so misinterpreted. "We try to listen to what you think. You have ideas, we listen. We have ideas, we hope you listen."

Thomas persisted. The agency just liked to do the kind of work it did best, and ignored client suggestions. He thought a combination commercial that featured several models might be a good idea, and he'd said so, but he had yet to see one.

Clow was appalled. The agency had done a combo ad as part of the previous year's disastrous Stanza introduction, in an attempt to borrow glory from Nissan's better-known models. They'd sworn not to make that mistake again.

"Oh really?" he said, combatively. "Bob, I don't want you going to sleep at night thinking we're not doing what you want us to do, and getting up mad in the morning thinking we're ignoring you because of our omnipotence and arrogance. Just tell us you want a combo. We'll do it. Then we'll tell you we don't like it, but at least we'll have looked into it."

Once he got started, he couldn't stop. "I guess every time you suggest something, we better comp it up or you'll think that we don't listen."

Clow's outbursts had an odd purity to them. He was not a tactical debater. When he lost his temper, his voice rose in an insistent bray, a loud, high monotone that made it seem as though his very soul was complaining. He was defending his honor. He had devoted his life to understanding communication, so that he could teach companies that couldn't reach the consumer how to talk. He was offended at the accusation that he'd acted out of petty, selfish motives.

No one in the room, least of all Thomas, had expected Clow to take his comments personally. People lobbed conciliatory niceties into the air. As they all got up to leave, Thomas said, with some concern, "Somebody calm Lee down."

Hours later, Tom Patty checked in with Thomas. The question of right or wrong aside, someone had to make sure that the client hadn't taken offense.

On March 5, Chiat/Day officially announced the financial consequences of the previous month. New York and San Francisco had instituted salary and hiring freezes. All the North American offices had put a temporary end to spot bonuses. The creative conference was postponed.

In the spirit of austerity, the 320 Club addressed the issue of food. Laurie Coots, Venice's director of administration and business development, and self-proclaimed den mother, reported that the $1,000 monthly pizza tab was only part of the problem. Unauthorized employees who had to work late were using the office charge account to order dinner from the trendy Rose Café across the street. Maybe there ought to be some kind of food rule—like dinner on the agency only if people worked until eight, or cookies only at meetings of an established minimum size.

Patty could not stand the idea of nickel-and-diming people, no matter how bad things got.

"We've got $32 million in income coming in from Nissan and we're arguing over $1,000 food bills for people who are here seven days a week?" he said. "That's insane."

"I just want to know who's getting cookies," said Kuperman.

Media director Hank Antosz offered to bake them at home.

Coots didn't like being teased. "The rule is, to eleven A.M., muffins, eleven to one, lunch, one to five, snacks," she said, brusquely. "We're spending about $4,500 a month on food. If you don't care, fuck it. Fine."

Kuperman listened in disbelief. So this was part of his presidential responsibility—determining whether a meal policy would strengthen office camaraderie, establish a brotherhood of suffering, or demoralize people to the point that it affected their productivity.

C H A P T E R

As the escalator descended to the California Lounge of the Century Plaza Hotel, eight hundred voices rose up over cocktails in a torrential, overwhelming roar of compliment, insinuation, and glad-handed anxiety.

"Haven't you cut off that fucking ponytail yet?"

"Don't worry. No onions, no garlic."

"There's six million people here. I can't remember names."

"Hi, howya doin'?"

"Hi, howya doin'?"

"Hi, howya doin'?"

"Jesus. It smells like somebody died. I mean, it smelled like this in London, but not until the end of the evening."

Thursday, March 8, was the night of the twenty-fourth annual Belding Awards, the West Coast advertising Oscars for creative work, a black-tie gala that was an orgy of self-congratulation, an evening of unchained ego. For one night, the agencies formed a closed society dedicated to the glorification of the advertisement as an art form. No one felt like a vendor at the Beldings. They were the creators of miniaturized entertainments, of images that were as potent a part of popular culture as any feature film or music video.

Nationally televised commercials were drama, condensed into as little as fifteen seconds, which happened to have a product as the central character. Print ads wove similar fictions—they showed the kind of life a woman might expect to lead if she wore a particular line of clothing, or the new respect a man who owned the correct luggage might hope to command. The people crowded into the lounge were proud of the compressed universe in which they had to function. The thirty-second spot or half-page ad was a discipline, not a diminishment. Clow liked to brag about how there wasn't a frame wasted in a Chiat/Day television commercial, and he couldn't think of a feature film that could make that claim. Advertisements had to create a world in no time at all. The Beldings celebrated the advertising agency as if it were a studio that just happened to produce very short features.

Every one of the nominees, in fifty-eight categories, would have its moment of glory, projected simultaneously on five oversized video screens that played to all corners of the banquet room, the television commercials accompanied by their soundtracks, played at brain-numbing levels, the print work displayed to booming rock music. Some were ads that clients had killed, and the ad agency, confident it had a prizewinner, had bought time or space to run the ad once, so that it qualified for deserved glory.

There was no room for memories of the belligerent client, the shot that didn't come off right, the five dozen executions that had died before an exhausted creative team stumbled upon the right one. Even the handful of clients who had been invited were respectful.

The buzz was that the Energizer Bunny was going to do very well—that it had a good chance to win the Grand Sweepstakes. Chiat/Day had purchased $125 tickets for every creative, as well as anyone who was at the management supervisor level, 126 people in all, in addition to $30,000 spent on entry fees. While that might seem extravagant, considering the agency's recent belt-tightening, it was viewed as a prudent investment in morale. Every winner would get to march up to the podium in person, tracked by that spotlight, to collect his bowl, and the account executives would feel they had shared in the victory.

The Chiat/Day people trembled with the effort to stay just the modest side of cocky. Clow buttonholed the *Los Angeles Times* advertising columnist, Bruce Horovitz, and teased him about what negative things he would find to write this year. Clow's mother, who had been so unnerved by the announcement of Wolf's promotion, had blamed the messenger for bringing her what she thought was bad news.

"If you ever see an eighty-four-year-old woman with a walker coming toward you," Clow joked, "you better run."

You were where you sat in the Los Angeles Room. Clout rippled out from a large, sunken center ring, reserved for the likes of Wolf, Kuperman, and Clow, to two crescent-shaped tiers on either side of the main floor. Not that anyone sat still: there was never a moment, from the chilled salad to the chocolate cake and coffee, and on through the awards presentation, when everyone was seated. There were new contacts to be forged, old acquaintances from previous jobs to greet and size up, gossip to be exchanged and rumors laid to rest. One pocket of people at a time would quiet down, as their agency's nominee was announced, only to explode with applause and cheers if it won. Around them the chatter continued, unabated.

The first presenter was actor and commercial spokesman Pat Morita, his arrival onstage preceded by a screening of his most recent Crest toothpaste commercial. There were two awards in the category of single commercial, ten to fifteen seconds, one silver bowl, and one finalist's certificate, both to Chiat/Day for Energizer battery commercials. The Chiat/Day crowd erupted. Clearly, this was going to be their night.

By the time Wheat Thins' Sandy Duncan bestowed a bowl on Chiat/Day, for the thirty-second Fantasy campaign truck commercial, there was only a smattering of applause from the increasingly envious crowd. It was past ten thirty. Patience and goodwill were wearing thin.

The main Chiat/Day table, where Wolf, Kuperman, and Clow and their spouses sat (Chiat had not attended in five years, since his attention shifted to New York), was a jangly, manic mass of bravado. Chiat/Day's fabled arrogance was really little more than a different way to dress up nerves. For all the talk of research and strategy, these men were in the business of selling attractively arranged sand as an appropriate foundation upon which to build a commercial enterprise. Their ebullience tonight was a reaction to the worry that underwrote their daily existence.

Each man saw himself vindicated. To Clow, a Beldings sweep meant that Chiat/Day was still a creative powerhouse. To Wolf, it was fodder for Peppers and the new business mill. To Kuperman, the awards signified that his reign as creative director had been a productive one, however unpopular, and they were a splendid calling card for a new office president looking for accounts. He used to needle Chiat about winning lots of Beldings in all the wrong categories, the dinky ones, like newspaper print. Now they were winning for sixty-second national television ads, high-profile work, and Kuperman had helped to guide the agency there.

He was all cranked up, and not about to tolerate any reminder of his mortality. Kuperman had inherited from his father a stubbornly high cholesterol count, which he battled by adhering, as much as possible, to the strict Pritikin Diet. This was not the night that he wanted to be confronted by Florence Henderson, the spokeswoman for Wesson Oil—a liquid that, he believed, would kill him if it got the chance. Her very presence impinged on his ecstatic mood. When she began to speak, he shouted, "How many people have you killed with too much Wesson Oil? Where are the rolls? This is the time there ought to be rolls flying up there."

He booed a competitor's commercial for the television shows *Wheel of Fortune* and *Jeopardy*, and he complained that Dick Sittig, the recipient of nine bowls, wasn't in his seat with the bowls piled up in front of him. Winning a bowl in every category would have been a perfect night. Short of that, it made a nice impression to stack them so high that people couldn't see around them.

When the agency won the Grand Sweepstakes for the Energizer campaign, as predicted, Kuperman got his chance to speak. "It's nice to get the bowls, and recognition from the community," he said, "but a lot of the work we did I really think was terrific, and it didn't get noticed. The real judge of what we're doing has to be us, not award shows. If we are, then we'll just keep winning awards."

He'd meant to inspire his own creatives to keep working whether they'd won or not, but as soon as the words were out of his mouth he wondered if he'd sounded pompous. He hadn't meant to imply that Chiat/Day was too important to worry about whether it won the Beldings or not.

*　　*　　*

The camaraderie at the Beldings masked a concern that was starting to nag at both Wolf and Kuperman, which was how to police Clow without making it seem that he was being held in check. Clow's problem seemed to be that the new hierarchy was perfectly vertical, save for the ledge built out to one side upon which he was supposed to perch. He had a commanding view, but access was a problem. He was looking to reclaim a piece of territory as his own.

Clow's perfervid devotion to the work, his quest for the grail, might draw clients to the agency, but it could cost both goodwill and dollars if it got out of hand. Kuperman found Clow's behavior particularly disconcerting, since he was such a quick-moving target. He had lost his temper at Bob Thomas. He stole creatives from the account work they should have been doing to help him with the copy and layout on a new business proposal he wanted to present at the April quarterly board meetings. He assigned himself the task of producing video tributes to Chiat, for the April 3 dinner honoring him as the Western States Advertising Association of America Leader of the Decade.

The next time Kuperman looked, Clow had adopted a stalled seven-month effort to devise a corporate campaign for Nissan, a frustrating speculative effort that had so far chewed up one hundred people in various departments at the agency. The problem was that customers perceived Toyota and Honda as the companies that made reliable, quality automobiles, from the top of their product line to the bottom, while Nissan was somewhere out in vague third place, making everything from hot sports cars to mundane sedans. Customers aspired to buy a Toyota or Honda, and then purchased the model they could afford. There was little of that brand loyalty among Nissan owners, in part because Nissan lacked an identifiable personality.

Tom Mignanelli said he had $10 million he would be willing to devote to a corporate campaign, to solve the problem, so Clow had come in at the last minute determined to find him some executions to spend it on. The traditional hand-drawn storyboard would not do. Clow insisted on rough videotape versions of the spots, spliced together from existing footage and affectionately dubbed Ripomatics or Stealomatics. They cost between $2,500 and $3,000, and Clow quickly racked up $19,000 in expenses, which led Kuperman to joke that someone ought to move up the date of the meeting before Clow spent any more.

The problem was that there was no way to stop Clow without sounding like a penny-pincher. Was Kuperman really prepared to niggle over $2,500 if the next Ripomatic was the one that charmed a $300 million client? He reminded anyone who would listen that Bill Bernbach had likened a corporate campaign to a man in a blue suit, pissing: It made him feel warm and good, but no one else noticed. The creatives ignored him. Clow and his troops were the classic model of last-minute creative madness—manic, up all night, living on adrenaline fumes.

While the production department hurriedly assembled a reel, and the creative department art studio comped up ten print ads, Clow and Sittig rehearsed their presentation in 3 Mile Island. Then they reviewed a reel of the competition's corporate commercials, designed to show Nissan what the company ought not to do.

They watched Chrysler's Lee Iacocca talking about the difference between Japanese and American product.

"We got more airbags," said Iacocca.

"We got more *windbags*," hollered Sittig.

"And who's done more about safety than we have?" asked Iacocca.

Clow and Sittig answered in a single voice. "Volvo! Audi! Mercedes!"

The day after the Belding Awards ceremony, Clow, Sittig, Rabosky and Patty drove south to Nissan's Carson headquarters to present the work, with a three-foot cushion of pride between the soles of their shoes and the ground. They'd swept the Beldings. Surely they could sell a corporate campaign to Nissan.

They came home empty-handed. Mignanelli, Bob Thomas and Thomas's counterpart in the Infiniti division had rejected everything. The work was what the executives called "bottom-up" advertising, small stories that might humanize the corporation but did not evoke its substance and size.

"Expand the monolith," said Infiniti's Bill Bruce. He wanted to impress the consumer, not chat with him.

Just like that, any hope of a corporate campaign was dead, the money spent on it gone, irretrievably. If Clow was unconcerned about how much this exercise in integrity had cost, both financially and in terms of the agency's credibility, Kuperman was deeply worried. Thomas's accusation that the agency didn't listen haunted him. What else could the people at Nissan think, if the best creatives in the office offered up a completely inappropriate set of corporate executions? Kuperman began to think he might have to assert himself, as president of the Venice office, and remind Clow that, at least in terms of Nissan, he was in charge. He resolved to mention the problem to Chiat. No one else could challenge Clow.

CHAPTER 9

Don Peppers *looked* disconcert-
ingly, if appropriately, like a
computer print-out come to life. His flawless, milky skin was as
smooth as fine paper, and his piercing eyes darted like animated
pin-dots. He had hyphen eyebrows and a small, straight mouth set
between two parentheses. Thin, dark brown hair shot back from an
impossibly clean hairline. His elegant, uncluttered clothes were in
solid colors, neutral tones, simple shapes in gradations of hue, something even the most rudimentary graphics software program could
generate.

Peppers appeared at Chiat/Day's Venice office a week after the
announcement of his hiring, ready to put plans into action, and held
court in the Boathouse, sitting on one side of the long narrow table
while a handful of locals—representatives of media, account services
and account planning—lined up across from him.

His very presence retired the question of whether Chiat/Day should
be getting bigger. "An agency that isn't growing is a dead agency," he
said. "If you're not getting new clients, something's wrong." Peppers
was there to tell everyone how. One of the best ways was the "door
opener," a presentation that had nothing to do with advertising but
might help Chiat/Day get invited to a pitch. It wasn't possible to tell
a major client anything about his business that he didn't already
know, not without spending $100,000 on research. Better to walk in
a smart side door with a provocative topic for discussion that related

tangentially to his business. Someday, a client would respond favorably; it was just a matter of knocking on enough doors.

Peppers fervently believed that the time was right for an assault, because he anticipated a revolution in the way the industry functioned. For the past thirty-five years, broadcast television—the three major networks and the independent stations—had been the dominant advertising medium, and advertisers had bought sheer numbers of viewers. All that was changing. Cable television gnawed at the broadcast audience, taking it down from over 90 percent of prime-time viewing in the 1960s to 60 percent in 1990, and tempting advertisers with smaller but more select audiences.

"As long as media is mass—when the consumer had no choice, when it was networks—you could fuck the consumer all day long with ring around the collar, because she had to get up and turn off the set to avoid it," he said. "With cable and interactive sets, with that remote control, you can't do that. It's got to be the polite invitation, instead of the harangue."

Advertising was going to have to change with the media it used. If Chiat/Day jumped ahead of the pack with an understanding of how to speak to consumers who no longer *had* to watch their ads, disaffected clients would turn from the competition to them.

What the agency had to do, immediately, was build a computerized network of contacts and start sending out mailings. The one trick was to have only the right people contribute names. "I don't want bozos mailing out," Peppers warned, "or kids, or short termers. One qualification also might be, a person who's willing to make more contacts. You meet at a meeting, a pitch, in a cold call, in a cold letter. Any of those can be transformed into a first-name contact.

"Any voice contact is an acceptable first-name item. People at a conflicting account we'll track but not contact. Then, if we lose the account and lose the conflict, we'll contact them. It's all doable. Just think about letting it bubble up. You've got a month to put together a list."

The others filed out, somewhat numbed by what they'd heard. It was as though they'd been driving along at a respectable sixty miles an hour when all of a sudden Peppers passed them doing an effortless ninety-five.

*   *   *

Before Peppers could get his program up and running, a $25 million opportunity walked in the door, costing no more than the price of a local phone call and ten minutes of an executive's time. Jim Weinstein, director of account services at Chiat/Day, had heard a rumor that Century 21 Real Estate was unhappy with its agency, McCann-Erickson, and at Wolf's instruction he made a cold call to see what he could find out. Weinstein despised cold calls—they were such transparent supplication—but he managed to be properly glib, and to remind his contact that Chiat/Day would be the perfect agency for the account.

To his amazement, the contact agreed, said that Century 21 was going to hold a review, and Chiat/Day would be invited to participate. Simple as that.

There was something grumbling in the creative department about the choice of targets. Century 21 was a franchise operation whose realtors, like the Nissan dealers, dictated the kind of advertising they wanted to see. It could be a difficult account, requiring ads that spoke to two disparate groups at once—the prospective home buyer or seller as well as the agent who wanted to do the selling. It would not be inspiring work. The creatives got hold of a Century 21 reel and dismissed most of what they saw as beneath their dignity.

But the excitement of going after a $25 million account won out. This was the new administration's first opportunity to pitch. Every-one—even those who wondered about going after such an account—had a reason to want to win.

A week later Wolf was back in New York, trying to convince Chiat, Jane Newman and the account executive on Reebok that the agency ought to participate in that pitch as well. The Bungee spot had aired during an NCAA basketball game on CBS on March 17, and the following night on the Fox situation comedy, *The Simpsons*. The next day the networks and Reebok were deluged with calls from concerned parents who feared their impressionable youngsters would try the death-defying stunt themselves. NBC refused to run the spot, and ABC worried about whether the Nike logo was too easy to see and the typed disclaimer too hard. Every aspect of the controversy found its way into newspapers and onto the nightly television news. Chiat/Day had gotten Reebok a priceless amount of publicity, the sort of extravagant press coverage that all the media dollars in the world couldn't buy.

But the agency had to be cautious, since bravado never won a piece of new business. Wolf wanted to address three questions: Did they still want the business; if so, under what circumstances; and how could they get it back? The first question was easy. Wolf wanted the business. He was satisfied with the circumstances, since he believed the client's promise of a level playing field.

How to get the account back? They made up a list of rules. First, someone would talk to Duerden to make sure Chiat/Day had a real shot—that being invited to the pitch wasn't part of a public humiliation scenario. Second, the agency wasn't going to turn itself upside down producing new work, but would continue with the work in progress. Third, Chiat/Day would seek reassurances that the relationship would be less rocky than it had been in the past.

Wolf caught up with Duerden back in Los Angeles, liked what he heard, and convinced the others to get back into the pitch. The only dissenter was Tom McElligott, who had gotten caught up in the intramural competition and worried about what the effort would do to New York's exhausted creative teams. Wolf reassured him. The agency had always done well as the underdog—better, ironically, than it was doing as the Agency of the Decade. A long shot might be just the thing to rejuvenate people.

Chiat/Day was scheduled to present in three weeks, on April 11. Creative teams in New York, San Francisco, and Venice went to work on executions with the tag line, "How far can you go in a pair of Reeboks?"

The executives who had been at this long enough knew that they were essentially helpless, that even their best efforts could fail with a client who had his own agenda—someone in middle management looking to clamber up the ladder on the back of what he decided were bad ads, someone with a relative at another agency who was providing a running critique of where Chiat/Day was going wrong. The best relationship with a client could be broadsided by a new hire who felt like cleaning house, by a hungry competitor who offered discount commissions, or by a more socially adept agency offering ski weekends.

In the weeks before the pitch, Wolf found himself reminiscing about the first time he had lost and won Reebok. The agency had pitched the account in October 1986, just months after losing Nike, but the presentation—the twenty-eighth pitch Chiat/Day had competed in that year—had been so stale that midway through his speech Wolf realized he was boring himself.

Reebok went to Ammirati & Puris Inc., which resigned it four months later. The client asked Wolf for help on the back-to-school project, and accommodatingly he flew to Boston—but his real intent was to corner CEO Paul Fireman.

Fireman invited Wolf to join him on a plane ride to Chicago. Wolf still savored the details of that two-hour flight. "I figured, my mission on this plane is to get the account, sell them on a campaign idea, keep them focused—and not just get some audition for Chiat/Day. I talked to him about how they had hired the wrong agency for the right reasons. I told him we had done terribly in the pitch, but we were really the best agency and would do the best work. There was no way I could go back and ask my people to get all pumped up on some audition. He wouldn't get the best work. Anyway, if he hired us that day, it certainly would look like they had the agenda and not Ammirati & Puris. No one picks an agency that quickly.

"So he said okay. Before we hit the ground."

The story was not parallel to the current situation—Wolf had not convinced John Duerden to hire the agency without an audition. But the content was not as important as the outcome. Things had worked out well in the end. That was all that mattered. Wolf had started out thinking, it could be Chiat/Day. He proceeded to, it will be Chiat/Day. By the time he'd gotten on that plane with Fireman, Wolf had known, it *is* Chiat/Day.

He needed to convince himself of that, again, by April 11.

Home *Savings approved* the "Us versus Them" television commercial, but the client's eye was bigger than his wallet. The final script required five locations: three handsome homes, a pig farm and a mansion that could double for a foreign dictator's palace. Richard O'Neill instructed George Winston, "Pick two out of three—good, fast, and cheap," only to be told, without hesitation, that fast and cheap were the priorities. The agency had figured that the spot would cost a half million dollars. Winston told O'Neill he had $300,000. Maybe $350,000.

He also refused to spend money on weather insurance, which would have bought him a free replacement day. The message behind his decision was clear: Chiat/Day had to figure out how to shoot all the scenes in two days, whatever the weather.

On the first day out, it poured. The crew was supposed to shoot three locations on Monday and two on Tuesday, but by late Monday afternoon, when the rain stopped just long enough for a single shot, it was clear that they would have to shoot four locations on Tuesday. There was no longer any question of shooting the three homes in the most flattering afternoon light. They would be shot in whatever light nature provided.

By early afternoon on Tuesday the crew was camped out at the home of Pam Gilbert on Shadybrook Drive, a quiet, secluded street above Sunset Boulevard in Beverly Hills. The three families appearing in the commercial were all Home Savings customers, hand-picked to reflect the cross section the client wished to reach. In addition to Pam Gilbert, the sunny single mother, there were the Morriseys, a well-to-do white middle-aged couple with a dog, and the Carruthers, a prosperous black couple with two children.

Gilbert's house was ranch style, set into a gentle slope, surrounded on that bright afternoon by equipment trucks, production troops and agency representatives. The idea was to show Pam Gilbert, her teenage daughter and young son standing proudly in front of their lovely home, their security provided by Home Savings, their dependability in reassuring counterpoint to the marginal investments favored by less trustworthy lending institutions. They were the beneficiaries of Home's largesse, and they were the foundation of its business.

The director, British photographer and director David Bailey, stood across the street, consulting with art director Mas Yamashita while a camera truck with a large crane edged into position. He had decided that he wanted to shoot each family in the same distinctive way, with a swooping shot that began high, and to the left, and then pulled down and across to where they stood. He tried the shot again and again, coaxing different expressions from the children, working on the son to effect nonchalance until his sister nudged him to attention.

Once satisfied, he dismissed the youngsters and focused on their mother. Pam Gilbert was the star of the spot. Her face would appear a second time, alone, as Home Savings spokesman George Fenneman intoned, "We put our faith in Pam Gilbert. Home Savings. America's largest. We know a good investment when we see one." The hairdresser fussed over Gilbert's tailored short hair, the make-up person ministered to her natural look to make it appear even more natural, and then she was ready. Bailey peered at her from behind the camera. He turned to Mas Yamashita.

"What's her look? Quite happy?" he inquired.

Yamashita nodded.

Bailey turned toward Gilbert and yelled across the street. "Okay. Quite happy! Sweet smile!"

A week after the shoot, after a weekend sacrificed to the chance to work with a favored editor, Butler and Yamashita had a rough cut of "Us versus Them"—which meant they had physical evidence of just how much trouble they were in. They had two problems they could not fix: the light wasn't as gorgeous as it might have been, and Bailey's swooping shot showed a lot of house but never gave the viewer a good look at those reliable mortgage holders. The two of them hovered uneasily outside Steve Rabosky's cubicle to show him the tape, careful not to betray their misgivings. Maybe they were so tired that they'd overreacted.

Rabosky popped the tape into his VCR, and O'Neill joined the group.

"It needs music," Rabosky said, glumly. *"Bad."*

"It needs glue," allowed Butler, cautiously.

Rabosky watched the spot three more times in quick succession.

"I think you ought to look—and maybe you did—at the pig scene," as something that needs more movement," he said. "The other black and white stuff has activity. I wonder if you ought to look at the first scene and make it do more than it does, so it fits in."

O'Neill explained that he'd asked the editor to fit the footage to the copy, about investing in pork bellies, which was why they had so many static broadsides of the pigs.

"That's a noble cause, but I don't think you're going to get anything but 'pig,' " said Rabosky. "Either change the pig or change the other two, and you can't do that."

He sighed. "The people. We never shot static shots, did we?"

"Don't look at me," said O'Neill. "I'm pissed as shit."

"That camera move is real distracting. You never show me the people long enough for me to see them."

"But then you wouldn't see the house."

The more Rabosky thought about it, the more gripes he had: He didn't like the people, he didn't like the pigs, he didn't see where they could wedge in a reference to $11 billion in loans that the client now wanted to include, and he couldn't think of any satisfactory way to cut between the color and black and white segments.

"Right now, you know what it's like?" he asked. "A Century 21 commercial. It needs something to give it character. What we needed was a locked-off portrait of the people."

As far as he was concerned, "Us versus Them" lacked humanity. Like Clow, he believed that there had to be a personal message inside this ad, an invitation to trust Home Savings with the biggest investment in most people's lives. A home was an emotional as well as a financial commitment. He had to find away to appeal to the consumer's heart, not his head.

"However you do it fucks it up," he said. "What you want is the widest contrast—a dictator and then a family. As soon as you bring in a house, it's not a family, it's a business proposition. It dilutes everything. You have to put it in human terms, not business terms. If it's business, you're the same as everybody else."

He watched the spot one more time and got an idea. If they slowed the color footage of the families down to six frames a second, from the normal twenty-four, and cut off the swoop at each end to use just the footage of the families, perhaps it would work.

A week later, after another weekend in the office, they were ready to show the rough cut to Winston. Rabosky, the creatives, O'Neill, and the account team packed into a tiny editing room, surrounding Winston, and showed him the spot. The pigs were much more active than they'd been the first time around, and the families appeared in portraits, moving very slowly, almost frozen in time.

"Are you guys happy with it?" asked Winston.

A chorus of voices responded, "Yeah."

"Nah. It stinks," said Butler.

They watched again.

"Very nice," said Winston. "Very nice."

Yamashita requested one more showing.

"Many more," said Winston, graciously.

After the last viewing he had one question. "Why are the portraits in slow motion?"

"It's more dramatic," said Rabosky, who had had a week to come up with an excuse. "Regular speed is boring."

"And it's romantic," said Butler.

"It distracted me," said Winston. "I was more taken with the motion than the people."

Rabosky could not afford to let Winston dwell on the motion, since they had never shot the families with a stationary camera. "I don't know if I agree with you," he said. "I don't think there's enough motion to be a distraction."

Conversations about a rough cut were always tricky. Chiat/Day's reputation for not listening often made clients more stubborn about their point of view. They came to the debate on the defensive, wanting to be heard, yet hoping that the agency had an answer for every complaint.

Winston yielded to Rabosky on the slow motion, only to find fault with the third shot of the pigs.

"Maybe it's too contrasty," he suggested. He studied a freeze frame. "Is that—a *snout?*"

"We love that snout," said Yamashita.

Patiently, Rabosky explained that it was a carefully matched shot, a close-up of the face of the pig seen in the preceding shot.

Winston was not impressed. "You work hard to match that shot?"

Rabosky bristled. "Yeah. We . . ."

". . . and directing that pig," laughed O'Neill, hoping to avoid an argument.

"Well," sniffed Winston, "it's not the shot I would have chosen, but I'll defer to your judgment."

They watched one more time.

"This is a great spot," said the client. "I think you've got a winner here. Good work, gang."

Outside the editing room, Baruch cornered Winston.

"You think Chuck's going to like it?" Baruch asked.

"Yeah."

Kuperman dreamed of retiring to a perfect little cottage in the countryside near London, someday, to paint and linger over tea with his wife, but that was years away. Still, he wondered if it was worth dying for. He had done what an office president was supposed to do. He had accepted an invitation to accompany fourteen visiting Japanese employees of Mitsubishi for a night on the town. He'd hopped from one bar to the next, drinking gamely at each one. Now it was one o'clock in the morning, and he found himself loudly singing Doobie Brothers songs off key and waiting to die.

The Japanese contingent had insisted on a blowfish feast at a Gardena restaurant, and, while Kuperman was as adventurous an eater as his health regimen allowed—married to a woman who owned a cookbook store, himself an accomplished amateur Chinese chef—he had never eaten anything that could kill him instantly if it was prepared incorrectly.

He had also never purposely insulted a client, and turning down the blowfish would rank as a serious affront. When the platters came out he looked at his companions, and they at him, hoping that someone else would take the first bite. Finally, one brave soul tried the fish, and lived. The rest, including Kuperman, dug in.

The next day he came to work feeling immortal, facing what he anticipated would be the first of many wonderful meetings with the agency's newest client and Kuperman's personal pet, the $5 million Taylor Made golf club account. He was an obsessive golfer who built weekends and vacations around the sport whenever possible, and he had pursued the account for almost a year, devising a campaign himself and politicking until he succeeded in prying it loose from its old agency, Ketchum Advertising.

He was going to nurse this account through the process himself, sitting in on everything from creative sessions to today's media planning meeting. If anyone wondered what the office president was doing, devoting his time to such a tiny account—or what the office was doing with Taylor Made at all, given Wolf's dismissive attitude about small accounts—Kuperman patiently explained that this was just the kind of small account Chiat/Day ought to have. It was an account with potential. The baby boomers were about to become arthritic. He expected a lot of runners, touch football casualties and tennis veterans to switch to golf in the coming decade, and when they did, Chiat/Day and Taylor Made had a golf club to sell to them.

C H A P T E R

The *mandate from Nissan* was clear, although it was unlikely that anyone in the scrubbed hallways of the company's headquarters, nestled between two major freeways, had ever boiled it down as succinctly as Sittig had: As he saw it, all the agency had to do for the 1991 model year was change the public perception of the Nissan Sentra—"from shitbox to dreamcar."

The problem was that the Sentra had been too successful at the bottom of the "basic small" car category, the kind of $5,000 bargain that attracted price hunters and first-time buyers, not enthusiastic motorists. The discount shopper, or the kid getting his first car, was a notoriously fickle consumer who couldn't even be counted on to replace one Sentra with another. If his income stayed the same, he'd buy whatever was cheapest the next time he needed a new car. If he ever got any money, he'd buy what he wanted, and since his Sentra had been a practical, not a passionate choice, he had no qualms about switching brands. To get people onto the Nissan aspirational ladder, to latch onto loyal consumers on the bottom rung—so that they could spend their car-buying years moving up to other Nissan models—the company decided to pursue a new, somewhat more affluent consumer. Clive Witcher, the head account planner on Nissan, estimated that 40 percent of the current Sentra market was comprised of what Nissan called "enthused" drivers. It needed to be higher.

The Toyota Corolla and Honda Civic, which were Sentra's primary rivals, both attracted young professionals at the beginning of their earning curves, while many Sentra buyers were blue-collar workers whose income potential was comparatively flat. Sentra buyers tended to look at Corollas and Civics and decide they were too expensive, but Corolla and Civic shoppers rarely deigned to consider a Sentra. The cross-traffic from Toyota was from entry-level Tercel buyers, which was something of an insult.

To get those Corolla and Civic consumers, Nissan had redesigned the 1991 Sentra, smoothing out its boxy lines and adding what everyone referred to as "European styling cues"—a generally more rounded design, as well as specific features like wrap-around side moldings and color-coded bumpers. The basic model would cost $7,995, and a sportier version almost $12,000, facts that had not yet been shared with the nation's Nissan dealers. The Sentra was still far from being an expensive car, but a lot of price-driven showroom traffic was going to disappear. Nissan and Chiat/Day had to embark on an education program, to prove to the dealers, and to consumers, that the 1991 Sentra was a better choice than the firmly entrenched competition.

The one thing that had not changed was Nissan's sales expectation. The Sentra had always been the company's high-volume model, with sales of over 217,000 in 1989. Half the Nissans on the road in Los Angeles were Sentras; nationwide, they made up one third of the company's sales. Although Nissan reduced its sales goal slightly, to allow for discount customer defections, Sentra was still supposed to be the sales leader. Nissan wanted to sell 660,000 cars in fiscal 1991—165,000 of them new Sentras.

It was time to begin work on the advertising for the 1991 model year—the planners had already been staging clinics and focus groups for six months, and the creatives needed to start up in March in order to have a finished campaign in the fall—but the Nissan account was in an unnerving state of flux. Just when people should have been thinking about cars and target consumers, they were wondering about basics like structure and chain of command. Everything that could move—executives, budgetary allocations, even the physical space from which the work was to be done—did, and then moved again.

No one at Chiat/Day was entirely certain who had the last word on creative work—Sittig, Rabosky, Clow, who continued to look at everything, or Kuperman, who intended to do so—and a memo from Tom Patty anointing Dick Sittig as Nissan creative director only increased the tension. For that matter, no one knew what to make of a new chain of command at Nissan. Ronald Hannum, late of the parts division, had been named the new marketing manager, and was supposed to assume much of Bob Thomas's responsibility for advertising, leaving Patty with a crumbled primary client relationship and Sittig with a bad case of lowered expectations. Sittig normally gained a good deal of his momentum by pushing off against the perceived dullness of the people he worked for, but there was a fine line between inspiration and suffocation. "It used to be a joke," he complained, "that the guy in charge of advertising used to be in charge of wing nuts. But in this case, it's true."

The regional side of the account was even more of a mess, though the extent of the problem was being kept secret from the people who would be most affected by the solution, the ones who worked on the account out of the Venice office. Nissan had informed Chiat/Day at the end of February that regional wasn't working. Taking the advertising away from regional agencies and plunking the whole account down in Venice had turned out to be too drastic a move, so Nissan wanted a compromise: the agency had six weeks to figure out how to set up a network of satellite offices in Atlanta, Dallas, Chicago, San Francisco, New York and Los Angeles, to become operational on August 1.

Everyone who worked on the Nissan account had a case of the shakes, except for Patty, the one man who arguably had the most to do. Singlehandedly, he compensated for all the melodrama that Chiat, Clow and Kuperman supplied. No matter what happened, Patty never got ruffled; a monstrous challenge was not a crisis, but merely a welcome test of his mettle.

The only visible excess in Patty's life was his rigid discipline. He awoke at five each morning to meditate, take a run on the beach and, if weather and time permitted, go for a swim in the Pacific. He was at the office by seven-thirty at the latest, in his standard uniform— white shirt, dark slacks, tie and one of several pair of extravagant cowboy boots. Twelve hours later he went home, usually chatting with Bob Thomas by car phone on the way there. After dinner he settled in to read, usually a history or biography. Patty had been known to throw Churchill at a reluctant client or a recalcitrant creative. The way he saw it, crisis was simply the result of poor planning. The long view was essential.

Patty's biggest concern was that the agency figure out how best to spend the $800 million Nissan was prepared to spend on all the aspects of its marketing plan—national, regional, dealer co-op ads and discount promotions. For the past three years, Nissan had pulled the financial rug out from under the national brand advertising in the final months of the year, and switched funds over to regional discount programs, like contests and incentives. It was necessary to improve short-term sales figures, but Clow called it a "vicious cycle." National built the brand. Any discount ad diminished it by implying that there was something wrong with the car, that cut-rate prices meant a cut-rate product.

This year, Chiat/Day had implored the client to take a more task-oriented approach to budget allocations. The agency wanted to break down the budget on a job-by-job basis and get Nissan to guarantee each figure, to avoid a last-minute shortfall. Nissan agreed to let the agency come up with an overall spending plan for the first time, and Patty was determined to get it right.

On March 16, Patty and three of his account executives papered the walls of the Treehouse with their calculations to walk Kuperman through the process.

They'd drawn a pyramid and labeled it "Hierarchy of Needs." At the top was "brand/product," at a total of almost $110 million, with estimates of $63 million for brand and $44 million for miscellaneous. Next was national events at $24 million. Regional marketing got $165 million, dealer co-op ads got $50 million, and the discount promotions got a whopping, frustrating $445 million, for a total of 791 million.

Kuperman climbed up onto the conference table and sat, cross-legged, while he studied the chart.

"What the fuck is miscellaneous?"

"Niche. Motorsports," said sports car account executive Penn Pendleton, referring to special ads announcing racing victories.

Patty interrupted. He was not about to let Kuperman get fixated on bad news first.

"Wipe your mind clean," he instructed Kuperman. "Say for this exercise that you have $110 million for the brand. We've had less than that before. We've had $75 million."

Kuperman was equally determined not to be lulled by good news. As creative director, he'd had the final say on regional ads. He knew that the national money didn't mean a thing if the regional ads were junk—and he worried that decentralization was going to make policing the creative much more difficult.

"The problem," he said, "is that what we had was a regional effort under our control. Now we'll have $110 million for the brand against $165 million totally out of our control. A whole lot of shit's going to hit the fan. Our brand part is going to be an even smaller part of the whole the consumer sees."

"That's what Lee just said," said Patty, dejectedly.

"Great minds think alike," said Kuperman. "And there's going to be idiotic stuff. A lot of stuff out there's going to be idiotic."

"Okay," said Patty. "But look at that $110 million figure and tell me what your priorities are. To launch the Sentra? If you want to launch the Sentra in any way that's effective, you need $43 million." That would pay for producing television spots and buying media. The biggest, costliest purchase would be network television: the plan called for three week-long flights of television, a "flight" being a block of continuous advertising time. The first would be a three-hundred-point network buy on programs that potential Sentra buyers were likely to watch—a saturation buy, since each point represented 1 percent of the target audience. A commercial could be placed to reach every member of its intended audience three times, or 60 percent of that group five times—or, as media buyer Hank Antosz liked to joke, one member of the proper demographic group three thousand times.

"I want more money on the first flight," said Kuperman. "Bomb the hell out of them."

He could have it, explained one of the account people, but then he'd lose the third flight altogether. There wasn't enough money for both.

"What about print?" asked Kuperman.

Six million dollars, came the reply, for any one of a half dozen media models the agency had prepared.

Kuperman sprawled on the table and rubbed his forehead, as though trying to erase an unpleasant image. "So we've spent $49 million to launch a car that has nothing to do with the brand image."

"Don't *say* that," said Patty. "We'll have the same problem with Sittig we have on the Stanza, where he can't stand the car."

"This is my personal opinion. It's not communicated to anyone."

"It's communicated to us."

"Sentra's a great car," Kuperman recited. "Stanza's a great car. We've got $60 million left."

They debated spending money on the Maxima, one of Nissan's most popular models and an advertising success story for the agency. Last year's Fantasy campaign spot about the four-door sports car, which introduced a critically acclaimed, sporty redesign of what had been a nondescript sedan, helped to boost sales from 63,630 in 1988 to over 97,000 in 1989. Perhaps they could forgo a new Fantasy campaign spot for the Maxima, run last year's commercial and spend the money on another model.

The car that needed help was the Stanza, which was overshadowed by Honda's Accord and Toyota's Camry, but Sittig wanted to banish it from the Fantasy campaign because he figured the bland customers who bought the car were too dull to dream. A regional campaign, the Stanza Challenge, had boosted sales by offering $100 to anyone who test-drove a Stanza, and then an Accord or Camry, and didn't buy the Stanza. The creatives would just as soon the Stanza remain a regional project forever.

"How about the idea that if you support the Maxima, you help the Stanza?" said Kuperman. The Stanza was one step down in price and luxury from the Maxima, and a favorite theory was that promoting the Maxima would encourage people who couldn't afford it to settle for a Stanza.

"That's like saying the moon's made of green cheese," said Patty. "It makes no sense."

"It would only work," said one of Patty's men, "if Stanza's position were already established."

Kuperman explored his forehead again. "So we're doing Sentra and Stanza next year. What an exciting fucking year we're going to have."

"Unless in the Fantasy campaign you can put more than one car in an ad," said Patty, echoing the Bob Thomas suggestion that had so infuriated Clow.

At that Kuperman leapt off the table and started pacing back and forth, yelling. The benevolent executive act only worked up to a point.

"You sit and wonder how bad advertising gets turned out?" he screeched, so that people walking by the Fish instinctively moved a few feet out of the way. "You start with such a fucking pure idea, and then you're sticking more than one car in an ad."

Patty insisted. The customer demographics for the Pathfinder sport utility vehicle, the Z sports car and the Maxima overlapped. Why not advertise all three in one commercial, and then give Sentra and Stanza each their own spots?

"You can't have a dream with mixed images," said Kuperman. "It's confusing. The imagery is about a single dream of one car. That's why it works."

"Why can't people dream about a brand?" asked Patty.

"Because people don't dream about a brand. They dream about a specific thing they want."

"People don't dream about Mercedes?"

"We're not in that position, and we can't do it until we are." Kuperman suddenly broke off and turned to study the pages on the wall.

"What do we need to do this right?"

"A billion," said one of the men.

"And dump it all at the top of the pyramid," said another.

What they wanted was $100 million to spend on national brand advertising instead of $63 million; but the only fat in the figures Patty had worked out with the executives at Nissan was the contest and incentives allocation. That was the last place the dealers would tolerate a cutback.

There were really only two choices, neither one acceptable: to do fewer things, which would frustrate the agency, or to do them all in fewer places, which would upset the people at Nissan. Nissan had a 4 percent share of voice, which meant one of every twenty-five car commercials. The company did not want that number to decline. A third, unspoken alternative was to do everything the client wanted on a skimpier budget than Chiat/Day was used to, but no one considered that a plausible solution. Despite Chiat's lecture on cutting production costs, the creatives had gotten used to working with the best.

"What happens," asked Kuperman, "if we have a great creative idea to introduce the Sentra that doesn't work as part of the Fantasy campaign?"

"Then whatever size the Fantasy campaign is, as a bubble, shrinks to this size." Patty held up thumb and forefinger a quarter-inch apart. "How the creatives deal with this will have tremendous impact."

"What does Lee say?" asked Kuperman.

"That he can introduce the Sentra in the Fantasy campaign. It'll be a $50 million savings if we can do that."

"Fine," said Kuperman. "Tell Sittig you'll give him $1 million if he can do it."

"I bet we'll get it, if we do that," said Patty.

Dick Sittig had no patience for Patty's pyramid, nor for Patty, for that matter, who returned the younger man's contempt. As far as Sittig was concerned, Patty was a shortsighted pragmatist, a man who wrote the numbers down and then figured out what he could do within Nissan's financial limitations. To Tom Patty's mind, Sittig was a self-indulgent child who was on his way to alienating the client. Sittig said aloud what Patty would not even allow himself to think: incentives were a drug that tranquilized the company into thinking it was making progress when all it was doing was satisfying short-term hunger for profit. The real task facing Nissan—and Chiat/Day—was to strengthen Nissan's image so that the company would never again have to offer another incentive. To Sittig, every dollar stolen from national to plump regional's coffers was a dollar wasted. To Patty, it was the only practical solution.

Wolf wasn't surprised by the changes at Nissan, nor was he distressed by them. He was adept at forecasting where the industry was headed, and had been aware for some time that more and more accounts needed two-tier advertising, both image and "retail," which carried what Wolf called "a buy-now message, a sense of urgency." In a tight market, very few companies could afford to linger on the high plain of brand building. They had to enter the fray and sell. The creatives who thought they were sullying themselves by working on retail ads would either have to prove themselves indispensable, like Sittig, or they'd have to adapt.

Wolf was far more concerned with account management's role at Chiat/Day. Account management was a force in New York, thanks to Wolf and Jane Newman; given his background and her history as a planner, they had been able to attract people who could stand up to the creatives. Venice had always been the reverse. Clow embodied the imbalance. Only a few members of top management had the nerve to contradict him, even though he relished a good debate. It was like disagreeing with God. Unfortunately, many of the creatives who had learned at his knee had mastered a superior attitude before they'd earned the credentials to support it. What was an informed point of view, in Clow's case, was too often just thin, sour condescension from the younger creatives. That, combined with weak account people who bought into the myth and accepted their own inferiority, made for an agency that wasn't balanced enough to handle the big accounts.

As president of the Venice office, Wolf had done what he could to recruit stronger executives. As CEO, as the caretaker of an extremely ambitious plan for growth and diversification, he had to do more. Wolf fervently believed that account management, not creative, was the key to the agency's future. So he gathered the three dozen members of the department in the Arcadia Ballroom of Loews Santa Monica Beach Hotel at eight thirty in the morning on March 26, to tell them what they needed to do to take over.

The agency seemed sound enough. Chiat/Day in Venice had enjoyed roughly a 35 percent increase in income over the past five years, while the rest of the industry grew at 9 or 10 percent. The agency's profit margin was a plump 20 percent, compared to the public agencies Wolf tracked, which averaged about 13 percent.

But the rosy profile was deceptive. The only way to keep ahead of the pack was to change what the agency offered, and how. Wolf had carefully chosen the words that best described the new Chiat/Day: " 'The world's most creative communications and marketing resource,' " he intoned. The important words were "world" and "marketing"—the agency had to start to offer a wider range of services, to a larger pool of prospective clients. Ads were no longer enough.

He came close to heresy, suggesting that the agency had been guilty of arrogance—that breakthrough creative had been shoved down clients' throats with insufficient regard for the clients' corporate culture. It was time to stop telling clients what they had to do and start being more responsive to their stated needs.

"When it comes to advertising, there's a circle of acceptability," Wolf said. "At Home Savings, that circle of acceptability is taking money seriously and accepting the fact that their prime customer is an older person. If we bring them double entendre or ads written in small type that old people don't understand and can't read, it's not going to run no matter how creative it might be. At Nissan, the corporate culture is: I want to see the car. The car is the star."

Once the account people proved that they understood their clients' business, Chiat/Day would be able to attract the kinds of major accounts that weren't seduced by a clever ad.

"Why, with all this acclaim, aren't we getting $50 to $75 million accounts? The answer is, frankly and really honestly, those kind of clients don't see us as an appropriate business partner. They know all about the creative. But they have a profile of Chiat/Day which is very different from the reality of Chiat/Day."

He had the statistics to prove it. In 1988, Chiat/Day participated for the first time in the Louis Harris Agency Reputation Study, a poll of six hundred of the top marketers in the country, to get their perceptions of the top twenty advertising agencies in the United States. Chiat/Day dominated the creative section of the survey, ranking high on creativity, innovation, and even effectiveness of creative work.

"Yet on all of the other measures, the *important* measures," said Wolf, "things like 'knows my business,' 'fiscal responsibility,' 'research-oriented,' we were way down. The point is—if a client believes he can get, maybe not the zenith of creative but very good creative, at a couple other places that also have this solid-citizen kind of stuff, is he going to risk his job, his business, his budget, on something that he believes is a very high risk proposition? The answer's obviously no. And that's the way we're seen out there. We are seen as: 'They'll hit a home run—or maybe they'll strike out. They do great work, so why do they lose all those accounts?' They see this place as high profile. High risk. Out of control."

His last index card was labeled "Leaders, not cheerleaders." Wolf believed that creatives wanted to be led, and if they were out of hand at Chiat/Day, it was because the account people hadn't asserted themselves.

"We have this concept called 'delivering the agency,' " he said. "It's like, who do you trust. We're in a service business so we're always questioning, arguing. But there's always a point where the client doesn't want to listen. 'Do it my way or I'll find someone who will.' At that point the client is looking for someone to deliver the agency: 'I don't want to fire you, but I don't want to do it your way.' "

Chiat/Day clients traditionally appealed to creative or senior management, and too often, as far as Wolf was concerned, got a belligerent response. "We've got to get to the point," said Wolf, urgently, "where the account people can deliver the agency."

Creative director Steve Rabosky and his partner Ian Potter, the only creatives in the room, listened to Wolf's sermon imperviously. In his plain white shirt and stern black jacket, Rabosky looked like a petulant boy forced to attend a Sunday church service, impatient with the stodginess of the preacher's message, worried that the others might take it to heart and make his life difficult. Rabosky had a decent enough reputation for being able to listen to clients, but he hadn't yet achieved Clow's preternatural consistency.

Rabosky was combative, as though fearful that an aggressive foe might snatch his integrity from him. The way he saw it, too many of the account people were too eager to make the client happy to begin with, and here was Wolf telling them to pay even more attention to what the client wanted. When Wolf asked Rabosky if he had anything he'd like to say, the creative director was brief: He wanted everyone to remember that "understanding the client's business does *not* mean accepting what the client says. It means understanding—as though you had the client's job, as though you were the marketing director."

The last thing he needed was a squadron of yes-men.

While Wolf tutored his troops in the assertive arts, Clow directed Chiat's relatives in a videotaped message for the Leader of the Decade dinner. Clow and Chiat's assistant had gathered the members of Chiat's immediate family in the Boathouse, along with a producer, cameraman and soundman, and had plunked granddaughter Hannah into one of the corrugated chairs. She had been coached in the art of blowing kisses, which she began to do with abandon, but Clow was not satisfied. Random kisses would not do.

"Can you say, 'Hi Zadie? Hi Zadie?'"

Bewildered, Hannah looked around for her grandfather. Carol Madonna rushed to his cubicle, grabbed the color photo of Chiat leaning on a Yellow cab, sprinted back and held it up next to the video camera.

"Who's that?" asked Clow.

Hannah tried to mouth the word "Zadie," but it wouldn't come. Clow suggested "Grandpa."

"Hi Damp-uh," said Hannah. "Hi Damp-uh."

Next up was Chiat's infant grandson Francesco. His mother, Debbie, propped him in the chair and Clow inserted a sign that said,

"Grandpa of the Century," under his pudgy fingers. Francesco grabbed it, hid behind it, and finally dropped it on the floor.

"Perfect," said Clow. "He's done everything with that sign you can do."

Debbie was a more self-conscious subject, managing a clipped, "Only for you, Dad," and a couple of "congratulations." Elyse took her turn, and then Chiat's son Mark showed up, wearing a 1980 Agency of the Year T-shirt, accompanied by Chester, his eight-month-old silky-haired pit bull. Clow taped Mark, miked and taped the dog, and got the whole group together, all the while talking to himself about what the opening shot should be.

In the afternoon Clow met Guy Day in the War Room, a meeting room on the second floor of the production building, across the parking lot from the warehouse, to tape his video greeting for the party. Chiat's partner of eighteen years didn't like to come into the main building, where he might be seen. He stood awkwardly against the wall of the War Room, fiddling with the script he'd written, waiting to record his testimonial to a man whose goals had diverged from his own.

Day was a man who, like Clow, liked to work a reasonable week and go home at night to be with his wife, while Chiat enjoyed the excesses of the business. Day was happy in a boutique agency; Chiat had always wanted to see how much further he could go.

And Day, unlike Chiat, displayed the conventional ad man's disdain for his calling. While he waited for Clow to get set up, he repeated a joke he'd heard from Jerry Della Femina, who had been by earlier in the day to tape his tribute. "So Jerry gets a call, come to this bar and meet the world's best copywriter. By the time he gets there, the guy who called says the writer isn't there, but his work is. Go to the men's room. On the wall it says, 'Free Soviet Jewry.' Under that, it's scrawled, 'And win valuable prizes.' "

He tried one take after another, consulting his script in between, visibly ill at ease. He kept tripping over the same line, about what Chiat said were the three most important things in advertising. Day had written down, "brilliant advertising, a big budget and billings," but no matter how many times he tried, he always said "billings" first.

Finally he threw up his hands, helpless.

"Well," he said, laughing. "I can't *lie*."

Clow did not know how to confront Wolf directly about their differences, but the first three months of the new administration had convinced him that he had to do something. He had to remind people that Wolf and he were supposed to be partners. That had been the intention—the strategy—and if the execution had failed, if the advertisement for the new Chiat/Day hadn't communicated the proper message, then he had to set it right.

He could not count on himself to be persuasive; his feelings might well get in the way. So he decided to let his work speak for him. He'd been toying with a new business packet, something to leave behind at a pitch that would explain to the prospective client the kind of agency that Chiat/Day was. If he could get it ready for the upcoming April quarterly board meetings, it would speak more eloquently than he could, and perhaps the other board members would rally.

So he spent whatever free moments he had in the creative department art studio, watching over Amy Miyano's shoulder as she worked. Miyano, the fifty-year-old art studio manager, had been with the agency for nineteen years. She was an unlikely mother hen, a tiny woman whose stern features were accentuated by the black clothing she favored, but she was Clow's absolute ally. Her brusque perfectionism rivaled his, and she was an outspoken critic of anyone who failed to meet their exacting standards.

She was protective of Clow and of what she would always regard as his department, even if she understood more clearly than he that it no longer belonged exclusively to him. Miyano was always willing to let him hang around, ready to rouse him from a melancholy mood or give him a hard time about a political gaffe. Clow took refuge in the studio, where finite problems could be solved with glue, a marking pen or a new typeface, and prepared to say what he wished he had said months before.

13

The creative directors were the artists of the industry, or so they fancied themselves. They chafed at the constraints placed on them by businessmen, both inside and outside the agency—men who, they believed, would have them settle for less in the interest of earning more. Their chosen form of expression was, of course, subsidized communication, at best a mix of inspiration and profitable purpose. Commerce owned every imagination in the room; but for their minds to flourish, they had to believe it was not so.

It was becoming ever more difficult, particularly since there was a contingent within the agency which spoke with increasing authority, and said that restraint was an admirable trait, not at all the same thing as servility. The creative directors' quarterly review, which took place the day before the North American and World Board meetings, was, as much as anything, an opportunity for the trustees of the agency's legacy to make sure it was not being squandered or misused.

Clow had run the reviews since his days as creative director, and he chaired the April 2 meeting with the air of a lonely man reunited with loved ones. The others straggled into the Treehouse, as close to eight thirty as they could manage. They inhaled the steam from their coffee, impatient for caffeine's helping hand, and watched Clow circle the room, looking at the work pinned on the walls, greeting the out-of-towners, acting as the genial host. The men in this room—Tom

McElligott, Rabosky, Sittig, Nissan regional's Jeff Roll, Ross van Deusen and Mike Moser from San Francisco, Jeff Roche from Toronto—were all people Clow had worked with or admired.

Michael Smith, the creative director from New York, blew in fifteen minutes late, in the middle of introductions, clutching a couple of videotapes which he handed over to Amy Miyano as though they were gold bricks.

"This is 'Jay and Me,' " he gasped. Each office had prepared a videotaped tribute for Chiat's WSAAA Leader of the Decade party. The New York office had filmed its version of Michael Moore's documentary about his search for the elusive head of General Motors, Roger Smith. "Five minutes, thirty seconds."

"They're supposed to be two minutes," said one of the others.

"We couldn't help ourselves," said Smith. "It's so-ooo good."

That was just the sort of thing Clow liked to hear—a commitment to quality that went beyond the constraints of the prescribed job. Not flagrant irresponsibility, but the kind of passion that might wipe out a client's reservations and get him to take a chance. As the agency grew, the creative department faced a chicken-and-egg dilemma. More and more work was getting stalled in the system, killed by account management, hostile focus groups, or the client, resulting in low morale. Incumbent creatives quit because they weren't willing to tolerate a six-month dry spell. Senior people at other agencies who were job hunting looked at the creative roster, realized there was no room for them on big accounts, and went elsewhere.

Too often the new hires at Chiat/Day were relatively inexperienced hotshots who were used to the sprint and lacked the stamina for the long haul. Their loyalty was to their own careers, to building a book of their work, and not to any specific agency. If they didn't get produced, they left.

There had been a time when Chiat/Day was the only creative game in town. It was still the preeminent place for a creative to work, but it wasn't the lonely outpost it once had been. There were more places to go because the agency had spawned a generation of creative-driven boutiques, many of them founded by frustrated Chiat/Day alumni who were tired of bumping their heads on the Clow ceiling, or unwilling to deal with Kuperman. It was possible for a creative to make time stand comfortingly still, by turning to an agency that looked the way Chiat/Day had ten years ago.

Clow worried that the constant turnover diluted the department, and made it vulnerable to pushy account people and insistent clients. What was on the walls of the Treehouse was supposed to be the agency's top work for 1989, but the consensus in the room was that nothing was as good as it could have been.

Forty-five minutes into the session, Chiat wandered in, assured Clow that he had no intention of disrupting the meeting and silently took a seat. His resolve lasted less than five minutes. He wondered aloud why the agency's best work was up on the walls. It would have been more productive to look at the work that hadn't run and figure out why.

"There are a lot of issues if we're going to keep up the quality, the integrity," he said. "Was it an account person beating up on a creative? What kept something from being good enough? It's a real issue, especially as we get bigger."

"We brought the bad stuff," Smith broke in, impishly. "It's the stuff we inherited."

"Let's not be defensive about this," said Chiat. "What do you think? I just think sitting here patting yourselves on the back because there's good work on the walls is a waste of time. You're adults with great work and clout. If you don't have clout, we'll either change the person who's taken your clout away or get a new creative director."

Hesitantly, Smith complained that he was having trouble getting Jane Newman to address the work on the Royal Caribbean Cruise Line account. He didn't like it, but the client did, so Newman seemed frustratingly content to let him keep producing what he thought was substandard work.

Rabosky griped that Wolf had been equally inaccessible on the Home Savings account. He'd issued the edict to give the client whatever he wanted, period.

"But here's the way to use Wolf instead of having him use you," said Chiat. "Get *him* to talk to the client. Use him as a tool—instead of having him use creative as a tool in the account management sense."

*   *   *

When Chiat left, the others fell back into their round of complaints. Jeff Roll, who was Sittig's regional counterpart, joked that he had carte blanche to do whatever advertising would be effective, as long as it always said, "Nissan Values Now." His partner, Tony Stern, had taken to telling people that the first rule of decentralization was, "If a dealer wants his daughter playing the accordion and sitting on a pig, we better make sure it's a good-looking pig."

Clow listened with a mixture of dismay and resignation. The agency had built its reputation on a refusal to make concessions, only to take on a regional, sales-driven account that fairly demanded surrender. It was probably foolish to have thought that Chiat/Day could impose its standards on regional Nissan. What he had to do was make sure that the rest of the agency continued to consider regional a profitable aberration from the creative-driven norm.

"This is just going to be," he said, "one of the honest-to-God hypocrisies of a billion-dollar Chiat/Day."

Wolf ambled into the Fish, where lunch had been set up for the creative directors, and tried to shake hands with McElligott, who couldn't because his index finger was full of chocolate brownie frosting. It was an awkward moment, not just because of the thwarted handshake, but because the two men were as dissimilar as they could be, Wolf the smooth executive, McElligott resembling nothing so much as an Ivy League English Lit. professor, in his immaculate khakis, pinstriped oxford-cloth shirt and crewneck sweater.

But Wolf had an urgent request. He was looking for an ally in the enemy camp: he wanted McElligott to review the new business package Clow had been working on.

"I'm having some problems with it," was all he would say.

The first item on the creatives' afternoon agenda was small accounts. Wolf wanted to limit the number of small accounts and set a minimum dollar amount for new business, which upset everyone in the room. The creatives believed that obstacles increased as budgets grew, that doing startling work for Nissan, where so much was at stake, was more difficult than doing it for Soho Soda or Taylor Made golf clubs. Clow intended to raise the issue at the North American

Board meeting, which would mean going head to head with Wolf, so he wanted to rehearse in front of a sympathetic audience.

"My attitude is, if you can do some great work, break even, and give people the satisfaction of doing great work, then it's worth having the accounts for the spirit and the environment," Clow told the creative directors. "If you have a small account that's making you do shitty work, then you should jettison it. But the line should not be the size of the account. The line should be whether we get to do good work."

"You should definitely bring that up," said Rabosky, darkly. "Because the powers that be, that oversee the spread sheets, don't agree with you."

"And it isn't just morale," said McElligott. "This agency's reputation depends on a constant stream of interesting work. The nice thing about smaller accounts is that you can do brilliant work that gets noticed and wins awards."

"I had an argument with Wolf at our five-year meeting," confessed Smith. "He allowed we could have three small accounts."

"God," said Clow. "It gets harder."

"It does get harder, Lee," said Smith.

"Every silver cloud," said Clow, "has a dark lining."

The North American Board met the next morning in the Treehouse. Clow arrived early and took his seat at the head of the conference table, the center of a creative phalanx—McElligott on one side and San Francisco's longtime Chiat/Day loyalist, Mike Moser, on the other. Then Clow got up to get a cup of coffee—and in his absence Wolf strode in and took what he considered to be his rightful place at the head of the table. No one stopped him. No one pointed out that Clow had been sitting there. When Clow returned, he hesitated, and then wordlessly pulled up a chair at the corner of the table, in the half-space between Wolf and McElligott. This was, after all, Wolf's show, a day for looking at numbers and evaluating percentages, for judging performance rather than profile.

Wolf already knew what he was going to say, and to whom, but he wanted all the executives in the room to see the figures. Chief financial officer Pete de Vaux explained the good news and the bad: Chiat/Day in North America was off to a "very fast start" in the first third of its fiscal year, which had begun on November 1, but it wasn't going to last, and it wasn't going to compensate for losses in Australia and the Pacific. He projected North American revenues at $111 million, which represented an 8 percent increase in profits; but the Mojo arm of the agency was looking at a 20 percent drop, thanks to the state of the Australian economy.

That, combined with a failure to meet projections in San Francisco and the new Toronto office, was going to offset even the healthiest year for Venice and New York. Any new business win would improve the picture, but the year was one-third over, and the only possibilities on the horizon were Century 21 and Reebok.

"It's an interesting year for Chiat/Day," said de Vaux. "Basically, flat income."

"We haven't had a flat year since 1981," said New York president Jane Newman. There was a note of distaste and disbelief in her voice, as though she'd just found the tiniest moth hole in her impeccable navy double-breasted suit.

De Vaux corrected her. "Eighty-six. But the performance of an agency that's not used to a flat year is pretty amazing. Most agencies don't know what to do when the engine of new business slows down. Our margins are still at terrific levels."

Kuperman was the first of the office presidents to make his report, and he found it hard to keep from being boastful. He had cut $800,000 from his budget without firing a single person, by not filling open positions and not replacing people who quit. This year's plan called for income of $42,850,000 at the Venice office, and $10,989,000 in profits. Just into the second quarter of the year, Kuperman was looking at a $24,000 increase in revenues and over $1 million in added profits, a neat little sleight-of-hand made possible by his budget trims.

The only account he had that was losing money was Dep, the $6 million hair-care, toothpaste and skin cream account that was Kuperman's albatross, a work-intensive, demanding piece of business that had cost the office $250,000 in the first quarter. Kuperman was determined either to renegotiate the pay structure or resign the account, certainly proof, at the edge of a recession, of his confidence. He'd managed to get Nissan to agree to renegotiate its contract, to cover the $3 to $4 million cost of decentralization. He ticked off each hardship, and his defense against it, and then sat down, and waited for anyone else to beat him, to suggest that he wasn't the best student, the fastest learner, in the room.

There was no way New York's Jane Newman could massage her numbers to get them to look as good as Kuperman's did, but she behaved as though Reebok were a wound that had already healed over. She would find $1 to $2 million to cut, so that she could meet her anticipated income and profit figures for the quarter, and that was all there was to it. She wanted to dismiss the whole sorry episode and get on with business.

Fred Goldberg and Chuck Phillips were in no position to challenge either of the executives who preceded them. Goldberg had left New York to open Chiat/Day's San Francisco office in April 1980, and now found himself in an awkward position—his options closed down by Wolf's promotion, his fiefdom permanently reduced to an office in a city where there were too many agencies and not enough work. Three of his accounts had cut their budgets and cost him $4 million in income, and another had left the agency. He reported that he had "significant new business" from a couple of existing accounts, but significant, in San Francisco terms, was not enough to impress the others.

Even $1.5 million in staffing and expense cuts couldn't get San Francisco near its projected numbers. The office was supposed to come up with $13.5 million in income, and now hoped for $11.7. Profits were projected at $2.6 million; Goldberg hoped to be able to hit $2 million.

"We're down about $500,000," said Goldberg. "There's not a hell of a lot of new business right now, either."

There was no apology to his tone. Goldberg saw his office as a separate, small agency struggling in a parched advertising climate. On those terms, he was satisfied.

Only Wolf, Chiat and he fully appreciated how separate it was. The agency had always planned to shut down the San Francisco operation and relocate some of the staff, once the new Venice building was completed, but Wolf saw no reason to wait that long. He did not want to support a flagging operation for what would be at least another year. The agency had offered to sell the San Francisco office to Goldberg, but he was reluctant to go into business on his own. He wanted to remain part of Chiat/Day; failing that, he wanted the company to find a new corporate position for him. Neither alternative was acceptable to Wolf, but Goldberg continued to push for some sort of association—something, in this arid economic climate, the safe side of enforced independence. Wolf, in the meantime, proceeded with his own plan to abandon the San Francisco office, and Goldberg, entirely.

Goldberg had been placed in charge of the subsidiaries in January 1990, but it was not a project that interested him, a rather inadequate consolation prize. He reported, flatly, that the satellite companies were feeling financial pressure. They all were looking at budget cuts, because there didn't seem to be any new business on the horizon.

Wolf moved on to the Toronto report without commenting on San Francisco. He considered Toronto a frontier town, the agency's first outpost in Canada and a convenient resource for the profitable midwestern United States. But the shortfall there was even worse than San Francisco. Chuck Phillips, the office president and an old friend of Chiat's, looked like a condemned man as he presented his report.

"Our numbers on a fiscal basis don't look very good," Phillips admitted, "but annually, given our new Nissan deal, we're okay."

"Federal Express?" inquired Wolf, regarding a recent pitch.

"We bombed," said Phillips. "We made a terrible presentation."

"I was counting on $675,000, not $375,000," said Wolf, referring to Toronto's profit figures.

He had no questions. Replacing Chuck Phillips might take a little longer than getting rid of Fred Goldberg, because it would require relocating another executive, but that was what he would do.

"So what we have here is L.A. doing $1.5 to $2 million more in income than its original plan, on the basis of a little bit of new business and severe cost cutting," Wolf said, approvingly, "New York on target despite Reebok with a possible $1 to $2 million in cuts, San Francisco scrambling despite losses to hold onto $2 million instead of $2.6, Toronto at 40 percent of expectations and we have to check that figure. As for the subsidiaries, this was the year we expected these divisions to come to the party, and they haven't."

Given the numbers, no one would be able to argue with what Wolf intended to do. Chiat already knew of his plans for San Francisco and Toronto, and had decided to stay out of the fray, despite his skepticism over whether such drastic action was called for. Wolf felt a little bit like a hired hit man, brought in to do the dirty work that the others understood was necessary but couldn't bring themselves to do.

Jane Newman was a lifer. She had come to the New York office as corporate director of account planning in 1981, and had become its general manager in 1987. She had been president of the New York office since 1988. In an odd way, she was Clow's complement, even if she seemed his polar opposite, with her dark, severe suits and elegant pumps, her fashionable frizz of blond curls and noisy bangle bracelets, her impenetrably cool demeanor. She was a pure planner, in the same way that Clow was a creative. Newman was the only woman account planning trainee when the discipline was born at a London agency in 1968, and now she perceived strategies instinctively, just as Clow imagined ads.

Like Clow's, her social skills were underdeveloped; all that mattered to either of them was the task at hand. Newman was as shy as she was bright, a tall, raw-boned woman whose voice bespoke both intelligence and tension. When she spoke to clients, she was unassailable. It was only when she was expected to step out of her realm, to engage in social niceties, that she faltered ever so slightly. She pulled at her cuticles. Her pale eyes and soft mouth, comically out of sync with the rest of her appearance, took on a faintly vulnerable look.

Newman preferred to stick to business whenever possible. She had engineered the New York office's growth with Wolf, without ever becoming the kind of parental figure Kuperman aspired to be. She was a distant monarch, respected and admired, but not adored.

Newman was the first of the office presidents to deliver her five-year projections to the North American Board, and she did so as though she were throwing down a gauntlet, daring anyone else to meet her aggressive plan—or to suggest that she would be unable to do so. Her billing objective for 1990 was about $200 million, which would yield $30 million in income. She would be satisfied to stay even with 1989's earnings, since in that year the office had picked up almost $13 million in "windfall" business—accounts that increased their budgets or walked in the door without a pitch. In five years she expected to more than double that figure—$500 million in billings, with $75 million in income. New York currently had thirteen clients. Newman figured ten would stick around and increase their billings, including the $35 million Royal Caribbean account, whose income she expected to double. All she needed was seven to ten more, in the right billing range, to reach her goal.

She ticked off the items she was looking for as though they were entries on a grocery list, as though finding them would be as easy as piling potatoes into a shopping cart. She wanted "our Nissan," a $100 million plus account, two accounts in the $50–$100 million range, four at $30–$50 million, seven in the $15–$30 range (which the office already had) and three small accounts. Newman shared Wolf's disdain for the small account, but she was willing to take on a few, if they met strict guidelines—"if they're entrepreneurial, real quick in terms of their decision making, and with growth potential, where advertising could really make the company."

San Francisco had no five-year plan—Goldberg had told his staff he was too busy with new business to draw up projections in time for the board meeting. Chuck Phillips's wildly optimistic projections only made some of the people in the room squirm.

It fell to Kuperman to elevate the mood, which was fine with him. He seemed to enjoy competing with Newman. He began his presentation by talking about the need to preserve Venice's culture over the coming years, but he ended with the promise that he could turn $43 million in income into $75 million in five years—an acceptably smaller increase than Newman projected, since Chiat/Day already owned a bigger percentage of the West Coast market.

He gazed menacingly at Newman.

"We'd like to expand our market," said Kuperman. "Our feeling is that anything west of New Jersey is fair game."

"Fuck you!" Newman shot back.

Clow would have a captive audience for his complaints after the lunch break, when he reviewed the year's creative work for the board, but the office reports had made him too impatient to wait. Neither of the agency's two largest offices seemed the least bit interested in cultivating the small account. If he didn't speak up now, it would look as if he endorsed their five-year plans.

Without any preliminaries (Clow rarely bothered to ease listeners onto his train of thought; he expected them to jump on while he was in motion), he reminded everyone that small accounts enabled Chiat/Day to do the kind of cutting-edge advertising that had earned its reputation in the first place.

"It's a tradition at Chiat/Day," he said. "I think having a hard rule is a mistake."

Kuperman broke in, but not in the way Clow might have hoped. For all his talk of Doyle Dane Bernbach and how the inappropriate big accounts had been its creative undoing, Kuperman the administrator was undergoing a philosophical change. He was responsible for Nissan, the entire agency's largest account. How could he go around spouting that big accounts paralyzed the creative process, and small accounts set the imagination free? He found himself, instead, repeating what Wolf had so often said: The goal is to do great creative on the big accounts.

"I know that's the long-term mission," Clow said, "but there's got to be room."

Wolf cut him off. "We've got to limit the number we have . . ."

". . . I know you can't have twelve or thirteen," said Clow, "but . . ."

"In L.A. we have an $8 million minimum," said Kuperman, curtly, as though a harsh attitude would propel him a safe distance from his conscience. "Below that we'll evaluate on a case-by-case basis."

"I think you have to evaluate the opportunities," said Clow.

Wolf was impatient. As far as he was concerned, keeping small accounts for the sake of the work was a vestige of the 1980s. The goal for the 1990s was to become what he called an "active business partner," and the way to do that was through strengthened account management.

"Thanks, Lee," said Wolf, in a tone that meant the conversation was closed.

"You're welcome," said Clow.

Clow was hardly ready to give up. Right after lunch he assumed an evangelical stance and started to preach to the board members. Big, as far as he was concerned, was starting to get bad. Average work that would have been killed in the good old days was making its way to the client because the agency couldn't pay attention to everything. A "closet account" mentality was creeping in, allowing creatives to act as though certain accounts just didn't matter. Clients and planning sometimes formed an inadvertent, unpleasant alliance that kept the creatives from doing what Clow considered great work.

What he wanted, from the people in the Treehouse, was the promise that their commitment was still to maintaining creative excellence—that the work, not considerations of size or profit, was the engine that drove Chiat/Day. It wasn't as guileless a position as it seemed. Clow wanted to see the agency grow and, with a house in Marina del Rey, another on Catalina Island, a boat to ferry him from one to the other and a new custom-built home under construction, he was as interested as anyone in making money. He just didn't believe Chiat/Day could put money first and hope to make more. Profits followed great work. The reverse wasn't necessarily true.

Clow did not find the support he was looking for. The rest regarded him as though he were the cantankerous uncle within the agency family, the tolerated eccentric. Until now, power had clung to him like one of his worn, familiar shirts. He had never needed to think about keeping it, because he had never had to seek it. Now it seemed that Clow's fears had come true. The others would always admire him, but they no longer seemed to believe in him.

When he was done he looked around the room helplessly. Then he blurted out, "The year-end changes were gut-wrenching, but I listen to Jane. She uses these *adjectives*." He waved his arms above his head, chuckling. " 'It'll be *tremendous*. It'll be *exciting*. . . .' " He hesitated, as though waiting for someone to tell him that it would, in fact, be so.

Hastily, Wolf interrupted him. "I want to add one thing. A reiteration," he said. "We've talked about the need to upgrade account management and planning and make ourselves an appropriate business partner. *None of that is meant to erode creative*. We shouldn't hear that we can't do great ads on big accounts. It's meant to enhance, not undermine."

"I didn't mean to blame you," said Clow.

Their fragile truce lasted less than an hour. The agency's new rainmaker, Don Peppers, had sent one of his staff to make a new business presentation to the board, and her words were a wedge that drove Wolf and Clow apart. She talked about the key to the agency's future: "Positioning, press attention, prospecting and pitching." She talked about setting up a computerized directory of contacts, a ten-thousand-person prospecting pool. She recommended "eye coordination and a handshake" as essential tools for making contacts.

"Sounds very sophisticated," grumbled Clow. "I don't think it will work."

Then Peppers's staffer started talking about the agency's desired positioning, and how Chiat/Day ought to be seen as an agency that acted "most in the interest of solving its clients' problems," and another argument broke out. Wolf said that clients knew about Chiat/Day's great creative, but they needed to know about the agency's other resources. Clow responded that he did not want to be an "appropriate business partner," which was what Wolf and Peppers were promoting. He wanted to be a communications resource, which to him meant a creative-driven shop.

Wolf barked at him. "The world believes they can get pretty good ads without dealing with the pain of Chiat/Day," he said.

But Clow was not finished. Peppers had not addressed the issue of how to teach clients what the agency was all about, in terms of process. He did not seem to understand that there was such a thing as an inappropriate account, no matter how big it was.

Wolf cut him off. "What is the biggest fear you have?" he asked. "What's the worst thing that could happen?"

"We convince very mediocre clients to come to Chiat/Day," said Clow, without a moment's hesitation, "and once they're on our balance sheets, we can't walk away from them. We homogenize the brand—the Chiat/Day brand—and become the safe place to bring your account, because we don't argue."

Tom Patty often disagreed with Clow—and did in this case—but he respected him. They had worked together for thirteen years. Both men had grown up on the beaches of Southern California and now lived blocks away from each other on the Silver Strand, a spit of land, choked with expensive homes, at the southern tip of Marina del Rey. Patty and Clow had designed the fence for Patty's home together, a story Patty liked to retell because it provided the perfect analogy for their work relationship. Clow had purchased hardware to fasten the fence slats together, and Patty had to admit that the hinges were exceedingly beautiful. The only problem was, they weren't strong enough to hold up the fence. In the interest of beauty, Clow was willing to give them a try. Patty, who owned the fence and was the guardian of common sense, vetoed the experiment.

Patty knew that Wolf and Clow would butt heads forever, but he hoped he could make Clow realize that they didn't have to be adversaries.

"There's a fundamental reality," he said quietly. "I've never found a client's business problem that could be solved solely through advertising. What we're talking about is not in conflict with doing great advertising." It was, he explained, merely a question of expanding the agency's available services and strengthening the non-creative departments.

"I'm not talking about conflict here," said Clow. "I'm talking about emphasis. We're not an Oldsmobile. We're a Porsche."

"But we don't want to be a Jaguar," said Newman. "We're not arrogant assholes, but it's the world's best-kept secret."

Clow hesitated for a moment, and when he did speak his voice was shaking noticeably. "The job is to define the world's best communications resource," he said loudly. "There's nothing wrong with that. That *makes* you a perfect business partner."

"Look," said Wolf. "We'll massage the words. We don't want to have the wrong clients for the wrong reasons—but the other side is that there are a lot of negative connotations we have to clean up.'

Clow ignored him, reached for the new business materials that Rabosky had written up at his request, and began to read aloud. When he got to the section about why Chiat/Day wasn't part of a multinational conglomerate, entitled "Why we're not part of Mega-ComOmni Group," Wolf silently shook his head.

It was all, Clow recited, about "the most common byproduct of big: Bad.

"The bad that comes from three different agencies with separate cultures and identities being welded together by bankers. The bad that comes from the focus shifting from the headline to the bottom line.

"The bad that comes from a human being's name on the door being replaced by the name of a corporate machine.

"At Chiat/Day/Mojo, you get the big. Over a billion dollars in billings, nine offices worldwide, a dozen satellite offices, subsidiaries, the works.

"What you don't get is any of the bad.

"Because despite the meteoric growth and changes we've experienced over the last twenty-odd years, we still believe in the simple premise for the agency being founded back in 1968.

"Good enough is not enough."

Clow was adamant about their selling an attribute that Wolf considered last season's merchandise and more belligerent than Wolf had expected about the Peppers proposal. They were going to have to appeal to Chiat.

CHAPTER 14

Over seven hundred people gathered at the Beverly Wilshire Hotel on the evening of April 4 to honor Jay Chiat, WSAAA Leader of the Decade, but they saw not a sign of the divisiveness that gnawed at Chiat/Day. No one could have guessed that the agency was in turmoil, over issues so fundamental that the very personality of Chiat/Day—the outline of its future—was at stake. From the outside looking in, the agency was as feisty and irreverent as ever, revamping even the stultifying realities of the banquet circuit to meet its demanding criteria. The stark black table linens, the extravagant custom-ordered flowers, the video tribute and a guest appearance by the Ad Punks, instead of anything resembling a traditional dance band, put the guests on notice: The heady decade for which Chiat was being honored might be over, but his agency was still brash enough to think it had the right—no, the duty—to retool the real world.

The only hints of the day's strife were subtle ones. Dick Sittig, a three-year veteran who had never worked in the same office with Chiat, was invited to the dinner. His predecessor on Nissan, Dave Butler—a dedicated lifer, the man who had served informally as Clow's text editor during Clow's reign as creative director—was not. To some, it was a practical choice, since Sittig represented the agency's future; but Wolf's critics considered Butler's absence absolute proof of the new CEO's disregard for the agency's culture.

Clow partisans also fretted over the significance of the videotaped tribute, which featured one of Nissan's favorite sales conference devices, a sarcastic puppet who kept interrupting master of ceremonies Dick Cavett. The crowd seemed to like the wisecracks, but Chiat/Day creatives had been tutored to distrust any idea that found favor too easily with too many people. Maybe the puppet was fun—but maybe he was a symbol of the stifling effect of a big account, of popularity mattering more than quality did.

At the end of the program Wolf and Clow got up to speak. Wolf talked about having nine offices in four continents, and about becoming the best agency in the world. Clow quoted from a twenty-year-old newspaper clip in which Jay Chiat expounded on creative standards. One man looked forward and saw opportunity, while the other looked back and saw heritage. Neither one could convince the other to turn around for a moment—but in the sentimental glow of the evening, they appeared to be working together, each one contributing his resources to a single goal.

When Chiat stepped up to the podium, ostensibly to offer his thanks, he offered instead a challenge to the self-satisfied audience. Advertising had served them very well—but then, most of them were white. What of minorities? If the assembled crowd was really so concerned with the health of the industry, then surely people would respond to his challenge: Jay Chiat was going to ask his World Board to contribute $100,000 to a minority scholarship and internship fund. He would personally match that amount. All that the members of the WSAAA had to do was set up and participate in the program—or admit that they lacked the conviction of the man they had chosen to honor.

"Thank you," he said, sweetly. "I love you." With that he got down off the stage and let the Ad Punks set up. The rear two tiers of tables emptied out quickly, given the late hour, which was fine with the people from Chiat/Day, who could now have a private celebration of their founder's career. Chiat jumped back up onstage to join the band, on tambourine, for their rendition of the Rolling Stones' "Satisfaction," gave up his musical aspirations halfway through, and started dancing with his two assistants.

By the time the World Board convened the following morning, Chiat had reviewed Don Peppers's new business materials. He regarded the document with ambivalence, and not a little cold fear.

This was what he had asked for from Wolf—an aggressive strategy for growth—but it seemed more a curse than a promise. He wondered if the rewards would be worth the compromise.

Clow brought up the proposal as soon as the meeting got under way, and Chiat immediately made his feelings known. "Peppers assumes certain things as one hundred percent reality that just aren't so," he said.

"I think it's real close," said Wolf.

"That's your point of view, and Peppers's point of view," said Chiat. "The danger is that you're going to change the whole point of view of the agency. It's an *insidious* little piece. It assumes certain things are true that simply aren't."

Wolf answered in a low, calm voice. He tried always to keep his arguments grounded, never to respond to an irrational outburst with anything but reason. It was as though he were rooted deep in the earth, while Clow and Chiat swam about on the currents of their emotions. If Wolf could maintain his position, the others would eventually stop their ranting, see that he had not budged, and yield.

"We have a perception problem out there," Wolf said, slowly. "Given all the press and awards, we should have gotten a lot of action, and we haven't."

"We have," said Chiat. "I think we've gotten a lot of action."

"We've had no action," said Wolf.

"Have there been reviews since the press that we weren't included in?" asked Clow.

Chiat couldn't think of any. He didn't see a problem.

Wolf persisted. "There's a negative perception out there. It isn't one man's opinion. We've got to tell a total picture of the agency."

"The conclusion of the piece," said Clow, referring to Peppers's proposal, "that we've got to reposition as the safest agency, is where I take it to task."

"Fine," said Wolf. "We can say, 'best communications resource in the world.' But then we have to define that as something more than 'We do great ads.' "

They bickered about the sentence that would describe the new Chiat/Day—what it might mean to potential clients, and what it meant to the people in the room. Kuperman tried playing diplomat: use Clow's line, he suggested, but then define "communications resource" in a way that made Chiat/Day seem an appropriate business partner. Newman argued that all Wolf was talking about was telling the whole story of the agency, not just the creative side.

Nothing satisfied Chiat.

"I have a serious fear," he said, raising his voice, "that this is the beginning of a real change in the agency." He turned to Wolf accusingly and told him that one of the creatives had approached him, the day before, to complain that he'd been told to do exactly what the client at Home Savings wanted, no matter what.

At that Wolf lost his cool.

"Jesus, Jay," he yelled. "Who told you that? When?"

"Yesterday."

"Well, why don't you ask me? *Any* creative person gets your ear." A note of petulance had crept into Wolf's voice; there were times when being thought of as the bad guy was an intolerable insult. "And I think if you look at what we've done in the last year, you'll see maybe I haven't had such a bad impact on the agency."

Clow jumped in, hollering, *"This fucking document says we've got to be the safe and sane agency and I can't go along with that!"*

Newman scolded him for losing control and Clow fell silent. But Chiat was just as upset.

"It's not reality," he said. "I have a fear of this thing becoming an excuse for us to become another agency. Change is daily. Chiseling it in this document is my fear—and then putting it in the hands of people who haven't been here long enough."

Clow wanted to avoid a showdown. As long as the debate continued, he had a chance. "Nobody really disagrees," he said. "The problem is strategy. All we have to do—a lot of the remedy—is in terms of sheer doing it, of reaching people. Not in undoing things."

"We want to correct things that are correctable, not change things," said Wolf brusquely. He was tired of Clow's assumption that he wanted to build account management at the expense of creative. And Chiat had bruised him with that crack about Home Savings. Wolf felt he'd saved an account that was on the brink of firing the agency, by imposing boundaries where there had been none. It was old business, from last October, and it had worked. He'd mentioned it proudly at his account management meeting a week ago; yet somebody in the creative department had held a grudge for six months and tattled to Chiat.

Angrily, he said, "I know exactly what I said in the account meeting. I said, one thing you can do is learn more about your client's culture and present that to the creatives. I said, we're never going to do flip ads for Home."

Chiat said he thought the conversation had taken place at the creative directors' meeting two days ago.

"I wasn't *at* that meeting," yelled Wolf. "And what should we do? Ignore Dick Deihl," the chairman and CEO of Home Savings, "and lose the account? Great."

Chiat could hardly deny Wolf's logic, but he wasn't about to capitulate, not after a dispute over the agency's very identity. An apology would seem like surrender, and he wanted to stay in charge. So he changed the subject and presented his answer to the need for better new business materials, a quirky multi-screen video presentation designed by a New York graphics artist he had met at the Aspen Design Conference. This was new business as theater: a history professor lectured in Hungarian about Chiat/Day/Mojo, which he pronounced "Shee-oat Dei Moyo"; a perky chef put on a cake-baking demonstration and used it as an analogy for the way the agency's departments blended together; a friendly woman introduced Chiat/Day's culture by quoting the Chinese proverb about giving children "roots and wings."

The presentation began with the slogan, "We believe that good advertising empowers people to make up their own minds about a product." It ended with the text, "Big clients and small, equal rights for all."

Several people liked the presentation immensely, and said so. The others were speechless.

"I figured if I got involved in new business it would galvanize the rest of you," said Chiat, with a slow smile, "because you'd hate me."

The fireworks were not over. Later in the day Fred Goldberg presented a plan to the board for restructuring the San Francisco office. He had shown it to Wolf the day before in an attempt to build support, but when it came time for him to speak before the World Board, he realized he had made a terrible tactical error. Wolf attacked the plan swiftly, lobbing objections like grenades at the stunned San Francisco president. Goldberg was instructed to come up with a plan for closing the office. He had six weeks.

No one came to his defense. Clow was unhappy with the decision, since he liked the idea of a creative boutique within Chiat/Day, but he was not about to step into the middle of a power struggle between Wolf and Goldberg. Chiat was less sentimental about the office, and aware that the animosity between Wolf and Goldberg was insurmountable. Unless Goldberg changed his mind about buying the office, there was no other solution.

Goldberg was outraged, but Wolf remained firm. They would figure out how to parcel out the existing clients, and how to inform them without precipitating defections. There was also the question of how many employees the Venice office could absorb, though Goldberg clearly was not to be one of them. He no longer had a home at Chiat/Day.

The last item on the agenda, as always, was the question of compensation and stock allocations. Before Wolf's promotion, he and Clow had been worth the same amount to Chiat/Day—about $600,000 in base annual salary, plus another $100,000–$150,000 in executive perks and stock. The 1988 recapitalization had brought each of them $3 million; the planned 1992 recapitalization would yield even more. They were among the handful of executives who had benefited from Chiat's expressed intention to make his people rich when they were still young enough to do something with the money—to buy them new opportunities.

But Wolf had a new title and responsibilities, and Clow did not. On April 4, 1990, the World Board voted to give Wolf 1,000,000 Employee Participation Units, 500,000 immediately and 500,000 in 1991, in recognition of his new position. It was the perfect motivational reward. EPUs cost the company nothing—they were handed out with the title of vice-president, or bestowed, at the board's discretion, to worthy employees—but they were worth nothing as long as the agency's liabilities were greater than its assets. For Wolf to cash in on his increased equity, he had to make the agency grow. The board was prepared to wager 1 million shares of future profits on his ability to do so. For the first time, Wolf was officially worth more to Chiat/Day than Clow was.

CHAPTER 15

When *Dick Sittig* decided to get into advertising, he figured the best strategy was "work for nothing and be death on everybody above me." He'd read Jerry Della Femina's 1970 best-seller about the advertising business, *From Those Wonderful Folks Who Gave You Pearl Harbor*, and was struck by Della Femina's observation that junior guys had the chance to get ahead because they were so hungry. They'd work nights for one tenth the pay, they'd work weekends, they'd relocate, they'd do anything to get noticed. Sittig took that as his model—and had managed, in five years, to be death on quite a number of his superiors.

He was, at thirty-one, a vice-president and associate creative director at Chiat/Day, in charge of creative on the agency's largest account, having bought his ticket the previous year when he and his partner had come up with the Fantasy campaign. After only three years at the agency, Sittig was a senior guy, the sort who was supposed to be looking over his shoulder at the hungry twenty-five-year-olds, which only drove him harder.

The way he looked at it, he was scrambling up a pyramid. There was a pool of talented creatives at the bottom, and a handful of top jobs at the top—and like Wolf, he figured he had until he was forty to secure his place. The last thing on earth he wanted to be was one of the anonymous men who were left behind. He remembered with a shudder the day he'd been in an elevator with Della Femina, for whom he had worked briefly, and a middle-aged man had got in and said, " 'Jerry, Jerry, don't you remember me? I worked for you for twenty years.' And this guy doesn't have two quarters to rub together." The image haunted Sittig. He looked ahead and feared obsolescence. He looked behind and worried about the next hot kid.

Or at least he said he did. All the talk about anxiety might as easily have been a play for sympathy, an advertisement of his humility, since Sittig's meteoric rise had not made him a lot of friends. His manner gave no hint of insecurity. A tall, slim man with a lantern jaw and steely eyes, Sittig already strode around the creative department as though he owned it, shoulders back, chest high, the picture of rapid success. He mimicked Clow's preference for shorts, but with a spin. If Clow's anonymous khakis announced his distrust of costume, Sittig's collection of shorts—checked ones, cuffed ones, Italian designer ones—implied that he was exempt from the industry dress code, that his aesthetic flourished outside the rules.

Dozens of freshly sharpened pencils, taped in a row on a paper backing, stood like a machine-gun clip on the ledge of his cubicle wall. Sittig was an ad warrior. The slang around the office for somebody who would just as soon write ads as breathe was "ad hound," but he took it an aggressive step further. Dick Sittig had a private pact with his own muse. He had sworn to defend her honor in any petty skirmish with a lesser mind, a vow that required his constant vigilance, since he was quick to judge—and, usually, to find people lacking.

Sittig had two creative teams working under him on the Nissan account. Technically, he was partnered with Clow, but for the moment, given Clow's other responsibilities, he was running the account alone. On Friday, April 6, he called his teams together in the Treehouse to look at Sentra launch ideas for the first time. They'd been soaking up Sentra lore for weeks—first a trip to Nissan headquarters to drive the new 1991 model Sentra, and then a trip to Smyrna, Tennessee, the site of Nissan's stateside plant, to seek inspiration on the assembly line. When they returned, each team got stacks of studio photographs, "beauty shots" of the new Sentra, to put them in the mood to glamorize the car.

What they didn't have, though, was an approved creative brief— the strategic roadmap that guided every campaign—the absence of which guaranteed that today's ideas would be scattered all over the conceptual landscape. The account planners and executives couldn't crack the "single most compelling idea" that every brief called for. At the moment, it read, "The new Nissan Sentra gives you the style and performance of a (well-built) sports sedan in an economy car." Style, performance, quality construction and economy. No one could communicate four attributes in a single commercial.

Sittig had refrained from giving the teams any concrete direction— not because he couldn't figure out what to do, but because it was too early in the process to set artificial limits. In typical Chiat/Day fashion, the teams started work without an approved brief, or any sense of what their group head wanted. They didn't know whether to fold the launch into the Fantasy campaign or try a separate introduction.

They came armed with tissues and rationales. Each one had heard the by now legendary story of how Sittig and his partner had come up with the idea for the Fantasy campaign munching cookies at the Rose Café, and the next day had wiped the other creatives off the face of the map with their executions. Each one hoped he would be this year's hero—but it was essential to have defenses securely in place, so that falling short wouldn't look like falling short.

"This is real loosy-goosy stuff," said one art director dismissively. "We expect it all to be shitcanned."

His partner complained that he had written "grocery list spots," and blamed the multiple-item creative brief.

Sittig strolled the row of Johnnie's pizzas that had been set out at the back of the Treehouse, slapped a slice on a paper plate and slung himself into a chair. He tilted his head back and piloted the slice down toward his mouth. He put his feet up on the table. He was ready to go to work. As far as he was concerned, this first session was like a game of pool. All the balls were racked up at one end of the table. His job was to shoot the cue ball down there and break them up.

A frustrating hour later he was listening to embarrassed creatives making feeble sex jokes: Why not show one BMW on top of another, their needles moving, their radiators steaming, the garage shaking; a postcoital cigarette for each sedan and—cut to nine months later—a little Sentra pops out. The problem was that the creatives had imagined only the most mundane fantasies about the car. They saw it as a bottom-of-the-line BMW, an affordable alternative to a Mercedes, a car that would magically transform a young man into a taller version of himself, alongside a classier-looking girlfriend.

Sittig wasn't buying. "It's all real logical and rational," he said. "We need to try some emotional stuff too. Nissan's bringing you the thrill of driving. I'd like to try emotional—like, 'the sports sedan for the rest of us.' " The teams might also want to try a tease introduction, one that talked about a new car coming but never said what car it was.

He offered two examples. He imagined a fifteen-second spot using clips from old TV talk shows, all of which said, "Let me introduce to you . . ." or, "Let's have a big hand for . . . ," without giving away the identity of the product. Or they could try what he called "a reverse Infiniti spot," referring to what the industry called Infiniti's "rocks and trees campaign," a series of commercials that lingered on gorgeous landscapes without ever showing the car.

"Spend thirty seconds lovingly shooting every detail of the car," he said, "and not say what it is or who it's from."

"No logo? Nothing?" said one of the writers.

"No," said Sittig. "Just that it's available October 10."

The others were silent, awed by the ease with which Sittig rolled out big, imaginative ideas. Encouraged, he tried a few more. How about filming a staged event—put a camera inside a Testarossa, catch people's reactions, and use them without showing the car, as though they were responding to a Sentra. He'd heard about Pontiac's plan to send a car to Mikhail Gorbachev. One of the writers jumped in: Why not send a Sentra to Václav Havel, the playwright president of Czechoslovakia?

"I'd love a stunt," murmured Sittig, appreciatively. "Something bigger than advertising."

The others filed out, mindful that Sittig the administrator could decide at any moment to become Sittig the copywriter, and upstage them all. One of the writers had approached him weeks before to suggest that everyone in the group ought to get work produced, and that it was Sittig's responsibility to make sure that they did. Sittig had responded badly. This wasn't school, where even the tone deaf got a chance to be in the Christmas pageant. Creatives had to win the right to get their work produced—and if they didn't, he would step in.

*   *   *

A week later, after a second dead-end meeting, Sittig announced his intention to do just that. In fact, he was going to invite every creative in the department who had the time or inclination to take a crack at the Sentra launch. People might complain about "gang bangs," in which more creatives worked on an idea than could ever hope to see their work produced, but Sittig and Clow were in agreement. If someone else beat you out on a gang bang, it meant that his work was better than yours. Instead of moaning about how your work didn't get picked, you ought to be fixing it—so that next time, everyone would resent you.

In the first three months of his administration, Kuperman had been swamped by the Nissan restructuring, budget emergencies, and by his own determined efforts to get account services and new business into shape. But he was mindful of the agency's smaller accounts, none of whom liked to feel small, all of whom lived in Nissan's shadow. They needed tending. On April 18, in response to the client's invitation, Kuperman and account services director Jim Weinstein made a day trip north to Livingston, California, home of Foster Farms Poultry, Inc., to make sure everyone there was satisfied.

Kuperman's first reaction to the news that the client wanted to see him had been apocalyptic. "We're getting fired," he told Weinstein.

But his account services director denied that there was a problem. "Why would they fly us all the way up there to fire us?" asked Weinstein. As far as he was concerned, the four-year-old account was as stable a client as the agency had. The company's advertising challenge was fairly clear: in California, where state law required poultry to be additive-free, Foster Farms' fresh, hormone- and preservative-free chickens were a parity product with competitor Zacky Farms' birds, so the advertising had to make Foster Farms' freshness seem fresher, somehow, as well as introduce customers to the company's deli meat line. In Utah and Arizona, where people were perfectly happy buying frozen poultry, the ads had to convince the consumer that a troublesome fresh bird—which had to be cooked within days, unlike convenient frozen fowl—tasted better, and was better for them.

It was a nice, finite challenge. The Foster Farms executives were reasonable, pleasant folks who had complained only once, back in the first year of the relationship, about feeling ignored. There had been some shifts in personnel, on both sides, over the past year, but nothing major.

Kuperman was unconvinced. He and Weinstein arrived at Foster Farms' offices and were ushered into a room, to wait for general manager Tom Orr.

"We're getting fired," said Kuperman.

Weinstein ignored him. A few moments later Orr walked into the room, greeted the two men, and said he wanted to fire Chiat/Day.

Orr had a list of grievances. He'd found himself arguing about supermarkets with a British account executive who had been at the agency for two weeks; how could a recent immigrant understand California agribusiness? He did not like any of the radio scripts he'd seen for the past six months. Worst of all, he hadn't seen Clow in two years. Orr understood about the demands that a client like Nissan made on an agency, but perhaps Chiat/Day's size meant it could no longer service the small client. Orr wanted to be at an agency where he was treated like an asset, not a back-of-the-hand obligation.

Still, he liked Chiat/Day. He made one suggestion to Kuperman and Weinstein: If they would shift the account from Venice to the San Francisco office, Foster Farms would stay at Chiat/Day. San Francisco was closer, and so much smaller. In that universe, Foster Farms would be a substantial account.

In the weeks since the agency's board meetings, Goldberg had been convinced to purchase the San Francisco office after all, induced by a loan from Chiat/Day and three years' salary guarantee. There had been no formal announcement, as yet, but the San Francisco office of Chiat/Day was about to become a competing independent agency staffed by ex-Chiat/Day employees.

Kuperman could hardly promise to consider Orr's suggestion, but if he confessed the truth he would lose the account. He asked for a chance to think things over. On the way home, he instructed Weinstein not to tell anyone what had happened. He wasn't going to let people know that the agency had been fired, because as far as he was concerned, it hadn't been, not yet. Kuperman was going to figure out how to save Foster Farms.

*　　*　　*

For all the talk of restraint, Chiat/Day went after Reebok as though the agency was the acknowledged favorite in a pitch for a brand-new account. New York had ten creative teams churning out ads, while planners and account executives worked on applications of "How far can you go in a pair of Reeboks?" for everything from sales meetings to advertising to direct mail.

The night before the pitch, Chiat and the rest of the team were holed up in a bank of rooms in a Boston hotel. He reviewed the creative and strong-armed Smith and McElligott into a late-night session that yielded a half dozen executions. Then Chiat reworked some of the ads himself, to get the exact tone he was looking for.

They agreed that they had an unbeatable presentation. The rumor around town was that the two agencies who had preceded Chiat/Day had made weak presentations. The only strong competitor was the Boston-based Hill, Holliday, Connors, Cosmopulos, Inc., whose Los Angeles office handled Nissan's Infiniti account. The people at Chiat/Day believed that Hill, Holliday could not handle a combustible account like Reebok. The pitch team—Chiat, Wolf, Newman, McElligott, Smith, account executive Steve Friedman and a handful of others who had worked on the account—spent three hours with Reebok executives on Wednesday, April 11. They emerged confident and exhausted. Jane Newman announced that she was "one hundred percent sure" of victory.

They'd given the client a hundred executions, all in the context of what Wolf called a "total program" for marketing and advertising. It was just the kind of presentation Wolf wanted to see from Chiat/Day—great work framed by appropriate strategy.

On Thursday, word came back that Hill, Holliday had done a great job. Worse, Reebok CEO Paul Fireman himself had attended the Hill, Holliday pitch. He hadn't been present at any of the other agency presentations. Those two bits of information had a devastating effect. Was Fireman predisposed to choose the Boston agency? Could Chiat/Day have done something better? Newman wished they had rehearsed more, and reversed herself; now she was as sure of defeat as she had been of triumph. Wolf grumbled that the creative really hadn't lived up to the tag line. Given the chance to do it all over again, Chiat still would have revamped the creative presentation at the last minute. But now a nagging pest of a thought perched on his cubicle wall and whispered insistently: What if his meddling had so unsettled the creatives that their presentation seemed ragged?

Protocol demanded that Fireman or Duerden call Chiat to give him the official news, but on Friday, April 13, Steve Friedman got a bewildering call. One of the people at Reebok wanted to know if Chiat/Day could produce a spot the agency had created for Michael Chang, the young tennis star who had won the French Open in 1989.

"What are you talking about?" he asked. It was the whole account that was at stake. Why would Reebok want Chiat/Day to produce a single commercial?

"They don't have anything," said the Reebok staffer, conspiratorially.

So that was it. The "they" in that sentence was clearly Hill, Holliday, who must have won the account. All Reebok wanted from Chiat/Day was a single commercial.

"What are you, *crazy*?" said Friedman. Then he stopped himself. It was fairly clear that Chiat/Day had just lost Reebok for the second, and last, time, but he knew better than to say no to business.

"Fine," he said. "We'll do it."

Friedman, who prided himself on not getting depressed, was depressed. He started calling people at Reebok, and finally got through to an advertising executive who was particularly fond of Chiat/Day. She confirmed his fears: Reebok was going to move the account.

"Fine," said Friedman. "But what was the positioning? What was the line?" Having invested three months of work in the "How far can you go?" line, he found it hard to believe that anyone had come up with a better one.

Hill, Holliday's line, she told him, was "Reebok—It's time to play."

"That's interesting," he said. "I don't quite understand how that's what you were looking for, how that's a rallying cry."

They chatted about some of the things Reebok might do—like having vans drive down Wall Street with a loudspeaker blaring, "It's time to play—Reebok," or inserting paper airplanes in *Footwear News* magazine—and as they spoke Friedman found his mood lifting. All these ideas were fluff, as far as he was concerned. Chiat/Day might have been better off refusing the invitation to pitch, but the agency hadn't lost on quality. It was politics, just as they'd thought all along.

He decided to order a custom T-shirt for the executive, that read, "Reebok. It's Time to Pray."

Jane Newman consoled herself that at least she would not have to fire anyone right away. Like Kuperman, she had been firing by attrition for months. Between those savings, the end of spot bonuses, and the raise freezes, she might be able to get by without a wholesale housecleaning.

She had a deep emotional block about firing people. In Britain there was a terrible stigma attached to being fired; people who were let go often couldn't find another job. Whenever possible, Newman insisted on what she considered to be a more humane approach. She told people they had two weeks to find another job, provided them with the name of a headhunter and, if possible, a job opportunity. She always wanted it to look as though an employee had resigned his job to take another.

Advertising was a fickle enough industry. A creative was only as good as his last ad, and an account executive only as valuable as his current clients perceived him to be. Most executives, including Wolf and Chiat, accepted firings as a necessary evil, but Newman wanted the employees who left to do so without a stain on their records, and she wanted the ones who remained to be spared the anxiety of wondering if they were next. It was something of a private crusade: people who left Newman's employ did so with their dignity intact.

She was grateful to be spared personnel problems right now. Privately she anticipated that this was only the beginning of a rough year. A big loss always made existing clients skittish. That, combined with a tight economy, could make her sunny profit projections something of a stretch.

For all of his resistance to the inequality that the corner office represented, and his love of the wide-open architectural spaces, Chiat was a slave to Manhattan's vertical orientation. Chiat/Day's offices at 79 Fifth Avenue took up five floors, with a sunny northwest corner space on each one. The cubicles were no larger than anyone else's, but they did have two windows, and on each floor, they belonged to a senior executive. Chiat, who liked to move his employees around periodically to shake them up, had had other offices before, but at the moment he occupied the seventh-floor corner, in the shade of a tree made by artist Liz Bachhuber out of the office's discarded scraps of paper.

On Monday, April 16, he came to work and waited for the phone call from Reebok. He knew that the agency had lost the account. Friedman's call was only the first in a flurry of exchanges the Friday before, as disappointed Reebok employees called to commiserate. Still, Chiat had to endure the charade of the formal notification. He had to sit and wait for the phone to ring.

He felt himself shutting down emotionally. He'd learned, over the years, to get to the point where bad news couldn't touch him. His colleagues liked to kid him: Chiat was always calm in the midst of a crisis like this one. He only got nuts when the world around him was placid.

This was different, though. He believed he would have felt this numb even if Chiat/Day had won Reebok back. The relationship had been too draining, over the years, too hard to read. He'd grown tired of the temperaments on both sides.

Chiat was trapped between two grating truths: it had been a mistake to be seduced into pitching again, and the pitch, in his mind, had been "absolutely bulletproof." The friction was enervating. He knew too well that it was possible to do great work and still succumb to corporate politics and cultivated relationships—but then, how to find the energy to try again? If he dwelt on that, he would be too upset to function. The only productive option was not to feel at all.

When the call came, he quietly informed Newman and Friedman that he'd gotten the official news, and agreed that they ought to throw a Reebok party on Thursday, to give everyone who had worked on the account a chance to swap Reebok horror stories. Whenever the magnitude of the loss started to swamp him, Chiat reminded himself: "The key was, we did as good as we could have done. We did the best we could do. That's all I can measure the quality of this place against. I can't measure it against why they didn't pick us, because I have no control over that."

It was what he always told himself when faced with bad news, but this time he seemed worn out by the effort. He and his agency existed as an insular universe, bound together as though the agency were somehow a physical and emotional extension of Chiat himself, grown out of him and connected to him. Any business disappointment was a personal rejection, and being jilted when he felt he had done his best was particularly painful.

By the end of the week his frustration had risen. The calls about producing individual commercials kept coming, but they didn't please him. Quite the reverse. He wished the account would go away if it was going to go away. He teased Friedman about making more money for the agency now that they'd been fired than they had when Reebok was a client, but beneath the wisecracks he was bitter.

"It's a lousy business, essentially," Chiat blurted out late one afternoon. "The joys you get aren't from most of your client relationships. The joy you get is from doing good work, and you've got to get it out of the work. You love those clients who allow you to do good work, and you have them for a while. A moment in time. I'm certainly not unemotional about this. We were in, we were out, we were back, we were winning, we were losing. I don't know."

As though in memoriam, revised versions of the Bungee spot ran again on April 18, 19 and 20, twice on ABC and twice on CBS. The ABC version used a generic white athletic shoe instead of the identifiable Nike, with a voiceover and superscript warning that said: "What you are about to see is very dangerous. The sport requires special equipment and training. This dramatization was filmed without injury." CBS allowed the shot of the Nike shoe. Its disclaimer read: "What you are about to see is very dangerous. The activity requires special equipment and training. This is a dramatization." The commercial never ran again.

16

The consequence of Chiat's decision to defer to his new management team, and his preoccupation with expanding the agency, was that there was no longer anyone to stop an argument. Disagreements rolled on for weeks, with no resolution in sight, often because the two men who had inherited the agency, Clow and Wolf, could not reconcile their differences. It made even Tom Patty uneasy. There was still no clear chain of command on Nissan creative—only an elusive Sittig holding closed creative meetings and acting as if he were in charge, when Clow was the ranking creative on the account. Patty had asked Wolf and Kuperman to address the issue, to no avail, so he called Chiat, who was about to leave for Europe, and demanded that he come to Venice on his return. Chiat had to decide, once and for all, who was in charge of Nissan creative. Patty wanted Dad to slap Sittig's wrist and order him to develop the Sentra launch within the Fantasy campaign.

Chiat relished the invitation. Aside from his barnstorming visit to Venice to promote fiscal responsibility, and his cameo appearance in the Reebok pitch, he had been doing what he said he was going to do, traveling throughout Western Europe looking for established agencies that might want to form an alliance with Chiat/Day. He had found a likely ally in Brindfors, a twelve-year-old agency with offices in Sweden, Norway, Finland, West Germany and Belgium, a company with a strong print reputation to complement Chiat/Day's film production know-how. They had agreed to try a joint venture, to be followed by a merger—the eventual goal being offices in Milan, Barcelona and Paris.

But prospecting was an isolated business, the excitement of it dulled somewhat by the sluggish economy. The era of lightning raids and acquisitions was over, replaced by a more methodical pursuit. It was nice to have an invitation to meddle. As soon as Chiat arrived in Venice in late April, he scheduled meetings with Patty and Sittig, and by the end of his first afternoon in the office he was in a fine, familiar rage. He called Clow in Auckland, where he was in the midst of a tour of Mojo's offices, and started to yell, sounding for all the world like an angry father who has come home from work to find his children tussling on the floor and his wife out getting her hair cut. *"It's seventy-five percent of our business!"* he shouted. "What are we doing with two junior teams on this account?"

The next morning he pulled Wolf, Kuperman and Patty into 3 Mile Island. "As of yesterday, there was no work on the Fantasy campaign in the agency," he began, without any preamble. "According to Lee, this is not a problem because he's responding to Bob Thomas, and he and you"—he gestured toward Patty—"are handling this the way it's supposed to be handled. Now, I don't see how you can be handling this the way it's supposed to be handled, if there's no work done on the Fantasy campaign.

"And the other issue is, I asked Sittig yesterday how many people are working on the account. He said two teams. I don't understand why only two teams are on an account that's over fifty-eight percent of *all* our business. What's going on?"

He kept talking. He didn't actually want an answer until he'd recited his complete list of grievances. "I'm trying to be calm," he said, "but I get this call from Patty who's nervous that nothing's getting done. What kind of magic was supposed to be done between yesterday and next week's work session?"

No one answered.

"I am assured," said Chiat, allowing sarcasm to creep into his voice, "that this is *not* a creative plot to abandon this campaign."

The others waited.

"Can't anyone else in the agency see the work?" Chiat asked.

No response.

Chiat sighed. "I don't understand how you're going to have a tissue session with the client in a week," he said, referring to the meeting where creatives presented scripts and tissue-paper sketches to the client, "when nobody's done any work on what I thought was a campaign with legs."

Kuperman observed, hesitantly, that while it might be a good campaign, it didn't easily expand to accommodate accolades and other special advertising. Those ads, in turn, drained media money from the campaign—and a campaign that didn't get seen was as good as no campaign at all. Perhaps they should change their definition of a campaign from a narrowly defined stylistic conceit to a broader attitude, or tone.

"Lee says, 'The attitude is the same,' " said Chiat, unconvinced. "That's one of those great lines. But what does it mean?"

Chiat's fear was that the agency was indulging in the sort of creative grandstanding that had contributed to Chiat/Day's rogue reputation—that the desire to get noticed had eclipsed any sense of what was best for the account. Last year Clow and Sittig had promoted the Fantasy campaign as a campaign that was broad enough to cover all the client's needs, a campaign that would endure. Now they were complaining that it was stale, a limited idea that would not stretch to include the Sentra launch. They dressed up their objections to look like honorable concern, but Chiat feared their resistance was merely a cranky desire to try something new.

Wolf confirmed his suspicion. "I talked to Dick yesterday," said Wolf, "and he said, 'Who would fantasize about a Sentra?' And, 'How do you fantasize about a car that doesn't exist?' "

Chiat was curt. "I have a fantasy," he said, "about getting another team on it that can fantasize."

"There are two issues," said Wolf. "One, who's the creative director? Two, what's driving this lack of work? And I really think it's this philosophy of 'Don't block me in.' Sittig doesn't want this campaign. He wants to do famous spots."

The more important issue was leadership: If there were a strong guiding hand on the account, Sittig would not be able to indulge himself. The reason there was no discipline was because Clow didn't impose it, and he didn't impose it because he seemed to think he was running his own exclusive fiefdom.

Wolf had gotten to the point where he thought Clow made both a very positive and a very negative contribution to the agency. The creatives thought of him as a guru, and his ability to inspire was invaluable. But he didn't fit into the Venice office's organizational structure. He had the authority to do whatever he wanted and there was no clean line of accountability.

No one had any qualms when it came to complaining about Wolf. Perhaps it was time for *him* to speak up. "You have a guy in Lee," he said, addressing Chiat, "who doesn't feel responsible to *anyone*. Except you. And maybe me." As a result, the agency risked disappointing its biggest client on the company's most important product launch. The first internal creative review was scheduled for the day before the client work session. Wolf thought it was suicide. What if none of the account people liked the work they saw on Wednesday? What if even the creatives were unhappy? How could they turn around and show that work on Thursday?

Chiat's mouth was set in a grim line. "Since when has that stopped us from presenting?"

Wolf was adamant. He instructed Patty to move the client work session back, to buy an extra weekend.

"Is Sittig capable of being a creative director?" asked Chiat.

Kuperman wasn't sure. A group head, certainly.

"If you have any doubt at all . . . ," said Chiat.

Kuperman was comfortable with Sittig as long as Clow was working with him. He agreed with Wolf: the real issue was, who would ride herd on the two creatives? Kuperman nominated himself, in a move that consolidated his power as office president and gave him the right to police Clow. He would assume formal control of the regional account, while Clow remained in charge of the national account; but on a practical level, Kuperman would run the whole show, since the office president had authority over any working creative. Clow might be the agency's creative conscience, second in rank only to Chiat, but on Nissan he was the art director, and Kuperman would be his boss.

Patty liked the arrangement because it meant that he could deal with Clow, whom he much preferred to Sittig. He reminded the others that he and Clow worked well together, only to be cut off by an enraged Chiat.

"*Fine!*" Chiat exploded. "*Then where's the fucking campaign?*"

Patty calmly explained that he had given Sittig a list of spots that were supposed to come under the Fantasy campaign umbrella, which only made Chiat more upset. Sittig had the list, knew what to do, and still hadn't come up with any Sentra Fantasy spots?

"The Fantasy campaign is going to disappear," Chiat said, "into the asshole of the Sentra introduction."

That day Chiat's edict went out: the 1991 Sentra launch was to be incorporated into the Fantasy campaign. The agency was not interested in teasers, an independent launch, or any of the other ideas the creatives had been working on for the past month.

Dick Sittig resented the postponement of the client work session, and the implication of doubt in his ability, but the May 2 internal meeting—the first to which the account staff was invited—was sorry proof of just how far the creatives were from a decent Sentra launch. One writer was dismissed for writing what Clow called "Mensa test" commercials, scripts that tried the intellect with references to everything from the atomic weight of boron to the Andromeda star cluster. Another team had what everyone agreed was a great line—"Your car has a body. Does it have a soul?"—but the execution was outside the Fantasy campaign and off-strategy, since it ignored the Sentra's affordability. Even Sittig had his ego handed to him. His first effort was an animated spot, "a cross between *Fantasia* and Santa's Workshop," he explained, that took the viewer on a tour of the Nissan design studio. Clow listened to the script, looked at the tape of sample animation styles, and turned down the idea.

"Just unusual visuals don't qualify as a dream, I don't think," he said.

"I thought part of the strategy was to say it's been redesigned," said Sittig, unable to hide his disappointment. He was not used to being found wanting in front of junior creatives.

The next morning Patty sat Clow down and told him they were nowhere. If Sittig wasn't going to be more enthusiastic about what he was doing, Patty was prepared to name a new group head. Having put Clow on notice, he marched back to his cubicle and called John Rinek, Nissan's national advertising creative manager. Patty wanted him to drive up to Venice that afternoon, to help clarify the client's position for the creatives.

"We're running out of time," Patty said. "We're sinking in quicksand, and while we're drowning they're shooting at us from the trees."

At the same time, a somber Clow pulled Sittig into his cubicle and suggested that the honeymoon was over. Sittig was going to have to learn to get along, which meant working within the framework of the Fantasy campaign. He chided his young partner.

"You guys just didn't do it," he said. "You didn't do dreams. You did lots of pretty pictures, but it wasn't dreams."

John Rinek was a valued ally at Nissan, a man whose loyalty to the agency predated his loyalty to his employer. Chiat/Day had recommended him for his current job, having worked with him years before on the Yamaha motorcycle account. It was easy to be frank with Rinek, a boyish, slightly built man whose auburn hair swooped across his brow in an adult version of a bowl cut. He was an eager, likable man—and he took the agency's problems seriously, since they would, if left untended, reflect poorly on him.

Clow, Sittig, Patty, Rabosky and his partner Ian Potter were waiting for Rinek in 3 Mile Island. The first thing he wanted to do, given the urgency of Patty's call, was reassure them that despite the seeming confusion over positioning, the agency and Nissan were talking to the same customers. The only disagreement was one of style.

"It's how we're doing it, not what we're doing," he said. "There's no disagreement on who our target is."

He showed them two lists of words. The way Rinek saw it, Chiat/Day wanted ads that were:

Confident
Smart
Sophisticated, understated, upscale

The people at Nissan had a different idea:

Confident
Smart
Bold, upbeat, enthusiastic, aggressive

Sittig couldn't restrain himself. "I'd like to talk to you about confident," he said. "A confident company, to me, can speak to the consumer in this tone of voice, but I think you want," and he raised one arm over his head, the other out to the side, "*marching to war!*"

"One thing we have in common," said Rinek, refusing the bait, "is our belief in the Fantasy campaign."

"Yeah, the Fantasy campaign," said Clow, chuckling. "Except we can't launch the Sentra in it. Just kidding. Just kidding, Tom."

Patty screamed in mock anguish.

Rinek tried again with an analogy about styles of architecture. "Nissan can say it wants to be Mediterranean. That Tudor isn't a good house, because Honda lives there. But it's okay to pick a style."

"It seems you don't care what the style of house is," said Sittig, "as long as the color paint is loud and the lawn ornaments are huge."

"If Bob wants a Mediterranean house," said Clow, referring to Rinek's boss, Bob Thomas, "the question is, will he let us be the architect and build him a bitchin' Mediterranean house, or is he going to keep telling us where to put the balcony?"

"Lee Clow?"

"Yes."

"Milton Glaser calling. Just a minute, please."

He was on hold. It was the one telephone maneuver that most enraged Clow, since it implied that the caller's time was more valuable than that of the person he was calling—that Clow could afford to sit and wait, while Glaser, the renowned New York graphic designer and member of New York's prestigious Art Directors Club, could not. He had to stifle the urge to tell the secretary that he'd wait to talk to Glaser until he had learned to dial the phone himself. When Glaser picked up, Clow wanted to say, "Hey, Milton, your finger broken?" but he thought better of it.

He would be eternally grateful for that moment of self-control. Glaser had called to inform Clow that he had been named to the Art Directors Club Hall of Fame, a clique of seventy-three members, most of whom were many years Clow's senior, venerable members of the East Coast design establishment. Clow was an outsider in terms of age, geography and aesthetic bent, which made the selection even more remarkable. He was the first Chiat/Day art director to be inducted into the Hall of Fame.

Kuperman didn't like the way the Venice office was running. Everyone who had any power seemed to be on the attack, while the masses tried to stay out of target range. There was none of the work-all-night camaraderie he recalled from the Nissan pitch.

It was May 1. The Century 21 pitch, Kuperman's first as office president, was scheduled for June 6. He had to figure out some way to motivate people, to get them to extend themselves rather than just working hard enough to stay out of trouble. Chiat joked that his most significant contribution since he'd handed over the operation to Wolf was fear. People were afraid of Wolf, too. Kuperman reflected on his own behavior. He was still short on patience and too quick to bully people.

He called his department heads together that afternoon to make a short speech about perception and reality. His perception, he told them, was that there was too much fear at Chiat/Day, too much finger-pointing. He'd managed that way himself, in the past, and sometimes he still fell into blaming people, but he thought it was an easy out, a dangerous attitude. It had to stop.

The reality was that the recession was going to get deeper and money was going to get even tighter. He didn't want the Venice office to be touched, so he instructed his department heads: "Get smart. I can't go around watching every dollar. Everyone has to watch it."

That was it. The next day he scheduled what he called a Century 21 "assault meeting" in the Boathouse, with Weinstein, Rabosky, Rob White, Laurie Coots, two account planners and the head of the non-Nissan media department. He announced that he had canceled his vacation to devote himself to the pitch—no small loss, since he had planned a dream trip, ten days of golf on the best courses in Scotland. He had done it to set an example. How could anyone complain about late nights or lost weekends when Kuperman had given up the trip of a lifetime?

They complimented him on his dedication.

"It may not be dedication," he said. "It may be preservation." But he was pleased at the effect. Those involved in the pitch would have to go some to match his level of commitment.

Century 21 faced a complicated challenge. The client needed to address three distinct constituencies: the franchisees who comprised its network of real estate agents, who needed the kind of inspirational message that would make them hunt more aggressively for listings; sellers, who wanted a realtor who could show their homes to advantage and command the highest price; and prospective buyers, who were looking for a realtor with great listings that they could afford.

The pitch, which required speculative creative work, was going to be expensive. Century 21 was prepared to pay $25,000 to purchase proprietary rights to the competing agencies' creative work, but Kuperman expected to spend an additional $100,000 to $150,000 to do the work right. In effect, the agencies subsidized the client's right to own material for less than it would have cost under normal circumstances. There was nothing to stop a client from producing a losing candidate's commercial, if that single idea was appealing.

An agency had the right to refuse to do speculative creative work—to try to win an account purely on the basis of strategic thinking, with perhaps a few rough executions to talk about—but the Century 21 field included major competitors like BBDO and Young & Rubicam. Such a tactic would likely be interpreted as insecurity.

Kuperman rattled off a list of things that had to be done immediately. He'd already talked to McElligott about getting creatives from New York and Toronto involved long distance. He wanted Rabosky to pick the creative teams today, and get them working. He didn't want to hear from the account planners, who had already spent $8,000 on focus groups, about how valuable more groups might be. He wanted the creative brief right now, and only grudgingly gave them an extra day. He wanted the planners to provide the creatives with a fact list of every claim Century 21 had ever made—or rather, the ones that could be substantiated. He wanted estimates for music, voiceovers, print work and three Ripomatics—the video collages they used to convey the way a finished commercial might look—so that he could appeal to Wolf for funds.

The only remaining issue was one of control. Who was running the pitch—Wolf, Clow or Kuperman? Since this was to be a creative-driven presentation, was Rabosky the last word? Given the disarray Kuperman had seen on Nissan and Foster Farms, he was determined to resolve that issue at the outset.

"I'm going to be the lead guy on this," he said. "Everything should filter through me. I'll be talking to Tom and Steve, but everyone should come to me."

He smiled at the people seated around him. "So let's get this sucker," he said, "because I'm not going to Scotland because of it."

Kuperman had a plan for another pitch, but only a half dozen people in the office knew about it. On May 8, Tom Orr and a couple of other Foster Farms executives came to Venice to meet with Kuperman, Clow and Weinstein. Kuperman sprung a surprise on the client. He wanted to pitch the Foster Farms business with a completely new team out of the Venice office, to prepare as though this were a formal review, but to limit the process, for the moment, to the office that already had the account.

"Please don't," said Orr. "We told you, if you want to keep the business, give us a San Francisco team."

Kuperman ignored the request and explained that he wasn't ready to lose an account so early in his tenure. Clow promised to serve as "creative watchdog" for a year, if only the client would go along with the idea. Then they waited. If Orr insisted on moving to San Francisco, they would have to confess that the San Francisco office was being sold, and a $4 million account would walk out the door. If he acquiesced, they would have to put together a secret pitch.

"Okay," said Orr, skeptically. "We'll give you a shot. If you want to pitch an L.A. team, okay, but it's your only shot. If it doesn't work, don't come back and say you want to try a San Francisco team."

Image advertising tried to convince people that they could buy fulfillment. A man might never attain the station in life to which he aspired, but he absolutely could purchase a symbol of it, one that others would understand and appreciate. What bothered Dick Sittig was that the Sentra lacked status. It was hardly anyone's dream car. The advertising had to concoct an aspirational image for the car, and to acknowledge the buyer's financial limitations without ever implying that these were permanent restraints. The Sentra had to look like the first in a string of ever more impressive automobiles the buyer would own.

Sittig was tired of the assignment, and weary of managing the creative teams. The first work session had been a disaster, despite Rinek's last-minute counseling, and since then Sittig had kept to himself. He knew he should have been dropping by to see how the others were doing, the way Clow always did, but he was getting testy. Sittig had always hated the kids in elementary school who asked the teacher what was going to be covered on tomorrow's quiz. He had always wanted to say, "Hey. I've been studying all the chapters. If she says, 'Pay special attention to Chapter Three,' I feel screwed. Figure it out for yourself, guys." That was how he felt about his teams. If they couldn't get it, he wasn't going to show them the way.

He sat alone in his cubicle late one night, a second client work session just days away, and thought about the car. Powerless people bought Sentras. He had to make them feel that that was a temporary condition—not to resent that they had failed to get further in life, but to assume that they were at the beginning of a grand ascent. He liked to call them "will-be's," as opposed to "wanna-be's." What he needed was a script that would make them believe in their own potential. Someday they would be in charge. Sittig had to communicate that.

Finally, the idea came to him—with no fanfare and fully formed, just the way the Fantasy campaign had appeared over cookies. He typed up a script and showed it to Clow the next morning. Clow drew up some rough boards and described the idea by phone to Chiat, who said he liked it. By mid-morning, a triumphant Sittig was staging impromptu performances in his office.

The commercial was called, "If I Owned a Car Company," a black and white dream in the expressionist style of the 1926 German film *Metropolis*—all angles and shadows, with the narrator seen only from his broad shoulders down. Sittig struck a pose—chest up, elbows out, fists at his waist—and became the narrator, a young man who dreamed that he owned a car company called My Motor Company. After he snared the biggest office for himself, he got down to the business of designing and manufacturing a great little sports sedan that even a young dreamer could afford. It debuted to wild acclaim.

"You know. Flash bulbs. Poppa-poppa-poppa. Poppa. Poppa," said Sittig.

The last line of the commercial was, "The 1991 Nissan Sentra. If you're tired of rich guys having all the fun." It was the synthesis of everything the new Sentra owner was supposed to be—ambitious, irreverent, on the move. Sittig spent much of the day doing repeat performances and accepting congratulations, as word of his idea spread throughout the building. Clow was already talking about adding the tag line to other executions, making it the line that held the launch together.

"All we need," Clow said, his eyes fairly dancing, "is 150,000 of them," meaning people who were tired of rich guys having all the fun, "who have $12,000 to spend. *Yeah.*"

Clow took charge of the May 14 Nissan work session with the air of a man who knew he had a delicious secret. He introduced Sittig's commercial by saying, "We think we've thought of something really neat, because it's from the point of view of the consumer." In Clow's pyramid of praise, "really neat" sat near the pinnacle, just down from "cool." He described the visuals, and then Sittig read his script, striking a new pose at every step of the dream.

"I think this could be a quite noticeable commercial," said Clow.

The client—all four of him—stuck to meeting protocol and chose not to comment until all the work was presented, so Clow played both sides of the dialogue, imagining the objections the client might have, and refuting each one in turn.

" 'Because rich guys shouldn't have all the fun,' " he said, savoring the line. "I think it's a really cool way of saying 'Affordable sports sedan,' which we all balked at."

He explained that they could use the line on print work, as well as on some of the other television executions.

"What it translates to is, 'I'm smarter than all those guys who're paying a lot for their cars,' " said Clow. "So it nets out to be a smart decision on a neat little car to drive. We got really excited about this. A fun attitude. It's poking fun at the minority—pushing it up high enough so that you're not Yuppie-bashing."

He presented four other executions, including a jovial spot called "Bob's Road," about a Sentra owner who enjoyed special privileges that included his own personal toll booth, his own freeway exit and a custom parking place. Then the people from the agency stared across the table at the quartet from Nissan, and waited.

"Lot of progress in one week," said national advertising manager Tom Hushek.

"The tonality is up and exciting and fun, and more credible," said Brooke Mitzel, national advertising manager for sports cars and trucks. "The only thing is, we don't want people to think they're driving a cheap car, and with these I don't think they will."

Rinek was more enthusiastic. "You've gone the step beyond to the essence of this car," he said. "The feeling. 'The affordable sports car' is more rational, but this is feeling. But you're not overpromising. You're telling them the feeling they're going to have, which is terrific."

"We tried to position Nissan," said Sittig, "as having graciously opened the sports sedan category."

"The democratization of the category," said Clow.

BOB: If I could afford a sports sedan . . . the road would belong to me . . . Bob. I'd have one of those multi-valve engines . . . independent suspension . . . . . . and of course, a spoiler on the back. Yeah . . . if I could afford a sports sedan . . . life would be a cruise.

COP: Oh, it's you, Bob.

ANNCR VO: Presenting the Nissan Sentra SE-R. Because rich guys shouldn't have all the fun.

The new Sentra SE-R

The $165 million Nissan national account transformed Chiat/Day overnight, from a renegade boutique into a major agency. "Bob's Road" was part of a $40 million effort to launch the redesigned 1991 Nissan Sentra. The "econobox" sedan got a facelift—and Chiat/Day had to convince the consumer that the new look was worth a hefty price increase. Advertising Age magazine named the spot Commercial of the Year.

Chiat/Day introduced another new Sentra model with a commercial called "If I Owned a Car Company," featuring actor Ron Pearson as a young man who dreamed of designing an affordable sports sedan. The tag line, "Because Rich Guys Shouldn't Have All the Fun," was supposed to make the Sentra owner feel that he had a bright future—that his tight budget was only a temporary constraint.

YOUNG GUY VO: If I owned a car company, first I'd snag the biggest office . . . then build myself a sports sedan. I'd make the body aerodynamic . . . like even the door handles would be cool. Then I'd give it a 16-valve engine. And, just to cheese-off the other car companies, I'd make my sports sedan affordable, 'cuz I'm tired of the rich guys havin' all the fun.

ANNCR VO: Presenting the 1991 Nissan Sentra . . . the first affordable sports sedan.

"Turbo Z Dreamer," a $1.7 million commercial directed by feature film director Ridley Scott, was the centerpiece of Chiat/Day's 1990 Fantasy campaign for Nissan. But critics who said that the spot glorified speed quickly killed it: "Turbo Z Dreamer" aired once on Super Bowl XXIV, and was never seen again.

TURBO Z DREAMER: So, I'm havin'

this dream—I'm in a Turbo Z . . .

. . . and these guys are after me . . .

. . . but they can't catch me . . .

. . . so they get a car . . .

. . . but they can't catch me . . .

. . . so they get a plane . . .

. . . just as they're about to catch me . . .

the . . . twin . . . turbos . . . kick . . . in.

SFX: Plane.

Extremely dangerous. Don't try this.

Extremely dangerous. Don't try this.

Extremely dangerous. Don't try this.

Extremely dangerous. Don't try this.

Reebok

Chiat/Day often got its clients into the headlines—and into trouble—with provocative creative work. Television networks that aired Reebok's "Bungee Jumper" were deluged with calls from concerned parents, worried that their children would try the dangerous stunt that professional jumpers John and Peter Kockelman, of Mountain View, California's Bungee Adventures, had executed.

ANNCR VO: The Pump from Reebok. It fits a little better than your ordinary athletic shoe.

Right:
The landmark Apple Computer "1984" spot, introducing the company's Macintosh computer, was so controversial that the client didn't want it to be broadcast. "1984" aired only once—and was named Commercial of the Decade by Advertising Age.

ANNCR VO: On January 24th, Apple Computer will introduce Macintosh. And you'll see why 1984 won't be like "1984."

SFX: Violin Music.

MAN 1: You know, there's just no substitute for a well-polished train.

MAN 2: Indeed.

MAN 3: (MAN 4 enters.) Roy, how nice to see you. (Shakes hand of MAN 4, who hands him a box of chocolates.)

MAN 2: Oh!

MAN 3: You shouldn't have.

MAN 2: Do sit down.

MAN 3: May I offer you a cup of tea?

MAN 4: Why thank you, Wendell. Listen, I do love what you've done with this place.

MAN 1: Yes, this fabric would look lovely in my caboose.

MAN 2: I must remember to pick some up.

MAN 1: Finger sandwiches, gentlemen?

ANNCR VO: If it's out there, it's in here . . . the NYNEX Yellow Pages.

SFX: Book slams shut.

ANNCR VO: Why would anyone need another?

The NYNEX Yellow Pages campaign, "Human Cartoons," is one of Chiat/Day's most enduring efforts, based on a series of puns on telephone directory listings.

Another long-time client, Home Savings of America, almost fired Chiat/Day because of staff turnover on the account, so a new team was installed and instructed to give the client what he wanted—which was a commercial called "Us versus Them," contrasting Home's conservative investment policies with those of less dependable savings and loan institutions.

ANNCR VO: While some savings institutions were investing in pork bellies . . .

Home Savings invested in Tom and Sharon Morrisey.

While others invested in junk bonds . . .

. . . we invested in the Carruthers.

When banks put their money in foreign countries . . .

. . . we put our faith in Pam Gilbert.

As America's largest . . .

Home Savings makes loans for one, simple reason, we know a good investment when we see one.

9

NutraSweet
Making the world
a better place to eat.

*By the fall of 1990,
Chiat/Day's New York
office had lost accounts
worth $90 million, and the
recession had chipped away
at the remaining clients.
The agency was a "ninety-
nine to one shot" to win the
$25 million NutraSweet
account, according to the
executive who ran the
review, but Chiat/Day was
used to being the underdog.
It beat out eight of the
largest agencies in the
country to win the account.*

ANNCR VO: This is the famous NutraSweet gumball. The first little product that introduced everyone to the great taste of NutraSweet. Well then we started thinkin', hey, this could be big, so we started talkin' to people. First to soft drink people, then cereal people and cookie people, and we talked to dessert people, and cocoa people, coffee people and cake people. Breakfast people and tea people and yogurt people, man, like, you'd be amazed how many food people there are to talk to, so you're probably saying, OK, you've been doin' a lot of talkin', now how many foods do you have to show for it?
NutraSweet. Celebrating ten years of making the world a better place to eat.

The Energizer Bunny, who "kept going and going and going," walked through parodies of traditional commercials to place second in Adweek *magazine's "America's Favorite Advertising" poll in 1990 and third in 1991.*

JINGLE: Chu Chu Chu Chug-a-Cherry Chug-a-Cherry . . . it's extraordinary Chug-a-Cherry.

SFX: BOOM . . . BOOM . . . BOOM.

ANNCR VO: Still going. Nothing outlasts the Energizer. They keep going . . .

. . . and going and . . .

Jay Chiat presided over Chiat/Day inc. Advertising, a $1.2 billion agency, with the taunting challenge, "How big can we get before we get bad?" In 1990 he came perilously close to finding out.

Bob Wolf, the newly named CEO of Chiat/Day's North American offices, had an ambitious growth strategy, including the pursuit of big clients once thought too conservative for Chiat/Day and the abandonment of the small accounts that allowed the agency to do daring creative work but didn't bring in sufficient profits. Chiat liked the plan enough to give Wolf the CEO's job— but then he began to worry that success would cost the agency its soul.

Lee Clow (left), the creative conscience of Chiat/Day, turned down the job of CEO and spent an agonizing year trying to wrest control of the agency back from Wolf. Venice office president Bob Kuperman tried to find common ground so that the agency could grow without losing its creative edge.

*New York office president Jane Newman found herself presiding over a
nightmare as the office's two largest clients—Reebok and Royal Caribbean
Cruise Lines—put their accounts up for review.*

16

By 1990 Nissan represented over $300 million in billings. The two men in charge were the agency's unnervingly odd couple. Account executive Tom Patty, a Chiat/Day lifer, was a model of discipline, from his early-morning meditation and exercise regimen to his daily chats with top Nissan executives. Thirty-one-year-old creative group head and resident whiz kid Dick Sittig was brash, outspoken, mercurial, as much an anarchist as Patty was a company man.

17

Steve Rabosky turned down a job paying twice as much, at another agency, for the chance to be creative director at Chiat/Day—but he had to fight Clow, Kuperman and Sittig for creative control.

Nineteen-year veteran Amy Miyano ran the creative department art studio and was Clow's ally and confidante.

19

In November, 1992 Chiat/Day moved into two floors of a three-story, $16 million building designed by architect Frank Gehry—and anchored by a set of binoculars designed by Claes Oldenburg and Coosje Van Bruggen.

Chiat/Day spent seven years in a warehouse, waiting for the new building to be completed. Gehry designed the interior to reflect Chiat's disdain for the traditional workplace: five-foot-high cubicles without doors, the same size for everyone; meeting rooms with big windows, to allow for easy eavesdropping; and conference rooms called the Boathouse (left) and the Fish (right).

Chiat/Day's battle cry, immortalized on one of the agency's countless commemorative T-shirts: "Good Enough Is Not Enough."

"You're aligned with the consumer," said a copywriter.

"It's really Us versus Them," said Sittig.

Rinek happily rode their crescendo of self-congratulation. "The great takeaway here is, people who see it on television want to know, 'What's in it for me?' You've given them a lot of that," he said.

The production schedule called for final approval of all Fantasy campaign work by June 15, so the spots had to go out to focus groups as quickly as possible. Clow wanted to make sure that the rich guys line didn't inadvertently make customers in the basic small category feel like poor guys—and everyone wanted to see which executions appealed to the newly defined target consumer, the young professional with a future.

Rinek's only concern was that the rough drawings he saw on the walls failed to convey the beauty of the new design. "We've got to show it off," he said, "so it pays off our line."

Our line. The client had taken ownership of the idea. Symbiosis had been achieved: the client and the agency had found a comfortable place to live together.

Having moved in, the client felt like tinkering. "Why is 'Car Company' black and white?" asked Mitzel.

Sittig had had ten minutes to enjoy his victory, and now people who knew nothing about creative were going to tromp on his execution. He answered very carefully.

"It's to distinguish his dream from reality," he told her, "and it's in keeping with the notion of industry on the march. It would be very handsome."

The rest of the meeting was devoted to a marketing presentation that one of the account executives had drawn up, showing in grim numbers what everyone in the room already knew to be true: Since 1985, Sentra had slipped from first place among imports in its category—outselling Toyota's Corolla and Honda's Civic, second only to the Ford Escort—to third place, selling for less than the competition and to less desirable consumers.

"We're has-beens," muttered another account executive.

The charts also served as a cold reminder that the dealers were the real problem customer. They relied on Sentra's rock-bottom price tag to help them make their monthly sales figures. They weren't going to be happy with a car that cost as much as $12,000, no matter how clever the advertising was.

Sittig studied the chart labeled "Demographic Trends." "If you're younger, poorer, dumber and your prospects for the future are bleak," he said, "you buy a Sentra. And you're ready to take a jab at the rich."

He smiled. "'Introducing the Sentra. Because we're tired of guys with jobs having all the fun.'"

Kuperman had nine people working on the Foster Farms presentation, but the day before the pitch he faced a diplomatic crisis that threatened to undo all their efforts. Stories about the sale of the San Francisco office were supposed to appear in the newspapers on May 22, the day of the pitch. It was monumentally awkward timing. The Foster Farms executives would suspect that Kuperman, Clow and Weinstein had known about the sale when they rejected the client's request that a San Francisco team work on the account. Kuperman would walk into a roomful of people who thought he'd been lying to them. Somebody had to get to them today with a plausible explanation.

He wanted Clow to do it, since Clow was the client's favorite at Chiat/Day. He coached Clow: Tell them the sale had been a year off and had been accelerated without the knowledge of the people in the Venice office. Clow asked Kuperman to jot down the proper line on a piece of paper.

Kuperman had put Bonnie Baruch in charge of the Foster Farms team because of her background working on the Vons account at J. Walter Thompson, and despite the fact that Home Savings believed it had her exclusive services. There would be time to deal with that conflict after he avoided being fired by Foster Farms.

The rehearsal convinced him that he had made the right choice. Baruch had ideas about how Foster Farms could break the stranglehold that Oscar Mayer and Louis Rich had on the delicatessen market—ideas that went beyond traditional advertising. She had understood Chiat when he talked about broadening the range of services the agency provided. Foster Farms needed to do in-store promotions, new coupon designs and celebrity and charity tie-in programs to elevate the brand.

She had research that showed poultry deli customers were older, whiter, smarter and had fewer children than shoppers who ate red meat. She even had a chart labeled "Personality of the Poultry Household," based on a computerized research program that asked interview subjects to rank their possessions in order of importance. Researchers analyzed the answers and came up with personality profiles that were much more specific than the usual demographic information about age, income and education.

She began to list the attributes of the target poultry eater:

Diverse
Doers
Practical
Family-focused (unlike the red meat eater)
Neo-traditionalist

But at that, Kuperman, the instinctive art director who had functioned for decades without such sophisticated research, lost his self-control. There was such a thing as useless knowledge. "We're talking to guys who need shelf space," he screeched, *"and you're talking about neo-traditionalism? What is this?"*

Then he collected himself, suggested that the presentation needed tightening, scheduled another rehearsal for 6:00 P.M. and left the room.

Minutes later Clow was on the phone with one of the men from Foster Farms. He told him that there had been talk at the board meetings over the past two years of consolidating the Chiat/Day offices when the new L.A. building was done.

"But with Bob Wolf and Fred butting heads, it was accelerated," he explained. "Last week Jay and Bob and Fred sat down and figured out a way for Fred to buy the office. Bob and I didn't know anything about it. Typical Chiat/Day weirdness."

He reported his speech verbatim to Kuperman.

For four years, from 1980 to 1984, Kuperman had been unable to set foot on an airplane. It all started when he was working on the Gallo wine account at Wells, Rich, Greene. The relationship was combative. Every week he flew north to Modesto, California, to meet with the client, and each time he came home feeling he'd been beaten up. Soon he started associating flying with being mistreated. That, and a couple of close calls, made him scared enough to start taking Valium and drinking to get through a flight. When it got to the point where he got off a plane, went to a meeting, and the next day couldn't remember the people he'd met, he quit flying.

But he had to fly to do his work. He tried hypnosis. He tried a psychiatrist. Finally he ended up in a UCLA Extension Division course called "Fear of Flying," taught by two pilots who helped people overcome their anxieties. Now Kuperman could fly, but he had to have a set pattern. He always arrived at the airport well in advance of the flight. He always had his seat assignment and his boarding pass in advance. Surprises unnerved him.

He did not consider it a good omen when he got to Los Angeles International Airport for an early morning flight to Modesto—his bad-luck city, by unfortunate coincidence the closest airport to Foster Farms' Livingston headquarters—to find the flight had been canceled. The eight other Chiat/Day people started suggesting plans—other airlines, to other cities with connecting flights—but Kuperman found himself rooted to the spot. All he wanted to do was stand still and wait for someone to say that this had been a terrible mistake, the plane was at the gate.

Failing that, he was willing to take the next flight on the same airline. Weinstein wouldn't hear of it. He was not about to start the day by calling the client to postpone the meeting. Everything had to go as planned. There was a U.S. Air flight to Modesto that was about to leave. If Kuperman really wanted to save Foster Farms, he would get on it. Showing up late was not the way to show the client how much the agency cared.

Twelve hours later, when Tom Orr lifted his glass at dinner and said, "We're going to stick with you guys, and we're looking forward to the new team," it all seemed worthwhile to Kuperman. No one even mentioned San Francisco.

The victorious team drove back to the Modesto airport, the smokers in one car, the non-smokers in the other, only to find out that their return flight had been canceled due to bad weather. The woman at the departure gate had a solution, though—a helicopter flight to the San

Francisco airport, where the team could get the last flight of the night back to Los Angeles. She had already located one of the two helicopter pilots, and was tracking down the second, who was off having dinner somewhere.

"Great," said Kuperman, who was not willing to contemplate a helicopter ride no matter how many pilots were on board. "Give me the keys to the car."

The others joined him, piled back into the rental cars and raced frantically to San Francisco, arriving just in time for the last flight. This time Kuperman endured the confusion with aplomb. He had saved an account. His run of good luck was still intact.

The next morning, Wolf strolled the aisles of the agency, singing "Old MacDonald Had a Farm" in a low voice. "Here a chick, there a chick, everywhere a chick chick . . ."

CHAPTER 18

On a deserted Sunday afternoon, the day before Memorial Day, the theme song from the baseball film *The Natural* echoed down the empty corridors of Chiat/Day, a stately crescendo—da *DAA*—followed by a stentorian march back down the scale—*duh* duh duh. Da *DAA, duh* duh duh. It was the inspirational music that had made moviegoers believe in an ailing, anguished Robert Redford as he stepped up to the plate, two out in the ninth, his team trailing by a run, in the final scene of the film. They knew, before he ever swung the bat, that he would hit the ball into the floodlights. The music said so. Steve Rabosky and Ian Potter kept playing the song, over and over. This was the kind of music that would make the Century 21 franchisees stand up and cheer. This was the inspiration for what they hoped would be the campaign that won the pitch.

Rabosky desperately wanted to win the account, despite his early misgivings about whether it was the kind of account that would allow Chiat/Day to do great work—and he wanted to win it with his own work, not someone else's. He had not yet asserted himself the way Kuperman had when he joined the agency, and Rabosky was suffering for his lack of political ambition. Clow, Kuperman and even Sittig overshadowed him, making him seem a caretaker creative director, one who maintained what other people created. He needed a win to remind the agency of why he had got the job.

He had wanted the position badly enough to back out of a $400,000 offer to become creative director at Ogilvy & Mather. The Chiat/Day job paid less than half that, but it was Chiat/Day; it was an invitation to wear Lee Clow's shoes. The problem was that Sittig, in the last year of Kuperman's administration, had devised the Fantasy campaign, the Energizer Bunny campaign, and helped out on the script for Home Savings' "Us versus Them" spot. With all that work in place, there was no way for Rabosky to make his mark until Century 21 came along.

For weeks, Rabosky and Potter had accumulated books, magazines, and reels of commercials, anything to jump-start their brains. They churned out dozens of tissues and sat through one internal review after another, to no avail. Today, finally, they had something that looked right. Rabosky wanted to adapt the idea behind the book *A Day in the Life of America*, which was a collection of photographs, all taken on the same day, meant to capture the spirit and variety of the country. They could do that on television and in print, a "Days of the Week" campaign using a different setting for each day of the week—a farmhouse, a suburban home, an urban train station—with copy that talked about how Century 21 was as predictable, as dependable, as the sun going down or the commuter train leaving on time. He played the theme music from *The Natural* to convey the mood of the campaign to Potter, who spent much of the afternoon drafting rough sketches. Now they needed a tag line to complete the concept.

It was the hardest part of the exercise. Rabosky always wanted a tag line to say everything, but in the end the best ones said very little. This one had to convey trust. Sales volume didn't mean anything to people who needed to buy or sell a home. They wanted a realtor they could depend on.

He tried out everything he could think of, no matter how awful it sounded. If Potter approved, he lettered the line on a piece of paper stamped with the Century 21 logo, to see how it would look. There were twelve tag lines already tacked up on the wall.

" 'We get it right, day in, day out.' " Rabosky wasn't happy with that one. The thought worked, but it just didn't feel right to him.

" 'We get it right every day.' "

" 'Because you can't afford to make a mistake.' "

" 'This is the one time you can't make a mistake.' " Rabosky rejected that one. It was an interesting line, but it didn't fit the campaign.

" 'America's real estate agency,' " he said.

"Homes . . . lives . . . trust," muttered Potter. "Anything with safe hands?"

" 'You're in good hands with Allstate,' " said Rabosky, ruefully. "Oh well."

" 'America's real estate agency.' " Rabosky lowered his head into his hands. "It's one of those lines that works, but you don't want to claim it. 'The client made me use it. I had no choice.' "

"If you're going to play this music and show these visuals," said Potter, holding up a drawing of an isolated house at sunset, "then we might as well say, 'America's real estate agent.' "

"But if we could put some strategic element to it, that would be nice. 'The reason why more people trust us is . . . (blank).' That's what it has to say."

"The line's got to be inspirational, hasn't it?" asked Potter.

"Got to be."

"The line should work on its own. It's not going to come by writing down words like 'smart' and 'safe.' "

"Yeah," said Rabosky. " 'Don't make a move without us' is too ad-clever. It's going to be a universal line that could go on any fucking campaign."

"Got to be a line that means everything," said Potter.

"Doesn't even have to be emotional," said Rabosky. "Just a statement on why we're smart. 'A smart choice.' 'A smart decision.' 'The smartest decision you'll ever make'?"

Potter scribbled the words down on paper and stared at them. "I don't mind that. Worthy of two push pins."

Then he decided to try. " 'When it's a big decision . . ,' " Potter said. He smiled. " 'When you can't afford to fuck up.' How's that?"

" 'Don't fuck up. Use us.' "

"That's what it wants to say," said Potter, as though a tag line was alive with a voice of its own. " 'It's too important not to choose us.' "

"Doesn't it have to be about 'us'?" asked Rabosky. "The agents? Us guys?"

" 'We're the best agents'?"

" 'Simply the best.' 'Day in, day out, the best'? Nah." Rabosky looked at the pieces of paper on the wall and his eyes glazed over. "I always wanted to do a tag line, whatever the company was: 'Century 21. What more do we need to say?' "

Potter drew "America is sold on us" on one of the tissues. It was Rabosky's favorite line, the one he wanted to use with the Days of the Week campaign, but it failed to tell the consumer why he ought to be sold on the company. The answer was "size," which presented a seemingly insurmountable problem for the creatives. Century 21 was the largest network of realty agents in the country, but it was not number one in each of its individual markets. Making a national claim meant nothing to the residents of a city who knew that there were three realtors bigger than Century 21 in their market; in fact, it might make them distrustful. Making local claims wasn't always possible.

Potter sat back in his chair. "It's a masturbatory line we're after, isn't it?"

"Yeah."

"Because tag lines aren't for consumers." Potter pointed at an invisible client in an empty chair. "They're for *you*."

Then he bent over his stack of tissues again, marking pen at the ready.

"What do banks say?" he wondered.

" 'America's largest savings and loan,' " said Rabosky, sounding bored. " 'We're everywhere you need us to be.' 'Not just a bank. A friend.' "

Whenever Kuperman had the time, he rushed over to the Riviera Country Club to play a round of golf. On Friday morning he joined a father and son, only to learn, by the second hole, that the kid was a New York copywriter who had come to Los Angeles because he wanted to work for Chiat/Day. For sixteen more holes he listened to the writer promote himself, and came home determined, from that day forward, to identify himself as a potato farmer from Long Island.

On Saturday morning his threesome included the western regional manager for Century 21. Kuperman couldn't believe his good fortune. He refrained from mentioning the pitch, lest the man think that Kuperman had planned the meeting, but the Century 21 executive was eager to talk business. Kuperman showed up for the Memorial Day creative review bearing nuggets of information that he arrayed in front of the others as though they were precious jewels.

Century 21 wanted its advertising to be elevated. Bigger. More important. Classier. Less specific. Grand. Like an airline.

A week before the June 6 pitch, these were the new criteria.

The Venice office was in thrall to Century 21—to the notion of having the account, if not the reality of living with it—and, temporarily blinded by love, was behaving in ways that were distinctly out of character. Kuperman, increasingly the pragmatist, chose to ignore the agency's avowed distaste for songs and jingles, and ordered the two Nissan regional creative directors, Tony Stern and Jeff Roll, to come up with a "sting," a melody for the words, "America's real estate agent." He wanted a song, too, so they stayed up all night and came up with a ditty called "A Place Called Home."

Stern kept singing the lyrics to himself. He confessed to Roll that he hated the song.

"It sounds awful," he said. "The meter sounds like, 'When Columbus sailed the ocean blue, in fourteen hundred ninety-two . . .' "

"I kind of miss things like 'Hey down, hoe down,' " said Roll.

Stern smiled a maniacal grin and sang, " 'Century 21, derry down derry down.' "

Rabosky, walking by, complained that it was impossible to sing the words, "America's real estate agent."

"Too many consonants," agreed Stern. "It's like trying to sing the word 'nougat.' "

Chiat had been careful not to impose himself on the pitch process—a trying discipline, given his propensity for last-minute raids. He told Wolf, "Use me as a tool," which conveyed his desire to participate but left the details to the man who was now in charge. When it became clear that the office was fully committed to winning the account—that the early reluctance Wolf had encountered from the creative department had dissolved in the heat of pursuit—Wolf invited Chiat to attend. Perhaps his presence would blind the client to what Wolf perceived as flaws in the creative work. He would communicate just how much Chiat/Day wanted the account.

Chiat had little to do until the day of the pitch, which as much as guaranteed that he would find a way to shake things up. The activity in the Venice office did not distract him. He could prowl around and see how the office looked with the Century 21 pitch peeled away. He was not pleased with what he saw. Too many people sitting around doing nothing; the ones who were doing something weren't doing it with enough verve. There was an indolence to the place, hardly the appropriate attitude in the wake of a $40 million account loss, even if New York was the specific casualty.

What frightened him was that these were the people who would hire the next generation. Having top management in place meant nothing if complacency was spreading through the ranks. He sought out Clow, the one person who would understand his distress, and suggested that they create a Chiat/Day/Mojo University, a week-long retreat for hand-picked members of upper management. They could load everyone onto a bus and get them out of town for workshops, speeches, even enforced exercise. By the time they were done they would be a team, bonded by the experience, infused with energy from above, ready to help lead the agency into the future.

Clow expressed his enthusiasm in his usual manner. He started to think about what the diplomas might look like, and who he could get to design the souvenir sweats, T-shirts, mugs and other paraphernalia.

On a more practical note, Chiat asked a woman in the finance department to compose a job description list. He wanted to know exactly who was supposed to be doing what in the Venice office, with an eye toward eliminating the unnecessary, or the underperforming.

The night before the pitch, Clow met with Wolf, Kuperman, Rabosky, Weinstein and the account planners in the Fish for a crash course in real estate. Wolf was going to make the introductory comments at the presentation, and Chiat the close, but Clow was going to do everything else—a departure from the standard pitch in which creatives talked about creative, planners discussed strategy and account management talked about all the things the client could accomplish with Chiat/Day. It was a grandstand play, designed to make Century 21 believe it was in Clow's legendary hands.

Clow grasped his mission. "They always like to see a creative guy who understands their business." But he had a jumpy mind that ricocheted off ideas at unpredictable angles. Wolf and Kuperman had to rein him in, to make sure that he wrote down what he needed to know on his yellow legal pad, and that he didn't write down anything else.

Kuperman watched him take his diligent notes and got edgy.

"You're writing down stuff you don't need to say."

"I'm just trying to get up to speed," said Clow. He referred to his notes and smiled brightly. "So an interesting thought is, 'You can be middle America without being Ward Cleaver.' "

"*Whoa,*" said Wolf. "We're getting off the mark here." He wanted to talk about asserting Century 21's preeminence in the field. He emphatically did not want to alter its corporate personality.

They were still disagreeing on basic issues that should have been resolved weeks ago. This was Chiat's restlessness codified: an accepting brain is a dying brain. There are always challenges, up to the last minute.

By the end of the process nerves were worn thin. Kuperman pulled out a pack of Stim-U-Dents and methodically poked at his gums. Wolf started checking the finished storyboards. Coots chewed her cuticles. Weinstein studied the decks, the pages of computerized print-out that were the foundation of the presentation. Rabosky was in a trance, the result of too many sleepless nights. Clow made up for his inertia: under the conference table, his legs jiggled up and down.

Clow ran through his presentation, but every time he took a breath, one of the others broke in to prompt him. He hesitated on the question of what Century 21's goal should be, and Weinstein quickly stepped in.

" 'To align your share of transactions with your share of preference,' " he intoned.

Everyone started to laugh.

"Why can't we say that in English?" said Clow. " 'Everybody knows who you are, but you're not converting into more listings and more sales.' "

He went back to rehearsing.

" 'In the four weeks since we met in New York,' " Clow began, and then broke off. He couldn't say that. He hadn't been in New York.

" '. . . We wasted three weeks,' " said Kuperman, finishing for him with a grin, " 'and jammed for the fourth as usual.' "

Clow wanted to know if they could impress the client with the breadth of their research, but the agency had only conducted focus groups in Minneapolis and Los Angeles.

"How many states did we *fly* over?" Rabosky asked, to tired giggles.

Even Wolf was getting punchy. He suggested that Clow prove how genuine a place Chiat/Day was by listing the clichés the agency wouldn't use in the presentation.

"Words you will not hear today," Wolf said, puffing out his chest. " 'Viable.' 'Synergy.' "

" 'I will not interact with you,' " said Kuperman, " 'and you will not share with me.' "

Clow leered. "And they probably don't even want a fucking marketing partner."

It was getting late. Everyone headed back to their desks except Wolf, Clow and Kuperman, who continued to fret over the presentation. Wolf had not given up his quest for a better tag line than "America's real estate agent."

" 'Working harder to earn your trust,' " he said.

"Put that in, damn it," Kuperman instructed Clow. "It's generic."

Clow hesitated.

"It's generic but it's blended," said Wolf. "Emotional and rational."

Clow didn't move.

"*Write it down!*" yelled Kuperman and changed the subject. "What's Jay's thing?"

"The impassioned close," said Wolf. " 'This is the most important pitch we've done in years. We'll put all our resources behind it. Lee will be your creative gun, Wolf will watch over the account, we'll put all our best people on it, and we'll put national resources behind it. Not just L.A.' "

Clow started laughing. "The sun never sets on Chiat/Day as long as Jay's in India . . ."

Wolf picked up the cue. ". . . Wherever there's a bully about to beat up a guy in a gold jacket. . . ."

By now they were screaming with laughter, exhausted from weeks of hard work that had led them toward a solution, but not right up to it.

"And *then*," shouted Kuperman, "we *all* break into song."

Once the hysterics had subsided, Kuperman spoke again, but this time with a real edge of anger in his voice, as though he'd suddenly realized that he'd run, full-tilt, into a dead-end. Rabosky's work was too narrowly emotional, while the service ads the agency was going to present were too rational. They had failed to come up with a campaign that could meld the two aspects of the message. Kuperman didn't see how they could win the account.

"Then can I bring up the logo change?" he asked, maliciously. " 'Your logo sucks. Loud. On speakers. How much would it cost to change it everywhere?' "

Chiat, Wolf, Clow, Kuperman, Rabosky and Coots left the office at noon the next day for the hour's drive south to the Irvine Hilton. They had no idea if today was the first or last day of presentations, if they were first, second or third, or who else was pitching today. Position counted for a lot. No one wanted to be first overall, or last on a given day; the former meant the client had no context in which to judge, and might miss a great idea, and the latter meant a tired client who was already thinking about going home.

As they headed for their cars, they joked about what might really determine the victor.

"Make sure to mention Lee and the Hall of Fame," said Chiat. "Dusenberry isn't in," referring to BBDO's chairman and CEO Phil Dusenberry, "and he's older."

"I guess the whole question will be, does Clow look more impressive standing up in Las Vegas in front of the agents than Dusenberry does?" said Clow.

"It may all come down," said Rabosky, "to whether they like Lee's tie."

Clow had a new tie, a black and cream geometric print that he'd bought especially for the pitch. In the inside jacket pocket of his black and white tweed sport coat he carried the tie he usually wore to pitches, a dark red one, in case he changed his mind.

* * *

Parlor Eight at the Irvine Hilton was a small pink and peach room. There was a horseshoe-shaped table at one end, with nameplates for the Century 21 executives, and at the other end there were two short tables for Chiat/Day. Two large television monitors sat on top of skirted stands.

The Chiat/Day team bustled about the room, setting up. They were elated to discover an overflowing wastebasket, full of discarded evidence that McCann-Erickson had made the morning's presentation. They pored over its contents—posters and a couple of executions—looking for anything they might be able to use to advantage in their pitch. McCann had done an execution about the homeless problem, an approach Chiat/Day had tried and discarded. Kuperman would be sure to refer to it as a bad idea before the afternoon was out. When Kuperman realized he had brought along a storyboard that featured a rejected tag line, he stuffed it into the wastebasket. Let the next agency in line find it, think it was Chiat/Day's big idea and squander precious time trying to sink it.

His mood soured when Laurie Coots handed him his custom-made name tag. She had had pins made up for each man to wear on the breast pocket of his jacket, little brown and gold nameplate pins with the Century 21 logo. Kuperman affixed his to his elegant double-breasted black chalkstripe suit as though he were mounting a cockroach on his chest.

There was nothing left but to wait. Chiat and Wolf were already at a table in the hotel coffeeshop, complaining about the state of the economy. Clow, Kuperman and Rabosky sat at the next table swapping war stories to get their adrenaline pumping. Fortified, they all marched to the elevator and headed back up to Parlor Eight.

For three hours they told the Century 21 executives what they would do with the business. Wolf talked about Chiat/Day's national resources. Clow wore himself out being enthusiastic. Chiat made his emotional closing remarks. The client got to hear "A Place Called Home."

When it was all over, one of the men at the horseshoe-shaped table finally spoke up. He was surprised, he said, by the work he'd seen.

"You guys are always so *funny*," he said. "Ever thought of humor for our category?"

"No," said Clow. "It's too serious."

"Just a thought."

" 'Just be your funny selves. Just be yourselves.' " Kuperman's voice dripped with sarcasm. He couldn't believe that the Century 21 executive had wanted something funny. That was the problem with being Chiat/Day. Clients were always expecting weird stuff, even if it wasn't appropriate. It was as though the agency had been invited to participate as an entertainment.

Clow and Kuperman were in Clow's black Pathfinder, stuck in a traffic jam on the San Diego Freeway behind an overturned truck that had spilled an as-yet-unidentified poison on the road miles north of them. They had more time than they wanted to review the events of the afternoon.

"There's eighty-seven ways to do the emotional stuff," said Clow. "They probably can't distinguish the classy way from the rest."

"They loved the print," said Kuperman.

It didn't matter. Clow was furious that the client hadn't told the agency about its executional preference. Still, he clung to a small hope, or rather, he invented one. He thought about the roomful of noncommittal executives and decided they were just tired after three presentations in a row, or under orders to hide their feelings.

Kuperman wanted to believe Clow but he couldn't. "I don't think we were as sharp as we could have been," he said.

Clow was silent for a moment.

"We could have made more out of the alternative we are, being in town," he admitted. "If you think you can service them from out of town, you're nuts. But there's so much else going on. It's a personality contest."

"I was at a pitch once," said Kuperman, "and I thought we did great. We didn't get it because one of our guys smoked a cigarette and the client didn't like it. You never know why."

They sat on the freeway for an hour and a half, lurching five feet ahead and coming to a cold stop, torturing themselves over what the client did and didn't like, repeating the line about doing something funny. When a raucous commercial came on the radio for a new show at Sea World, they both stopped to listen. Clow started laughing.

"Every now and then I suddenly notice all these ads," he said, "and how stupid and obnoxious they are. And I realized how insane this all is. To get worked up about it."

Kuperman started to sing along with the first song that came on after the commercial, only to cut himself off and announce he was going to walk back to the office if traffic didn't start to move. Clow lurched onto a nearby exit, cut across a gas station to avoid a red light ("You can do that with a Pathfinder," he said, proudly), and snaked his way back to the agency on surface streets.

When they got back to the office Clow reached into his jacket pocket and took out the tie he always wore, the one he'd chosen not to wear today. He shrugged, as much as admitting defeat.

"Maybe it *was* the tie," he said.

CHAPTER 19

The Century 21 Real Estate announcement, awarding the business to Campbell-Mithun-Esty, came just a week after the pitch, on June 13, but in that brief time everyone involved in the pitch had managed a rationale. The disgruntled creatives blamed Rabosky for promoting his own work over theirs, he blamed the agency for going after the wrong kind of account, and Kuperman, as usual, blamed the client for not recognizing quality. Clow thought the loss proved that there were certain accounts the agency shouldn't pursue. To Wolf, it proved that there were accounts the agency had to chase—but the creative department wasn't yet up to the task. Chiat realized, too late, that the new management structure had effectively demolished the successful Venice pitch team of Wolf, Kuperman, Clow and White. They all had theories, but no one expressed regrets publicly.

Unfortunately, there were few reviews on the horizon to distract them. The $22 million Carl's Jr. fast-food account was up for review, but it was not much of a temptation, since Carl's Jr. chairman and CEO Carl Karcher was a difficult client who had donated heavily to the anti-abortion group Operation Rescue, and would want an agency to staff his account with like-minded conservatives.

The National Basketball Association, which had always produced its own commercials in the past, had $10 million to spend on commercials and promotional programming, thanks to a new $600 million contract with NBC Television. The NBA needed someone to make it an international sport—to make it famous, which was just what Clow liked to do for clients. The agency decided to participate in the pitch, but Wolf disdained it from the start. It was a "glamour account," a high-profile business that had too little money and too little opportunity for growth.

His rainmaker was hardly prepared to surrender to the exigencies of the moment. Don Peppers was in Los Angeles to rehearse a presentation that he and Rob White were going to make to Nintendo, the computer game giant. Nintendo had just hired Foote, Cone & Belding, but Peppers had prepared a door-opener on the fiber-optics revolution, and there was an executive at Nintendo who was willing to listen to it.

Peppers wanted to talk about a time, about fifteen years in the future, when there would be tens of thousands of television signals, when households would sign up with brokers who would protect them from commercials they didn't want to see and provide them with the ones they were interested in.

Meekly, Rob White wondered whether people would choose to pay for the privilege of not seeing any commercials at all. Peppers reassured him. People were addicted to advertising, despite their griping. They used brands to define themselves. They were members of what Peppers called "image tribes," concocting a public identity based on the brands they acquired or wished to acquire—brands whose value was, in part, their symbolic meaning to the rest of the community.

"People don't really want to be different," said Peppers. "They just want to be the same as certain kinds of people."

Neither man expected the effort to yield tangible results, but Peppers took the long view. If Nintendo went up for review in three years, the company would have to invite Chiat/Day. He had something interesting to share. Nintendo would be in his debt.

Lee Clow, back from a meeting at Nissan, was hurrying across Main Street when a woman saw him and shrieked. "*Long pants—my God!*"

He was on his way to the kind of meeting he might, under less unsteady circumstances, have chosen to forgo: a discussion, at Chiat's request, of why the agency wasn't being inundated with new business opportunities. The *Advertising Age* Agency of the Decade award had made everyone feel proud, but had yielded little. So far in 1990 Chiat/Day had participated in only one pitch, and had lost it. Southwest Airlines had just dismissed the agency from a pitch at the preliminary credentials stage, after hearing case studies intended to prove that Chiat/Day could handle the account. It was a slap in the face for an established agency with credits like Nissan and the Energizer Bunny, and a painful sign that something had gone terribly wrong. In the preceding eighteen months, the agency had had five victories in six tries. The discrepancy was too stark to ignore.

The benign explanation, what everyone called "the prettiest girl in school who doesn't have a date for the prom" theory, was that clients assumed Chiat/Day was too busy to bother with them. Wolf's less pleasant theory was that the agency still seemed a troublesome proposition to most clients. Whatever the cause, the agency had to do something to change the business community's mind—and if Clow failed to participate in the defining the solution, he could hardly complain about what it would be.

Chiat, Clow, Wolf, Kuperman, Peppers and Coots crammed into Hardy and immediately began sparring. Peppers said he could have saved the Southwest presentation. Clow insisted that Southwestern was one of those inappropriate clients who was intimidated by a strong agency. "We can't wear a mask and pretend we're not," he said.

Kuperman believed that the agency had to convince prospective clients to go through an abbreviated version of the Chiat/Day process, including work sessions, so that they would understand and appreciate the agency's assets. Wolf cut him off: the issue, for new business, was first impressions. He wanted to talk to some of the consultants who orchestrated reviews for clients, to find out their opinions of the agency. He wanted to know specifically what he could do to improve the agency's reputation.

At that, they grew quiet. They were back to the fundamental issue: Was there something wrong with Chiat/Day that needed to be corrected for the agency to grow, or would tampering undermine its considerable strength? Peppers had talked to a consultant in the Midwest who said that the agency's greatest asset was also its biggest weakness. "People believe they're playing with fire when they play with Chiat/Day," Peppers reported. "If they're strong, they'll get brilliant advertising. If they aren't, they'll be run over."

"They don't want to be beat up," said Chiat, reflectively.

Clow jumped. What people thought of as beating up clients was often just a case of the agency being smart.

"Some of the people at the agency do beat up clients," Chiat said.

"A roomful of smart people intimidates most companies," said Clow, resentfully.

Wolf thought that the agency suffered because of all the "baggage" it carried, after years of grandstanding.

"So what," snapped Chiat. "It's been out there for twenty-two years. We haven't done so bad." It was all right for Chiat himself to criticize his agency, but he was not about to let Wolf denigrate its past.

"You're being defensive," replied Wolf.

Peppers took that as an encouragement. "There's smart, and then there's arrogance," he said. "You're arrogant. You try not to be, but you are. The only thing worse is justified arrogance, and yours is justified."

"We probably don't even understand the arrogance in what we say," said Chiat.

"Self-confidence is arrogance to some people," Clow insisted.

"The baggage is *not* arrogance," said Wolf. "It's 'These guys are in it for themselves and not for you.' "

"That comes," Kuperman said, quietly, "with being a creative agency." He agreed with Wolf on the issue of small accounts, and he was eager for a big win, but there was an essential difference in their approach, born of Kuperman's history at Doyle Dane Bernbach and his enduring respect for Chiat and Clow. He wanted the wins, but not at the expense of the work. He was trying to make a place for himself, to string a tightrope between Wolf's ambition and Clow's dedication.

"The only answer," said Chiat, "is a handful of word-of-mouth clients saying it isn't true."

"But you've got clients saying it *is*," said Wolf. "Either they believe it, or they have to, because they fired the Agency of the Decade."

"How do you deal with it?" asked Chiat.

"You don't sit back and say, 'Fuck you,' " said Wolf. "It's public relations. We've got to tell the whole story; not just the creative awards, but how we improve business for our clients."

"We're the Donald Trump of advertising," said Peppers. "Everyone wants to take a shot at us."

Then Chiat delivered his diagnosis. What the agency needed, rather than another round of arguments about identity and goals, was simply a better pitch team. Wolf, Kuperman and Rob White had been "crackerjack," in his estimation, particularly with Clow along for the ride as the agency's mythic creative hero. The administrative shuffle had broken up that team: Wolf wasn't around enough, and Rabosky and the planner who often subbed for White were both rather reserved, straightforward men. It didn't matter if they said the same things Clow, Kuperman or White said. They lacked verve.

"How we used to win it," he said, "was, we *liked* each other at the pitch."

"They saw our enthusiasms," agreed Clow.

"And now I think people don't like each other," said Chiat, his voice growing louder. "They're all adversaries. Our pitch teams have gotten older. We're not enthusiastic. *We're jaded. We're pitching. We don't seem hungry.*"

"Yeah," said Clow. "I was listening to Jay at Century 21 saying, 'We want the business,' thinking, 'That's the *worst* way to do this.' "

"Pitch is theater," said Chiat. "You don't have a humble quiet guy, unless you think the client will respond to that."

Histrionics were Chiat's way of reminding the others that he was still around, that this was still his agency. What was unnerving was the quiet complaint, the urgent instruction, issued without melodrama.

While he was in Venice, he met with chief financial officer Pete de Vaux and let him know the extent of his unhappiness. Corporate overhead was out of hand, and de Vaux was not making cuts quickly enough to suit him. He wanted to see changes, and he wanted to see them before the next round of board meetings. There was no room for dialogue, no heated invitation to respond, only the expectation of swift obedience.

* * *

Chiat/Day's June birthday celebration, organized by the Nissan account staff with its typically militaristic zeal, was the perfect escape valve for the agency's collective tensions—a Tricycle Grand Prix that transformed the warehouse into a raceway and made it virtually impossible for anyone to avoid participating. A three-lane track ran down Main Street, out the front of the building, and back up to loop through the account services department and over toward Kuperman's office. The Fish became the Birthday Hospitality Tent, with VIP seating in front of it for June birthday celebrants and a bag of souvenir gifts on each seat: a "Nissan: Built for the Human Race" button, a sample of STP Sun of a Gun Protector, a VIP plastic badge, a program of the day's events and a racing flag. There was a grandstand directly across Main, complete with speakers pumping loud rock-'n'-roll, and a screaming master of ceremonies in a leather Harley-Davidson jumpsuit.

The relay teams lined up for the qualifying heats—the Radical Regional Racers from Nissan regional, High Heels on Wheels from the print production department, the Bean Counters from finance. Weinstein, in a wheelchair because of a skiing accident, was the pace car. The pit was in front of the grandstand. Refueling was essential to win the qualifying heat: each rider had to stop long enough to take a bite of a hot dog from a pit mechanic.

The senior executives rarely participated in the physical foolery of birthday parties, but they encouraged the others to play. Chiat, Kuperman, Wolf and Clow stood at the sidelines and cheered on the helmeted racers, who clambered onto their tricycles and set off, some pedaling with the outsides of their feet because their legs were too long to jackknife into the proper position, some falling off as they headed around a curve. The ones who survived received their hot dog snacks and pedaled off again, either carrying the food in their cheeks like chipmunks or spitting it onto the floor. As soon as a chunk landed, a big yellow dog, smuggled in for the afternoon and delirious at his good fortune, darted onto the raceway and ate up every bite.

There were certificates for the fastest driver, the best crash, the most pathetic driver, the most dangerous driver, and the best use of fashion footwear, which went to the High Heels on Wheels team, for having raced in spike heels. The grand prize was a small trophy, to a man from the MIS (management of information systems) department whose knee was bleeding from a spill.

It was as much an initiation into the culture as a birthday party. Each month, another department tried to come up with a more outrageous idea for a party, to remind the employees that self-consciousness had no place at Chiat/Day. The true hero was the one who surrendered to experience, who refused to let image stand in the way of a good time.

CHAPTER 20

Dick Sittig took his girlfriend to Cannes in late June for the International Advertising Film Festival—a pleasant enough break from the Nissan Fantasy campaign, particularly since the Energizer Bunny campaign Sittig had devised was favored to win the Grand Prix over almost two thousand other entries. Sittig was ready to celebrate. He checked into a $700-a-night hotel room, ate his share of cracked lobster claws, and waited for the official good news.

He was having lunch with Kuperman at the Eden Roc, on the day of the awards show, when they heard: Not only was the Bunny not going to win the Grand Prix, but the campaign had been thrown out of the competition on the grounds that it wasn't original. European judges complained that the Bunny parodies were derivative of a British campaign for Bass's Carling Black Label beer that featured a cowboy riding through a series of fake commercials. No one accused Sittig of outright plagiarism, but the suggestion was there, along with the public humiliation.

Kuperman was furious. That night at the awards banquet, fueled by more Scotch than he was used to, he had to be physically restrained from jumping onstage and giving the audience a piece of his mind. Sittig, who had never seen the beer commercials, decided to take the high road and keep his mouth shut. He figured anything he said in his own defense would sound like sour grapes. He attended the awards ceremony, but he left his tuxedo at home in favor of his Chiat/Day Babes in Baja T-shirt, commemorating an annual women employees' retreat. Then he waited for the screening of the Grand Prix nominees and the announcement of the winner. When the Bunny appeared on screen, the four thousand Cannes delegates applauded wildly. When a three-year-old British agency won the Grand Prix for a Maxell audio tape campaign, some people booed and howled.

Sittig returned home the injured martyr and walked right into a production budget crisis on Nissan, hardly an exercise to improve his sense of self-worth. Bob Thomas had approved "Car Company" and "Bob's Road," with only one ego-bending request: he wanted "Car Company" to be in color, not black and white. Production was supposed to begin in two and a half weeks, on July 23, but so far everything was costing more than it should. Chiat/Day had given the client a generous ballpark estimate of $4,850,000 for the entire Fantasy campaign—thirty- and sixty-second versions of "Car Company," "Bob's Road," and spots for the Stanza 240SX, Pathfinder and Nissan truck. To everyone's frustration, the estimates from directors and production companies were coming in higher—$133,000 over budget on "Car Company" and $213,000 over on "Bob's Road."

Sittig huddled in the production department's War Room with a couple of account executives and Richard O'Neill and Elaine Hinton, both of whom were running figures on their calculators. There was little conversation—just the staccato clackety-clack of the calculator keys, punctuated by the occasional announcement of a revised figure. They needed final approval from the client in four days. If they couldn't cut the production companies' figures, they would have to pare down their own ideas.

Or they could eliminate the sixty-second version of Sittig's spot. One of the account executives reminded him that the only reason to do a full minute was to tell viewers that the Sentra launch was a big event. It wasn't really necessary; the shorter spot, which got 75 percent of the television air time, would sell the car.

Sittig shook his head in disgust. "So much for the biggest event in Nissan's history. 'Big, big, big, big, big, big.' Thirty seconds."

He was not going to suggest sacrificing the spot. He intended, instead, to act contrite about the overages and hope for the kind of sympathy that translated into a few more dollars. "We go in and say, 'We've been a little bit bad,' and they scold us, and we come back next Tuesday having cut a little. And they'll say, 'Good for you,' and sign off."

The strategy backfired. Sittig was in his cubicle looking at magazines when two members of the account staff came back from the meeting where they should have gotten budget approval, and informed the creative group head that the client wanted to cut 20 percent from the production costs. John Rinek had chided the agency people. Had they forgotten? Nissan expected the spots to be in the $700,000–$750,000 range. He wanted to see "Car Company's" $1,133,000 costs cut to $850,000–$900,000, and he wanted other commercials to come in under $700,000, to make up for that over-budget allocation.

The good news was that the agency had no trouble saving the sixty-second version of Sittig's commercial. The client loved the idea, as long as it was $250,000 cheaper.

"Tell him," said Sittig, "to *fuck off and die*. It's like a guy's wanting a Z, going to the dealer, asking for it with the options, the dealer says, '$29,000.' And the guy says, 'Okay. I want it for 16.'"

He stood up, assumed a threatening stance, and started yelling. *"Get real. Grow up. Be an adult. Smell the coffee. Get out the résumé!"*

Suddenly Kuperman appeared in the hallway. Sittig's behavior was not becoming—and all too familiar to a man who had thrown his own share of tantrums. He decided to set an example: in a calm voice, he admitted that he had heard talk of a $700,000–$750,000 average cost.

Sittig protested. The spots *were* in that range, if you took an average.

"So, pick up the phone and call Rinek. What he's afraid of is, he'll okay these," said Kuperman, referring to the two Sentra spots, "and then the rest won't come in for the right money, which is what happened last year."

Sittig slumped in his chair, grabbed a pad, and started adding figures. He tried one calculation and got an average cost of $840,000. He tried again and got $751,000. He turned to his computer and used its calculating function: $808,000 average, including his Sentra commercials, "Bob's Road," and spots for the Pathfinder and the 240SX. Kuperman encouraged him to review the estimates with O'Neill again, looking for items to cut. Why go on location to Africa for the Pathfinder, when they could approximate the look of Africa at San Diego's Wild Animal Park?

"Great," muttered Sittig, as he wandered off to look for O'Neill. *"You're* the art director on it. Make it fabulous."

It was the time of year when he liked to have his letter of resignation ready.

Sittig was not the only one feeling cranky. One woman decided that her department boss didn't appreciate her contribution and quit. A Nissan copywriter who had one too many ideas torpedoed left to join an agency in Chicago. Mike Mazza, the art director on "Turbo Z Dreamer," figured that Sittig and Rabosky stood between him and a promotion, and decided to give notice.

Laurie Coots, whose job it was to poll the rank and file, was worried about the defections. The turnover rate at the agency had always been high—this year it was 46 percent—but this was different. More people were leaving, and grousing loudly about their bad experiences as they headed out the door. Coots had always conducted exit interviews to explain severance benefits to departing employees. Now she expanded the interviews to include a conversation about why people had chosen to leave.

Her fear was that the agency no longer offered people the opportunity it had offered to her seven years before. Coots had come to work at Chiat/Day, leaving behind a frustrating career in hotel management and a faltering marriage, because it seemed the kind of place where a hardworking employee could accomplish anything. She had taken a 40 percent paycut and a demotion to secretary, and then worked her way up to vice-president. She was proof that Chiat/Day was a place where an employee could create her own future—an avid defender of the culture, determined to protect what had become her home away from home.

But what she heard, from the disgruntled departing, was that the spirit of the place had evaporated, and that what was left was little more than an idiosyncratically fun place to work. Too many people lacked expectations, so they did just enough work to survive at their jobs, when what the agency needed, what it had always depended upon, were people who worked to propel themselves into a promotion.

Coots reported her findings to Kuperman and Wolf, and found a resistance that surprised her. Kuperman was willing to admit that the creative department was "running on fumes," for which he blamed Rabosky's lack of leadership, but he wasn't averse to more people deciding to quit. Resignations were a tidy alternative to firings, which were still a threat. Besides, Kuperman had troubles of his own, though he was not about to admit his exasperation. He had put Rob White in charge of the National Basketball Association pitch, only to find that White was insufficiently dictatorial. Kuperman was now working harder on a $10 million pitch, and caring more about the results, than he wanted to.

Wolf dismissed the notion that Venice had a morale problem. There were always employees with gripes. If Coots wanted to see a real morale problem, he recommended New York, where budgets were drying up, creatives were doing work that never got produced, and Jane Newman's normally cool detachment was starting to look like its cousin, denial.

In the midst of the general malaise, the man who arguably felt the worst said the least about it. Eight months into his tenure at Chiat/Day, Tom McElligott remained something of a misfit, at odds with New York creative director Michael Smith over issues of taste, and uncomfortable with Newman, who seemed to regard him as an intruder. More significantly, he was ill at ease in his role as a top-level troubleshooter, even though it was one he had devised himself. McElligott considered himself a copywriter who had become an administrator against his will, a hostage of his own reputation. He longed for the linear relationship between written words and produced work. Being an airport-hopping overseer, even at a creative shop like Chiat/Day, was an exercise in frustration.

In early July, McElligott found himself in the cavernous dining room of what was officially known as the Ennis-Brown House, a 1924 Frank Lloyd Wright home that hugged a parched hillside curve above Hollywood. McElligott and Smith were in Los Angeles to supervise production on the first television commercials for Obsession, the Calvin Klein fragrance—an odd venture in itself, since McElligott had not written a single word. The scripts were abridged excerpts from the writings of Ernest Hemingway, F. Scott Fitzgerald, Gustave Flaubert and D. H. Lawrence, all on the subject of obsession. All

McElligott had to do was make sure that their words were treated with respect.

Smith scurried around with the special effects men, who had spent all morning setting up a storm, complete with electronic lightning bolt, outside one of the bedroom windows. Director David Lynch, best known for the television series *Twin Peaks* and feature film *Blue Velvet*, sat by the pool and collected his thoughts. McElligott was left to wander the house, a happy enough endeavor for a fan of Frank Lloyd Wright, but not enough to distract him from his distress.

He wandered outside, where the heat guaranteed him some solitude. The view from the courtyard next to the house was of the smeared top of a thick layer of smog. The others darted out to the canopied buffet table, or to grab a quick smoke, and then disappeared inside.

McElligott leaned on a low wall. There were problems back in New York—he was dissatisfied with the work for Royal Caribbean Cruise Lines, he was frustrated with Newman, who found the work acceptable, and he was tired of working with creatives who were preoccupied with the threat of further cutbacks. It was all a function of his executive position, which he would have traded happily for the chance to write ads.

"It gets harder as you get older," he said. "I'm arrogant enough to think I have the answers, to think I can look at something and devise an intelligent solution. But there are so many other people involved— which is probably why so much of what you see is so awful. I assume that, once, there was a guy in a little office who had a good idea. But so many people get their hands on it.

"I was much happier when I was a copywriter."

Then he walked back inside to see if the lightning was working right.

For most people—those who had not yet succumbed to despair— production was the agency equivalent of summer camp, the one point in the advertising cycle when the agency enjoyed a measure of autonomy. The client knew his product. The agency knew the flattering illusions that would transform that product into something more than its physical self.

This was what made all the months of meetings worthwhile. Jennifer Golub, the producer on the Energizer battery commercials, willingly sacrificed her summer to the Bunny's production schedule for the chance to make what she considered to be her contribution to the visual arts. The fact that the Bunny financed her work was an insignificant detail, at this point. She was making little movies and solving problems; the communication, now, was between her and her own perfectionism.

"Dance With Your Feet," a parody of a foreign film trailer, was her particular obsession, because, at sixty seconds, it was the advertising equivalent of an epic movie. She had spent an exasperating year trying to get the Bunny into movie theaters. At first the client thought that "Dance With Your Feet," which mimicked romantic foreign films about tempestuous first love, was too expensive. Sittig came up with a cheap alternative—Golub could piggyback on a martial arts feature film two of his friends were producing if she was willing to change her concept. She agreed, but halfway through a long night's shoot an obstinate third producer suddenly materialized. She negotiated with him for weeks, until the actors' contracts came up for renewal, and then, faced with additional payments and feeling little hope, she walked away from the project.

Golub went back to Energizer with a smaller budget for "Dance With Your Feet," and the client approved the project. She invested all her deferred enthusiasm in the production. She auditioned four hundred dancers for a ballet scene, paid $500 per day for a perfectly trained sheepdog, and had prop people stapling sheaths of wheat in place to cover up the track on which the Bunny was supposed to roll through an open field. She hosed down the young female star to make it look like she had been caught in a downpour, and she filled a plastic tent with smoke to get a lighting effect that didn't look like Southern California. The Bunny was peripheral. Golub was enjoying the cinematic sleight-of-hand that led up to the punch line.

A week later, Golub was one of three dozen people, all of them at least temporarily on the Energizer payroll, who took over a mammoth soundstage on the Universal Studios backlot for the three days. They were there to shoot the fifteen-second "Chug-a-Cherry" spot—a parody whose reference, depending on the background of the person asked, was either a fifteen-year-old Dr Pepper commercial or Fred

Astaire's legendary dance number from the film *Royal Wedding*. A dancer selling the nonexistent Chug-a-Cherry brand was supposed to flog the soda pop by dancing up onto the ceiling, only to be interrupted in mid-air by the Energizer Bunny.

Early in the morning of July 18, dancer Adam Shankman was too nauseated to care about who had preceded him. He only wanted to know how they had survived the process. He stood in the shadow of Astaire's secret weapon—the Roundy-Round, designed specifically to make it look like Astaire could dance from the floor onto the wall and then onto the ceiling—and wondered how he could execute six seconds' worth of dance steps without either throwing up or crashing into the wall.

The Roundy-Round was a motorized cylindrical frame, fourteen feet in diameter, set on a metal base. It was capable of making a complete clockwise revolution in six seconds. An arm extended off the frame, upon which a camera and cameraman's seat were mounted. Inside the cylinder was a small room—a stage dressed as a small room—with a back wall, one side wall, a floor and ceiling. Shankman, who had won this part over 250 other dancers, was supposed to do what Astaire had done: As the machine began to spin, he entered at the open side of the room, where the wall was missing, and start to dance, while lip-synching the lyrics to the Chug-a-Cherry jingle. First the floor, then the side wall, and finally the ceiling surface rolled under his feet. The camera, spinning with the machine, made it seem that Shankman was dancing sideways, and then upside down. In fact, his feet never left the ground.

That was how it was supposed to work. The problem was that the Bunny had to enter the scene no more than seven seconds into the phony commercial, which meant that the Roundy-Round had to complete its spin at top speed. Shankman spent the first day rehearsing while technicians set up the lights, and after fifty attempts was convinced that it would be all he could do to maintain his balance. He went home, crawled into bed, and his head spun all night. He arrived for work the morning of the shoot certain that he would never be able to dance, sing and smile at the same time.

While the Chiat/Day brain trust—producer Golub and a production assistant, Rabosky, the account supervisor, two art directors, director Mark Coppos and two employees of Coppos Films—reviewed the test tapes from the previous day, Shankman rehearsed with the choreographer, trying to devise new dance steps that would make it easier for him to keep his balance.

At 10:30 A.M., everyone was ready. The cameraman was strapped into his bucket seat. The Roundy-Round's engine began to whir like a jet airplane, making conversation impossible. The "bunny-wrangler," one of three men who understood how to operate the Energizer Bunny's computerized controls, took his place next to the machine, ready to thrust his little charge onto the floor on cue. Shankman took his place at the edge of the set.

The Roundy-Round began to turn. The music boomed:

Chug-a-Cherry
It's extraordinary.
Chug-a-Cherry,
It's so very cherry.

Shankman never got his mouth open. As soon as the machine began to move he was transformed into a desperate hamster on a very fast treadmill, his carefully rehearsed steps dissolved into a mad scramble as he raced to keep from being hurled into the wall.

The engine stopped. The cameraman, dangling upside down in his chair, discussed the shot with the director. Golub and Rabosky worried about the tiny shudders they saw on the tape, because the speed of the revolution made the Roundy-Round bump ever so slightly. Shankman apologized for forgetting the lyrics, but Coppos, seeing a long day ahead, told him not even to try to lip-synch until he could remain upright.

They tried again. Shankman stumbled on the shift from the wall to the ceiling. He complained that he was slipping. He despaired of ever being able to hit the side wall on the proper cue. Golub and Rabosky began to plot a strategy for selling the client on a thirty-second version, so that they could slow the machine down to a manageable pace and then break up the dance footsteps with product shots and close-ups. There was delightful fantasy, and then there was physical reality. The dancing might never be right enough to sustain a fifteen-second commercial, but the agency was hardly going to admit a second mistake after all the confusion surrounding the movie trailer. They needed to have an alternative, and an explanation for why it was actually a preference.

Luckily, after a long day's effort, Shankman finally mastered the machine, retiring the need for any further negotiations with the client. The illusion worked; both the concept and the agency's reputation were preserved.

CHAPTER 21

On *Friday, July 20*, Royal Caribbean Cruise Lines made a numbing announcement: The $35 million account, the largest at Chiat/Day's New York office, was putting the agency on ninety-day notice, which meant that the client had decided to hold a review. If Chiat/Day failed to win back the account, or decided not to participate in the pitch, total New York losses for 1990—including Royal Caribbean, Reebok, and two smaller accounts, Bissell vacuum cleaners and Sara Lee—would come to $90 million, reducing the office's billings by almost half, to just over $100 million.

What made the news even harder to take was that the decision came as a complete surprise. It left the New York office reeling. If a seemingly stable account like Royal Caribbean decided to defect, one that had enjoyed the attentions of Newman, McElligott and Smith, what else might go wrong? The only question more troubling than why the client had decided to leave was why no one at the agency had seen the move coming. New York might be vulnerable on other accounts and not even know it.

The loss was doubly upsetting for both Chiat and Clow, who felt that there had been creative problems on the account for a year, and had said so, only to be ignored by the people who had stepped into power. Chiat had confessed his concern to Jane Newman and the Royal Caribbean account staff, but all he got was a polite—and, as it turned out, misinformed—brush-off. The client was completely satisfied with the work, they had told him. There was no reason to shake up a solid relationship.

Just three months earlier, at the April quarterly board meetings, Wolf had called Venice and New York the "horses" that pulled the rest of the agency along. Now, a week before the board convened again, Venice stood alone, steady, but not growing—nothing to show for all its efforts to chase down new accounts.

There was nothing unusual about its plight. In June, an industry forecaster had looked at advertising dollars spent during the first half of 1990 and predicted a disappointing year. He adjusted his expected annual increase down to 5.3 percent, almost a percentage point lower than his December 1989 figure. In the early and mid-1980s, spending had increased annually by as much as 15.8 percent, and only once dipped below 7.5 percent. In 1989, the slippage was dramatic, to 5.8 percent. What the industry had hoped was an aberration now looked like the start of the downward trend Chiat had anticipated.

In this climate, and compared to what was going on in New York, maintenance looked like vibrant good health. It was thin comfort, though. Like a wary visitor to an ailing friend, Venice seemed suddenly cautious, fearful of getting too close lest an errant germ infect the entire agency.

Five days after the agency got the news about Royal Caribbean, Wolf met with Chiat, Clow and accountant David Weiner. He had two items on his agenda: he wanted to get out of the subsidiary business, and he wanted to replace Jane Newman.

Chiat had dreamed of establishing a broad-based marketing and communications company that would strengthen the bond between agency and client, but Wolf confronted him with the nightmare reality: Chiat/Day had so far been unable to assimilate its acquisitions into a cohesive, synergistic network. The smaller companies still operated like independent contractors, occasionally taking on a Chiat/Day account, but too often failing to exploit the relationship. Clients did not perceive the subsidiaries as part of the agency.

Of the five subsidiaries, only two—Perkins-Butler, the direct marketing firm, and Bob Thomas & Associates, which handled public relations for Nissan—were worth keeping. Chiat/Day had mismanaged Keith Bright & Associates, the design firm run by a longtime friend of Chiat's, expecting long-term client relationships from a business that historically had worked on a project-by-project basis. The agency's relationship to Jessica Dee, an East Coast public relations firm, was plagued by personality conflicts. Anderson & Lembke, a business-to-business agency, was healthy enough, but the principals wanted to become a mainstream agency, which guaranteed client conflicts with Chiat/Day. It was time to admit defeat and get back to the business of advertising.

To Wolf's surprise and relief, Chiat offered no resistance. He might have let the subsidiaries linger for a while longer, and he resolved to cushion the blow, where possible, by arranging to accommodate executives, like Bright, who might want to buy back their firms. But he accepted without argument Wolf's call for a clean break. It was as though he knew what steps needed to be taken, and only hoped that someone else would act as catalyst. Chiat lacked the aptitude for this kind of decision; his yearning clouded his vision, making him believe he could accomplish the impossible. One of the things that had appealed to him about Wolf, from the beginning of their relationship, was that the younger man dreamed in a different vocabulary, the language of numbers and percentages.

The question of Jane Newman's continuing role at the agency was a more difficult one. Wolf recited the particulars against her. Morale in New York was low because people had lost confidence in Newman. They accused her of playing favorites, of not being a fair manager— and whether they were right or wrong, that was now the prevailing perception. She had failed to form partnerships inside the agency, and as a result people felt that they worked for her, not with her.

More to the point, in the case of Royal Caribbean she had failed to cultivate relationships with top-level executives. Incapable of small talk, unsure of how to elicit what a client was feeling, she stood back, banking on an efficient, businesslike demeanor to get her through. In this case, she had fooled herself into thinking everything was fine.

There was no remedy for her behavior, and no denying her equally formidable abilities as a strategist. Wolf was prepared to find another job for her at the agency, but he was adamant that she could not continue as office president. The only issue was how to move her out "and not cut her legs off."

Chiat thought Wolf was wrong, that relieving Newman of the presidency was extreme, a move that might cause more problems in New York than it would solve. He made a plea for continuity, but then he gave in. He would not contradict Wolf. There was no point in having given him a title and authority if he was going to take it back when they disagreed.

As he always had done in the past, Chiat turned to Lee Clow with his misgivings. They both understood Newman's reluctance to get involved in the client social whirl, her unease with the endless dinners, parties and weekend retreats some agencies plied their clients with. They shared her disdain for such marginal activities, Chiat because he lacked the attention span for an entire evening's conversation about shoes, Clow because he hated parties, period. In the early days, they had considered their unwillingness to do anything but work to be a proud badge of the agency's pure intent. Now it seemed evidence that the agency had failed to mature.

"We have no relationships beyond the work," said Chiat.

"We've never been any good at making friends," Clow agreed.

They might tease Kuperman about his golf weekends, but in truth that hobby was as close as the agency came to strengthening its bond with its clients. Kuperman played golf with the people from Nissan, Taylor Made, Mitsubishi and Home Savings. Patty took the client out on his sailboat. All Newman did was to attend to the work.

The board meetings at the end of July stood in somber contrast to the feisty, competitive atmosphere of April. Clow and his creative directors faced grim news when they gathered in the Treehouse on July 25. The Royal Caribbean loss guaranteed layoffs, but that was only the most public of the problems the agency faced. The recession was gnawing away at their clients. They were all cutting back their advertising budgets in anticipation of slimmer profits in the coming months.

New York was the hardest hit. The American Express Gold Card was on hiatus, in terms of ad spending, until 1991. New York Life Insurance Company had produced only one television spot, and had no plans to produce more before the end of the year. Arrow Shirts was dormant. The Calvin Klein television commercials had cost the agency $100,000 of its own fee, spent to correct mistakes, and there was no money to do the music that director David Lynch wanted to use. National Car Rental, Smith reported, had "gone away," a gentle euphemism for a client who wasn't spending any money. Whitney's Yogurt had $100,000 to spend for three commercials, which the agency would direct in house.

On the heels of the Royal Caribbean defection, Newman had ordered Smith to cut $600,000 in salaries, which represented half of his twelve-team creative department. He worried that client cutbacks would mean even more pruning. How could he service existing accounts and chase new business if he had only a skeleton staff?

Clow overruled Newman. Smith was to cut the people he wanted to get rid of anyhow, the ones who weren't pulling their weight, and then stop, whether he had met the $600,000 figure or not. The rest of the cuts would have to come from account services, or someplace else.

But Smith feared that Wolf and Newman intended a housecleaning, one that would end the creative department's dominance of the agency. Newman had told Smith that she was planning to make a speech to the New York creatives to discuss the "area of acceptability" for each client—a speech that sounded hauntingly like the one Wolf had delivered to the Venice account services staff in March.

Clow sighed. Wolf did not seem to comprehend the role that an aggressive creative department was supposed to play at Chiat/Day. "He pays lip service to, 'You need to know when it's the right time to fight and when it's the wrong time,' " said Clow, sorrowfully. "But I think he thinks, 'If you're fighting, it's the wrong time.' "

He reminded the others of what Wolf had done when he became president of the Venice office in 1986. In Clow's absence, Wolf had scheduled a creative department meeting and told the staff that any work he didn't like would not leave the office. Clow had confronted Wolf: "That makes you the fucking creative director," he said, "and you're *not* the creative director."

Now they faced the same issue, in part because no one but Wolf had been willing to assume the responsibilities that came with power.

"I don't want to run Chiat/Day," said Clow, to himself as much as to the others in the room. "I'd like to impact the creative product, but I don't want to run it. Can we find people to run things who still have respect for the product? I guess we naively thought we could—not thinking that it would become a political thing."

He still clung to the notion that creative would once again prevail.

"We make what we sell, so we've always got the control," he said. "We just have to use it intelligently enough." What hobbled him was that he couldn't figure out how. After seventeen years, he was the agency's most sophisticated creative resource, and a country rube when it came to power. Clow was the personification of the Chiat/Day credo: "Don't take your work seriously, but take it passionately." He was Chiat/Day's greatest success, and he was its most highly evolved victim.

Wolf got right to the point the next day at the North American Board meeting. The central issue facing the agency was, he said, "our need to get lean." It was a matter of losing people or losing profits—and Chiat's challenge to his new CEO was to show that the agency could make its profit figures in bad times as well as good.

The numbers were down everywhere, even in Venice, where Nissan had so far spent less than anticipated and speculative new business work was the office's single largest expense. Venice's profit margin was a flat 28.6 percent. Toronto anticipated a break-even year, and London now expected losses of $1.48 million—perfectly acceptable numbers for start-up operations, but an unfortunate drain on agency resources just as the New York office was in a seemingly bottomless decline.

Wolf presented the New York report for Newman, who had stayed behind in New York to prepare for an emergency meeting with Royal Caribbean, in the hope that she could convince the client to stay. Taking into account the cuts Wolf planned to make, New York would manage $5.5 million in profits on $25 million in income, down only $300,000 from the year's estimate. The real damage would show up in fiscal 1991. If New York failed to win any new accounts its income would be cut in half, from $25 million to $12 million. It was enough, Wolf said glumly, "to have ramifications for all of us. Even the fat cats in L.A."

Michael Smith tried to reassure the board members about New York's prospects. The office was already on the trail of several accounts—including, to everyone's surprise, the United States Marines, as well as the Centers for Disease Control and the Chemical Manufacturers Association.

"We've got war, pestilence and famine," joked Smith.

"Great," said Kuperman. "If we just stick with the military-industrial complex, we've got it made. Get ourselves a cigarette account and we're set."

Everyone laughed, but Kuperman did not intend to let them off the hook. It was all too tempting, when money was tight, to give a conservative client the kind of work he wanted, and then use profits as an excuse to churn out more mundane advertising. In the past, Chiat/Day had taken a principled stand against cigarette advertising, and employees had voted against taking on Northrop Corporation as a client because of its defense contracts. The agency had to maintain those standards, no matter how hungry it was. The wrong accounts could change Chiat/Day's personality overnight.

Halfway through his first year as Venice office president, Kuperman was confirmed in his initial belief that it was up to him to preserve the spirit of the office—and by extension the spirit of the agency, since attitude seemed to emanate from Venice. Wolf was in place because Chiat felt he could attract a greater variety of clients, but someone had to be prepared to stop him, to protest when he went too far. Clow lacked the stamina to stay with the debate; he exploded and then lost interest. Kuperman saw himself as the terrier, the one who had to grab hold and hang on for dear life.

"Just change the flag," Kuperman said. "From a skull-and-crossbones to a swastika."

He wondered if it was wise to embark on a European expansion program, given their money problems. Didn't they need to have some kind of master plan?

Peppers affected a German accent. "Zee master plan?" he said, laughing. "Today, it is Chemical Manufacturers. Tomorrow, zee world!"

Kuperman was not amused. "You may think it's funny, but. . . ."

Wolf cut him off and suggested that he raise the issue at the World Board. There was more bad news to plow through today. Pete de Vaux's director of financial services, Simon Bax, who had taken on the subsidiaries after Fred Goldberg's departure, recited the figures that had led Wolf to recommend a death sentence: losses of $500,000 on $15 million in income for the eight months that ended on July 1, with projected losses of $1 million on just over $20 million in income by the end of the fiscal year. The board agreed to sell Bright & Associates back to Keith Bright, and to sell Jessica Dee or shut it down.

"Our issue," said Wolf, "is to not lose money and uncomplicate our lives."

Clow said little during the morning session. It was as if he had returned to the family homestead after a long absence, and was listening to the new owner of the property describe the improvements he wanted to make. Wolf had every right, of course—he held title—but Clow still had the emotional claim on the landscape. Everyone expected him to voice his opinion at some point. It was just a question of how far he was going to let Wolf go before he invoked history.

At the lunch break, the board members filed next door to the Boathouse, a more hospitable room for a meal than the stark, cold Treehouse. Clow stood in line for his lunch next to M. T. Rainey, the Scottish planner who had been made president of the London office after two years at Chiat/Day in New York.

"It's hard, being this big," Clow said.

She smiled helpfully. "Well, we're getting smaller."

Pete de Vaux overheard them. A puckish grin creased his face. He spoke loudly enough for all to hear: "We're trying to see how small we can get before we get good."

The confrontation came early in the afternoon session, in the midst of a discussion about how to find better account services people. The question of whether to raise them in house or recruit new talent was civil enough, but it led quickly to a debate over the role an improved account staff was supposed to play. Wolf complained, as he had many times, that even the most talented account executive met with disdain from the rest of the agency. What he wanted was to "empower" the account people. "Let people know they run the business," was the way he put it.

Kuperman couldn't restrain himself. Account services running the agency? Not in his lifetime. "I don't *want* them to have control," he blurted.

"*Beep*," said Peppers, as though Kuperman were a contestant on a game show. "Wrong answer. Wrong answer."

Kuperman all but bared his teeth. "It may be the wrong answer for you," he said, harshly, "but it's the right answer for me. I don't want to work at an agency where account people run it. Creatives have the final word."

"What if they're *wrong*?" asked Wolf.

At that Clow spoke up. He and Chiat were still available as the court of last resort. They could resolve any deadlocks—which effectively meant that creative would still run the agency. Wolf ignored him.

Clow began to yell. "*Accounts are not going to be run by account supervisors*," he said, his face flushed, the veins in his neck throbbing. "*That's not the way it's ever going to work!*"

Wolf stayed calm. All he wanted to do, he explained, was enable an account person to tell a creative, " 'I don't care if you think this is cute. It's wrong for the account.' "

Clow would not yield. Account people had to earn the creatives' respect. It didn't come with the cubicle, like a stapler or a computer.

"Then we don't disagree," said Wolf. "That's how the office should run."

But Clow was yelling. "If we *had* enough people who'd *earned* that respect, we'd run like that."

"I think the president of the office should be the final word," said Kuperman. He hadn't felt that way when he was creative director and Wolf was office president, because Wolf, then as now, seemed willing to trade in the agency's creative reputation on a new, more submissive model. Kuperman was in just the sort of position that appealed to his sense of drama. He was the only one who could navigate growth without compromise.

But when Wolf spoke again he addressed Clow, as though they were having a private conversation within the larger, public debate. It bothered Wolf that people still thought of Chiat/Day as a place where creatives won all the arguments. He feared that the agency's profile kept good account executives from coming to the agency— which meant that creatives, many of whom lacked Clow's maturity, ran the agency by default.

"Why don't we take away empowerment," Clow replied, "and talk about mutual respect instead?"

Exasperated, Wolf dropped the debate. The numbers would convince the board of the need for change more forcefully than any rhetoric.

The World Board would make any final decisions about fiscal strategy, but Wolf wanted the members of the North American Board to know what to expect. He had three plans for stabilizing the agency's finances, and he anticipated that the final strategy would be some combination of them:

- Salary cuts of 5–10 percent among employees who made over $200,000 annually, with a smaller cut for employees who made $150,000 or $100,000;
- Salary and raise freezes across the board, for as long as one year; and
- Hiring freezes.

There was silence.

"Frankly, we're in a tough state," he went on. "New York is taking a bath, London and Toronto are investments that haven't yet paid off, Australia's in bad shape and the subsidiaries are an experiment that's not working. It's not a question of why. It's a question of how to do it best."

Kuperman spoke first. He felt that a salary and raise freeze for all employees would be "a disaster." Let the people who could afford a cut, take it. The employees who made $30,000–$40,000 had to be protected.

"We spend $36,000 a year on flowers," he said. "I'd rather see the flowers go than deny a secretary a raise. We should try to keep this thing from affecting the people who make the agency go."

"I hear you," said Wolf. "Let me play devil's advocate. Sally's making $30,000. Her friend is unemployed. Hundreds of people would take her job in a minute. Isn't there some way to communicate that? That the industry's fallen on hard times?"

"Too many signals go against it," said Kuperman. "The palace across the street. Flying first class. Seven people serving food in New York."

"That's going to go," said Wolf.

"Is this going to affect morale?" Kuperman. "Yes. So keep it up at the top."

"There isn't enough money at the top," said Wolf.

Kuperman wanted to know how much money the agency would save with the pay cuts at $100,000.

One million, came the answer.

And if freezes were instituted throughout the agency?

Two million.

"It's *wrong* to do," he said.

"Relative to what?" Peppers inquired.

Kuperman wondered if they could save enough by cutting salaries over $50,000 but no one had done that computation. "I can't believe you have to go down to the $18,000 secretaries," he said. "You *can't* go in and say to them, 'There's a raise freeze.' It's not *right*."

Clow managed to speak without any of the emotion that usually betrayed him. Like Kuperman, he blamed the people who ran the agency, including himself, for its predicament. They had over-reached. They had turned away from advertising, which had made them a success, and now their expansionist dreams threatened everything they had spent two decades building. There was a note of chastisement in Clow's voice, as though he regretted having succumbed, along with the others, to the temptations of power and wealth.

"This is a business built on people and the environment," he said. "We have to find the line that satisfies the economic needs without decimating the environment. Management has to bear the brunt. Our environment is the most fragile ecosystem we've got. So let's make sure we get rid of dead wood and take cuts ourselves, before we cast a pall."

"This is not an insidious attempt to fuck the people," said Wolf. "This is the most generous agency in the country."

"We've never successfully communicated that," said Kuperman.

"Right," said Wolf. "We have to communicate this is not an evil plot to take food off the table."

"Is this in a month?" asked Kuperman. "Two weeks?"

"Nope," said Wolf, firmly. "Days. We'll meet Saturday, make our decision, and do it." He wanted staff cuts as well—and he wanted people out the same day they were fired.

Ira Matathia, the New York account services executive who replaced Chuck Phillips as president of the Toronto office, rehearsed what he expected to say the following Monday. "Take the afternoon off," he said, "but take your nameplate with you."

Word of Kuperman's defense of the masses traveled quickly throughout the Venice office. One woman walked up to him as he headed back down Main Street and hugged him wordlessly. Others gathered in small groups and spoke approvingly of his altruism. Kuperman had begun to take the small emotions that fueled his early career—the arrogance, competitiveness, and a rude anger—and expand them into something finer. He was still prone to the unexpected flare-up, still rage's hostage, but he was fast becoming a master of anger's more dignified, democratic relative, righteous indignation.

Kuperman represented not just himself but his office. He no longer had to sell an execution to his boss, or a campaign to a client. Now he was selling his vision of the agency, both to its employees and to top management. More and more people at Chiat/Day were buying his product: Kuperman's presidency was his most effective piece of work.

Sitting at a patio table at Loews Hotel the next morning, just a breezy half-block from the Pacific Ocean, Pete de Vaux was struck by how quickly the shock dissipated. He hadn't expected to be fired today over breakfast with Wolf and Weiner, but as soon as he recovered his equilibrium he realized that he had, in fact, expected to be fired at some point. He had known he was in trouble for a month, ever since Chiat complained about the corporate budget.

Wolf and Weiner had a list of complaints—including leases whose terms weren't as favorable to the agency as they might be, and $400,000 worth of problems on the Bright & Associates office renovation—but de Vaux doubted that any would be considered grounds for dismissal if New York weren't in such terrible shape. In hindsight, the $12 million debt repayment had been a mistake, but there was no way to anticipate the magnitude of the summer's losses.

He told himself: "The real reason they're firing me is that I've become obsolete." Simon Bax could do the CFO's job, with Weiner looking over his shoulder, and de Vaux's two other financial responsibilities, the subsidiaries and the international plan, were inactive.

If it had been up to him, he might have fired himself. But he wouldn't have stopped there. He would have fired Newman and not given her a new job, and then he would have fired Tom McElligott and Don Peppers.

At eight o'clock on Saturday morning a subdued Chiat escorted Newman into the Boathouse, where the rest of the members of the World Board were gathered, their carry-on luggage littering the floor behind the conference table. Newman's features were frozen in a sorrowful wince, her eyes darting, wishing for approval and expecting disdain. Everything about her was diminished. Her chic, streaked bob, a halo of sunny ringlets, was, this morning, a Medusa's head of flattened curls. She seemed to have forgotten her makeup.

She listened as Wolf presented the North American report. He expected revenues of $103 million, down from an operating plan figure of $120 million, and beneath the 1989 figure of $107 million. Profits would probably be $14 million, down from a projected $25 million, and lower than last year's $19,500,000. The profit margin for 1990, which was supposed to be 21 percent, would likely be 14 percent, down 4 percent from 1989.

He was terse. The dream of becoming a multipurpose marketing company was over. "We have to shift back to our core business, and what we do well, which is advertising," he said. "We don't have the depth of management to do more things well."

The trick, Wolf said, was to cut back enough to restore the agency's financial health, but not so much that the cuts "paralyzed" the company. Chiat/Day had to embark on a new business push, the kind of scouting expedition that none of them had thought would be necessary for the Agency of the Decade, and there had to be enough bodies around to mount the attack.

As he spoke, Newman methodically studied and nibbled each of her cuticles.

She made only one suggestion, just above a whisper, her eyes downcast. Whatever the board decided to do about pay cuts for the rest of the agency, Newman wanted salary cuts for every employee in New York. She intended to get rid of fifty people by Tuesday, and she was prepared, as an act of contrition, to order pay cuts for the ones who were lucky enough to remain.

"Cut it back," she said, in a flat voice, "and then build it up again."

The idea was rejected. No one office would be singled out for punishment.

Instead, the board instituted pay cuts for everyone who earned over $150,000, a salary freeze for people who earned more than $100,000, and a 5 percent raise ceiling for all employees. The new CFO, Simon Bax, was dispatched to ask for a $10 million line of credit from the Morgan Guaranty Trust Company of New York, the first time in the agency's history that such a move had been necessary. And the board decided against occupying all three floors of the Venice building. Chiat/Day would keep the warehouse and take one and a half floors across the street. The rest of the space would be leased. It was not at all what Chiat had envisioned, but there was no way to rationalize paying rent on the entire building, not unless business improved.

Newman approached Wolf as soon as the meeting was adjourned. If Chiat had been running the agency, Newman would have felt more secure. He knew how dedicated she was to her job and he valued that devotion. He would appreciate the difficulties she had faced over the past year, as her top executives had left, one by one, the creative director to a higher-paying, more prestigious position at Ogilvy & Mather, the account planning director and account services director to Chiat/Day's London and Toronto offices. Newman had been left with a crippled office. Chiat would have understood that and given her the chance to rebuild. Newman had increased billings from $108 million to $200 million in the first three years of her presidency. She deserved another chance.

She didn't know whether Wolf would give it to her. She had seen what had happened to Fred Goldberg and Chuck Phillips, and wondered whether Wolf was going to make her pay for a crisis she felt she had been powerless to prevent.

"Are you going to fire me?" she asked.

"I'm not going to fire you," said Wolf. "I might ask you to change jobs."

"Give me six months," she said.

"I'm not sure we can afford six months," he said. "But I'm thinking about all my options." Wolf had no intention of giving her six months. He had already decided on Newman's replacement—he was going to offer the job to Bob Perkins, of Perkins-Butler—and he had resolved to commute to New York himself at least two weeks out of every month.

Wolf had come to a strange pass. He believed that the agency could find someone to replace him, even though he was supposed to be the unique individual who would guide it into the future. The man who was irreplaceable—for all their arguing and despite their fundamental disagreement on what Chiat/Day was supposed to be—was Clow. Nobody else could do what he did, and with Wolf about to spend half his time in New York, Clow's full participation was essential.

Wolf told Chiat that they had to restore Clow's financial parity with Wolf, to give him concrete proof that Chiat/Day still considered him an essential asset. Clow had lost too much time nursing his hurt feelings over Wolf's title, and then his April raise. He had wasted valuable energy worrying about philosophical issues when he should have been making ads. If money made Clow less preoccupied with his position, then every penny would be well spent.

Chiat agreed. Clow would receive Employee Participation Units to match Wolf's. The two men now had an equal interest in the agency's future.

The firings began early in the morning on Monday, July 30, a day that quickly became known in the hushed halls of the Venice office as "Black Monday." A dozen members of the corporate staff and a half dozen account services employees lost their jobs. Account services director Jim Weinstein showed up for work, got a summons to see Kuperman, and an hour later was in 3 Mile Island getting a crash course in the legalities of severance from corporate administrator Sharon Stanley.

Rabosky took up residence in a small conference room and fired four creatives, one right after another, instructing them to leave the building immediately and come back at the end of the day to collect their belongings. He was trying to minimize the effect of the firings on the rest of the staff—the extended mutterings of a bitter ex-employee could poison morale—but the brusque dismissals only made the survivors frightened. People gathered outside their cubicles, listening for rumors, reminding each other of the great work they had been doing.

Kuperman insisted that the layoffs had nothing to do with the situation in New York, that Weinstein and de Vaux were expendable, the corporate staff was fat, and Rabosky was just reshaping the department in his own image. His pronouncements fell on deaf ears. Mass firings always meant an agency was in trouble. Until Chiat/Day started winning new accounts, no one would feel secure.

At the end of the day, Kuperman called the members of the account services department together and informed them that they now reported directly to him. He would find people at the agency to relieve him of some of the responsibilities he'd never liked in the first place, such as the number-crunching budget work. That way, he could devote himself to what he said was "the part of the business that interests me the most—doing the work with clients, helping them figure out their strategy, working through the advertising, solving problems. That's what I want to be involved in."

In the midst of the turmoil Clow sought refuge in his sanctuary, the creative department art studio. He hovered at Amy Miyano's side until finally her nerves snapped.

"What *is* it?" she asked him.

The past few days had crystallized the problem, and its clear solution, for Clow. "It has to come back to creative," he told her.

Miyano was speechless. She had been warning Clow for years that someone who cared about power was going to step in and take over the agency. He had turned down the Venice office presidency in 1980, when Chiat had given up the post to move to New York. By the time Wolf stepped into that job five years later, the office was in disarray. Wolf cared about position. He began to take charge.

Over the years, Miyano had predicted more trouble ahead, and each time Clow had chastised her for having a negative attitude. Now he was telling *her* exactly what she'd been telling *him*, that the agency had to be grounded in the work—when he was the one who had let it get away.

"That's right," she almost hissed. "But you gave it up! *You gave it to Wolf! You did.* You gave over the business."

Just once, she wanted Clow to take responsibility. Instead, he told her proudly of what he considered to be his latest accomplishment. He had convinced Chiat, over the past few days, that he, Clow, should be "the counterbalance to Wolf." As proof of that, the agency was going to restore him to financial parity with the CEO.

Miyano had to restrain herself. He was *supposed* to be Wolf's equal. The only reason he felt the need to reclaim his status was because he had given it away in the first place. Ever since January 1, 1990, he had behaved as though Bob Wolf did run Chiat/Day, and Clow was an accessory, an exquisite antique displayed on the corporate desk to impress the client. Miyano loved Clow and considered him one of her dearest friends. But she found it hard to forgive him his shortsightedness. His restored parity wasn't a prize. It was his birthright, which he had given away.

The next morning a letter went out over Chiat's signature, addressed, "To Everyone in the Chiat/Day/Mojo Family."

> *As you are probably aware, 1990 has been an extremely difficult year for our industry. Unfortunately, Chiat/Day/Mojo has not been immune to industry problems. It seems that the day after we received the Agency of the Decade award, things began to get tough. It wasn't that we didn't expect it. We had predicted client spending cuts almost a year ago. However, we didn't expect them to hit as fast, or to lose two of the biggest accounts in the agency within a 3 month period.*

Chiat anticipated resentment from Venice staffers who would wonder why they had to endure cutbacks when it was New York that was in trouble. "The agency has always functioned with a 'we're all in this together' attitude," the letter went on.

> *It helped us get through the Apple, Nike and Pizza Hut losses when LA was down and New York was having a good year. This attitude has been the reason the work coming out of each office is as good as it is. We don't have a "branch office" mentality.*
> *It's understandably frustrating that with everyone working so hard and some offices, particularly Los Angeles, doing so well, [we have] to institute austerity measures. However, when we look past the immediate future to 1991, our forecasts tell us the economy isn't going*

to get any better. That means getting in shape by paring down and having people in place who work hard and smart.

Effective August 1, the agency's board members, senior management and major shareholders would take a "significant pay cut." The letter didn't spell out the details, but it did lay out the future for everyone else: A wage freeze for those who earned over $100,000, and a 5 percent raise ceiling throughout the agency.

> *I believe the worst is behind us and I am quite bullish about the future. We are poised to win some significant new business.*
>
> *I just reviewed the work at the Creative Directors meeting in Los Angeles and its [sic] more good work than I've seen in a long time. And if we're going to be a great agency, it's the advertising that makes it that.*
>
> *This agency's strength has always been riding out the downturns and coming back stronger than ever. We've got the right people in place. We've eliminated all of the waste and energy-draining activity. We're focused. We know who we are and what our objectives are.*
>
> *Now it's time to get to work and deliver.*
>
> *Fondly, Jay.*

Forty people lost their jobs in New York, although Wolf indulged in a little "damage control," telling *New York Times* advertising columnist Kim Foltz that thirty people had been fired

As Chiat had feared, the press regarded the anticipated loss of Royal Caribbean as part of a disturbing trend. Worse, when reporters added up their figures for the year's losses, and subtracted them from New York's published billings, the losses plunged the office below $100 million—which, according to the *Times*, made its business prospects even dimmer.

"It is generally believed in the industry," wrote Foltz on August 2, 1990,

> *that agencies with billings of less than $100 million would not be considered by national clients for their large accounts. . . .*
>
> *. . . Some advertising executives said a primary reason for the problems at the New York office was the frequent absences of Jay Chiat, the agency's founder, who moved his office to Manhattan when the New York branch was opened in 1981. He recently has been*

spending increasing amounts of time at the agency's other offices in
the United States and abroad. . . .
     . . . The agency's plans to establish itself as a big international
advertising power seem to have stalled.

Clow, who knew nothing of Wolf's intention to offer the New York
presidency to Bob Perkins, had what he thought was a "neat" idea,
which he shared with Wolf: they ought to make Tom McElligott
president of the New York office. It would send the right kind of
message to the business community. An ex-creative director as president of the Venice office, and an ex-creative director as president in
New York. Everyone would know that Chiat/Day was back on track.

"Yeah," said Wolf, "but McElligott in New York is as crazy as you
being president in L.A. Kuperman has other goals. That's what makes
him a better president than he was a creative director."

Three days later, on Sunday, August 5, Wolf had dinner in New
York with Bob Perkins. He formally offered Perkins the job of pres-
ident and chief operating officer of the New York office, starting
immediately, to work in tandem with him. He was going to talk to
McElligott, too, about committing much more of his time to New
York. Together, they would solve the New York office's problems.

Perkins accepted.

The next morning Wolf had a breakfast date with Newman. He
knew he had to tell her cleanly and quickly. If there was anything in
his words or manner that allowed for debate, any ragged edge of
uncertainty where she could dig in and hold on, he would have
trouble. He was not there to have a conversation. He was there to fire
her and to offer her a newly created job as the agency's vice-chairman
in charge of strategic planning in new business.

He told her, showed her a draft of a press release announcing her
departure, and asked her what she wanted him to say about her future
role at Chiat/Day.

Her first reaction as to get up and walk away. She fought to remain
composed. "You could say I've been promoted to Pope," she said,
bitterly, "and it won't matter. They'll say we've made the move to save
a failing Chiat/Day." She refused the new job. She felt betrayed,
worse, betrayed by a man whom she had supported since the day she

interviewed him, at Chiat's request, to make sure that he was Chiat/ Day material. Newman felt that Wolf owed her the chance to turn the office around. He should have been loyal.

She went back to her office hurt and disbelieving, and within an hour the phone began to ring. Chiat called. So did Clow, Weiner and Sharon Stanley, all of them with the same message: Don't quit.

Newman thought to herself, "I wasn't going to quit. Maybe I should."

The public announcement of the management changes appeared in *The New York Times* and *Wall Street Journal* on Friday, August 10, the day Newman was scheduled to speak at the *Advertising Age* "Creativity" conference in Chicago. There was only one reference to her in the *Times*'s coverage: "While he praised Ms. Newman as a valuable executive, Mr. Wolf said she lacked the administrative and personnel skills to run the office successfully."

Reading that, Newman felt as though she had been slapped in the face. She was supposed to be onstage in an hour, having just suffered the worst humiliation of her career. She managed to drag herself to the room where she was supposed to speak, only to have one of the conference organizers rush over to her, exclaiming, "Oh my God, are you still here? We thought you'd left Chiat/Day."

The following week, she left for a month's leave of absence. Distraught over imagined shortcomings, Newman went to Barnes & Noble and bought $89 worth of business management books, to research what she had done wrong. She packed up her books and her nine-year-old son and headed for the farm she and her husband owned in Warwick, New York. She had no idea if she would ever come back.

A perfect irony sat, unnoticed, in the midst of all the confusion, ignored by men who were too busy trying to clamber out of a hole that seemed to deepen every time they took a step up. For eight months, Clow had labored to define his new role at the agency, daunted by Wolf's title and status. He had sworn, at the outset, to provide leadership to complement Wolf's management skills, but he had failed. Wolf, with his overt ambition and assured manner, had dwarfed him—and as the months passed Clow had retreated, working on Nissan, doing a star turn at the Century 21 pitch, chasing the glorious past.

He was about to be granted a wish he had made back in December, before the promotions had been announced. Clow had said then that employees needed a leader they could look up to, and an administration they noticed not at all. People needed inspiration. They did not need to see the wheels turning. Now, Clow was going to have his chance to lead. Management, in the form of Bob Wolf, was about to become invisible.

C H A P T E R 22

Tom Patty, who had escorted the Sentra strategy past the line of Nissan middle managers like a proud father of the bride, was almost to the pulpit when someone in the back of the church started complaining about her dress. In early August, just weeks before the agency was to present its Fantasy campaign to Tom Mignanelli for final approval, two Nissan executives who felt neglected balked. They weren't comfortable with the emphasis on sporty style and driving fun, nor convinced that the buying public would be. They wanted to stick with what had always worked—the well-built economy car.

Chiat's account people explained that the redesign and the price increase demanded a new point of view. The consumer would hardly pay more if he continued to think of the Sentra as a sturdy little bargain. He had to be shaken up. But the executives had entered what Clow called the "scared defensive mode." They would have to be coaxed out before they caught Mignanelli's attention and made real trouble.

The agency declared a thirty-day moratorium on all creative work until the malcontents were eased back into the fold. But Patty, realizing that a month's delay would mean cost overruns, did not intend to let the disagreement last that long. Coddling the two executives would be quicker and less costly.

He set up special meetings for them with the agency staff, extended briefings designed to make them feel part of the process. He exhorted them to "get back on the train." One of the men collected miniature trains, so Patty gave them each a toy train. The two agreed finally to endorse the slate of commercials. The agency's date with Mignanelli was secured.

The meeting had a tone of a royal audience. Mignanelli was a large, muscular man who looked as if he had been stamped out of the same sheet metal that went into his cars. He strode into the conference room where the top executives from the Nissan division and a half dozen agency people were gathered, listened to the commercials, laughed, and asked a few questions of Clow and Patty. He gave his blessing to the 1991 Fantasy campaign, and rose to leave. Chiat/Day had managed to satisfy its patron saint at Nissan, the man whose approval, though little more than a formality, meant that their relationship continued in good health.

What the agency people called the "real client" was harder to impress. The fifteen members of Nissan's Dealer Advisory Board, representing 1,100 dealers nationwide, had begun to complain loudly about the sorry state of their business—and they were deflecting their anger onto their bohemian cousins, the ad men. With a recession going on, the dealers wanted to talk about sales, not style. They were suspicious of words like "long-term image" or "aspirational choice." Dealer slang for the showroom was "the store"—and what they needed was more people coming in to shop.

It was dealer complaints that had precipitated the decentralization plan. If they continued to be unhappy with the new arrangement, the entire regional account would be in jeopardy. Chiat/Day had to make the dealers their allies, make them happy at the prospect of losing their largest-volume model to a replacement that could cost twice as much.

The agency and Nissan had scheduled their first roundtable discussion with the members of the regional council for August 6. The morning session would be held on neutral turf, Loews Hotel, followed by an afternoon meeting at Chiat/Day's Venice office. After a buffet breakfast in the hotel's second-floor lobby—the dealers in their sport coats and leisure wear, the agency staff in a funereal assortment of somber business suits—Bob Thomas, Kuperman and Patty faced the task of convincing their guests that the future was not as bleak as the present.

Patty attempted a Will Rogers quote: " 'Even if you're on the right track, you'll still get run over if you just sit there.' " Kuperman dismissed the bad press Chiat/Day's New York office was getting and explained that Venice was "way ahead of where we want to be." Thomas congratulated the agency on the Fantasy campaign, which he credited with the past year's increase in purchase intention—a consumer's stated desire to own a Nissan, whether he was in the market right now or not—from 2.9 percent to over 4 percent. New product, particularly the redesigned Maxima, had contributed mightily to that increase, but Thomas was here to sell Chiat/Day to the dealers. He generously gave all the credit to the agency, in the hope that he could warm up the room.

The dealers greeted him with the same stony silence they had shown Patty and Kuperman. When it was their turn, they introduced themselves and one by one recited their woes. A New York dealer who sold loaded Pathfinders to Manhattanites with country homes had been allocated the basic model instead. He predicted that Stanza sales would cannibalize the high end of the new Sentra market and cancel out any chance of a volume increase. A major Los Angeles dealer was very concerned about the Sentra pricing structure, and wondered if any advertising campaign was going to be enough to change the public perception of Sentra as a cheap little car.

The most anxious dealers were the ones from the Northeast, who were being hit from two sides at once: buyers had less money to spend and banks were buying less retail car paper than they had in the past. It was harder to buy and finance a car than it used to be. Given that painful fact, the last thing the dealers wanted was to lose their cheapest car, the one that lured the marginal customer into the showroom. The move seemed to run contrary to what other car manufacturers were doing.

"Everyone else is extending their ladder," said one dealer, "while we're pulling ours up. People will have a good experience elsewhere and not switch to Nissan."

Thomas tried to soothe the dealers with talk of Sentra's metamorphosis into an "image model," but one man broke in impatiently.

"You going to have something to get us enthused?" he asked.

"Something we can pull people in with, give them a Knute Rockne speech and have them wet their pants?"

Thomas chuckled and implored the dealers to watch the day's presentation. If they still had that kind of question to ask, they could ask it tomorrow.

One dealer looked at the printed agenda, which included a session at Chiat/Day's Venice headquarters, and saw the word "Fish" listed after the lunch break. Why, he wondered, would they be serving fish when they had already eaten lunch?

In the interest of credibility and rapport, Clow had worn trousers, an oxford-cloth shirt, and slicked back his wispy shoulder-length hair for his presentation to the dealers. He showed them the video of the 1990 Fantasy campaign, and then he posed a teasing question: "How does somebody dream about a car he's never seen and can't buy?" With that, he launched into a description of the "Car Company" storyboard, and followed with an impassioned reading of Sittig's script.

The dealers took notes, studied their hands, rubbed their chins, scratched their heads, and said nothing—and Clow, like a dying stand-up comic, just kept talking about what a great commercial it was.

The dealers, unconvinced, wondered if the agency had researched a possible name change for the car, whether the word "Nissan" could be mentioned more often, and when there might be a commercial that actually provided practical information about the car.

Would the line "Because rich guys shouldn't have all the fun" offend women?

Would it make Sentra customers feel they were doomed to be poor?

"Is there enough of a beauty shot of the car?" asked one dealer. "I know you can get carried away with creative, with wrapping a story around it. But we need to see the product."

Clow assured him that there were some beautiful shots of the car.

The interior, as well as the exterior?

Yes.

It wasn't until Clow ran through "Bob's Road" that the group relaxed. The spot was funny, there were lots of shots of the car, and it was more accessible than "Car Company." Then Rinek stepped up to discuss media. During the last week of October and the first week of November, it would be almost impossible to turn on a television set and not see a Sentra commercial. There would be another blitz in November, another in January, and another in February. Thirty-five percent of the company's television budget was allotted for Sentra commercials.

These were figures the dealers understood, and appreciated. The public would find it difficult to escape news of the 1991 Sentra. If the concept was right—as Nissan and the agency insisted it was—perhaps 165,000 units wasn't an impossible goal, after all.

Sittig devoted himself to the casting sessions for "Car Company," sitting through over 250 auditions for the part of the young dreamer. He suggested testing stand-up comedians for the voice of Nissan, instead of the announcer the company usually used. This was his chance to make a minute's worth of history. Now that he had been relieved of his more mundane responsibilities, he could spend all his time making sure that "Car Company" looked the way he wanted it to.

He found the actor he wanted for the job, but Clow liked another candidate, a tall, slender, blond man with a dancing background.

"He'll move well," argued Clow.

"He's not going to move," said Sittig. "He's going to strike poses. And if this guy stands next to the car, he'll dwarf it."

They met with Rinek and Mark Coppos, who would direct the commercial, and agreed to recommend Sittig's candidate to marketing manager Ron Hannum. Rinek was dispatched to show him the actor's audition tape. Unfortunately, both actors were on a single tape. Hannum preferred the wrong man.

When Sittig saw the actor who got the lead role in "Car Company" on film, he groaned, "Oh, shit!"

Not only was the kid too tall and thin, he didn't at all convey the captain-of-industry fantasy Sittig had created. His gestures weren't grand enough. He wasn't an imposing figure. He was corn-fed and lanky. Desperately, Sittig consulted with the director to see if they could figure out a way to convey the magnitude of his role to their star.

"Ronald Colman on amphetamines," suggested Coppos.

But twenty-four-year-old Ron Pearson, a stand-up comedian and actor, didn't know who Ronald Colman was.

"It's a combination of Mussolini and Yul Brynner," Sittig tried. Pearson drew a blank.

"*King of Siam*," said Sittig. Pearson had never seen *The King and I*.

The first day's work—matched shots of Pearson, first in a polo shirt and jeans, dreamily gazing skyward, and then in a suit and rakish hat, living his fantasy—was a complete waste as far as Sittig was concerned. Either they would have to reshoot it or salvage it in the editing room. He showed up on location for the second day of shooting, Sunday, August 19, to oversee Pearson's performance.

The crew prepared for a four o'clock shoot in front of Bullocks Wilshire, a 1929 department store whose facade had been transformed into the headquarters of the fantasy car company. Two men affixed bold letters that read "MY MOTOR COMPANY" over the doorway, as Pearson stood nearby, striking poses. Sittig watched the crew members—and, out of the corner of his eye, the actor.

"If this is a success people will be killing each other to get that sign," he muttered. "If it's a failure they'll weld it to my office."

The transformation of internal fantasy into physical reality was always a humbling process, but Sittig seemed particularly agitated. When Clow arrived, fresh from a Catalina weekend, Sittig grabbed the older man and spirited him off to a production trailer. He showed Clow the previous day's footage.

"Let's redo it," said Sittig, petulantly. "It would only take fifteen minutes."

Clow corrected him. "The set-up alone will take more than fifteen minutes."

They wandered back outside. A crane was in place in front of My Motor Company for a swooping shot from the hero's point of view up to the company logo and flag—a gear and a T-square. Sittig peered into the camera and sniffed.

"We need a helicopter," he said.

Clow ignored him. There was nothing to be gained from wishing for the moon. He was preoccupied with the task at hand, which was to make the film look as good as possible with the resources they had. He peered at the video monitor, cupping his hands to block out the daylight. When the director complained that the shot looked too busy, that Pearson seemed to be making one too many moves, Clow stood up, mimicked the actor, and agreed that yes, one of his gestures had to go. Sittig wanted the crane to carry the camera straight up the building, not on the diagonal, because the angle canceled out the power of the ascent, but Clow's concerns were more practical. As much as he wanted upward motion, he didn't want to see any wobble. Sittig might have the concept in his head. Clow, by this time, had a little movie running in his.

The sun marched defiantly down Wilshire Boulevard toward the Pacific Ocean, threatening to cut short the day's production in mid-debate. After two hours of trial and error, Pearson put on his customized suit, with its extra broad shoulders and nipped waist, and stepped up onto the dolly, a square wooden wheeled platform that would roll him into position for the opening shot.

Four pigeon wranglers perched on ladders and prepared to liberate two crates of birds. They were what Sittig called the "hero pigeons," who would fly heavenward, on cue, and lend a triumphant grace note to the opening scene. Actually, they would be tossed in the proper direction. These were not trained homing pigeons. They had been birdnapped that very day, and, having spent an unexpected afternoon in a box, would flee once they were set free. Too many takes, and the dream would have to do without them.

At 6:15 P.M., in what Clow happily declared to be "*wonderful light*," Coppos started shooting. Over and over again, Pearson rolled smoothly into place, clamped his hands to his waist and stuck out his elbows, and then gestured toward the clouds, as the camera and the pigeons guided the viewer up the facade of the building, toward the company's logo.

Across the street, a handful of onlookers mimicked Pearson's pose, to the delight of everyone from Chiat/Day. One production assistant imagined customers walking into dealerships nationwide, striking that pose, and asking to see the new Sentra.

The next night an overeager Pasadena police officer shut down the "Car Company" shoot at 10:00 P.M., even though Chiat/Day had the necessary permits to work overtime at the deserted Royal Laundry, whose vast rooms had been dressed to look like the executive office, the design studio, showroom and wind tunnel of My Motor Company.

The confusion cost the crew the night, which they needed for the wind tunnel shot.

They struggled to keep to their two-day schedule at the laundry location, but the limitations of time and space kept getting in their way. Pearson couldn't complete his carefully rehearsed movements fast enough to get from the door of his office to his desk on cue. A complicated tracking shot from the office into the design studio required the use of a stand-in for a shot over the dreamer's shoulder, and the stand-in was in costume, in place and on film before anyone noticed that his shoulders were not as broad as Pearson's and he was a good four inches shorter. The extras in the design studio scene were white and Asian, but Mignanelli was known to favor a racial mix in Nissan's commercials. The agency decided to add a black actor for the sake of heterogeneity—only to take him out later, once they realized that he blocked out too much of the set.

When the agency found a black actor to play a photographer who immortalized the unveiling of the new Sentra, O'Neill and the account executive worried that he was too prominent a minority presence. There was a difference between ethnic balance and overdoing it. The director shot alternative endings, one with a trio of photographers and one with a white actor. Clow and Sittig decided to use the black photographer for the rough cut, but no one expected him to survive.

The crew finally got to the wind tunnel shot late on Tuesday night. They finished at four in the morning, which gave everyone just enough time to race home and pack for a noon flight to Nashville, Tennessee, so that they could shoot at Nissan's factory in nearby Smyrna.

Wolf and Chiat were preoccupied with New York. Wolf had tried Kuperman's Foster Farms strategy on Royal Caribbean Cruise Lines, and requested a six-month trial period with a brand-new account staff. The client rejected the idea, but Wolf still thought he saw a glimmer of hope. Unlike Reebok, Royal Caribbean was a steady, predictable client. The problems had been on the agency side, and they had been remedied. Surely the agency could woo the client back. Both common sense and the financial imperative demanded that Chiat/Day make the effort. The New York office geared up to pitch the account on October 4.

That left Clow and Kuperman even more to themselves, just at a time when they could take advantage of the opportunity. Clow had available space in his brain, because production, however frustrating, was a finite universe, one of angles and lighting, of women's stockings pulled taut over camera lenses to soften what the lens saw and smoke pumped onto a set to make the light more flattering. Kuperman, for his part, would have shanghaied the parking attendant if he thought the man had something to contribute to new business.

They had lost the National Basketball Association pitch, which Kuperman blamed on their decision not to present speculative creative work, but there were new opportunities—Sparkletts bottled water, a $6 to $8 million account, and Toshiba portable computers, a $17 million piece of business. Clow was back to balancing spinning plates on sticks again, with Kuperman proving a deft associate, and their enthusiasm was contagious. All their prodding and meddling had an effect. Defensive alliances dissolved. Creatives ceased identifying themselves as members of either Clow's or Kuperman's aesthetic camp. They got caught up in the race to win a piece of business for the agency.

After months of uncertainty as to who exactly was running what at Chiat/Day, the agency had a practical model for proper behavior. Rather than worrying about power and position, the two senior creatives at Chiat/Day were showing up at pitch meetings, dissecting strategies and scribbling ideas for ads. Clow and Kuperman took tacit control, and by their actions encouraged others to stop bickering and get back to work.

The only one who failed to respond was Rob White, who seemed uncharacteristically confused and distracted. His co-workers chalked it up to overwork, given the array of new business projects he was working on, but client issues were not all that were on his mind. In mid-August, White had gotten a call inquiring whether he would consider leaving Chiat/Day to form a new agency, where he would be a partner, not an employee. He had always imagined himself a Chiat/Day lifer, but the suggestion of an alternative—of not just a new job but a new status—made him hesitate.

For all the agency's talk about how it cared for its people, White nursed a couple of grudges. He had had to ask for his promotion to vice-president, and had yet to be made a senior vice-president, even though the men who ran the other departments carried that title. He had asked to become a member of the North American Board, like the creative director and the head of account services, and was turned down. The offer of a partnership, of equity, made him take a look at what he had. Having to acknowledge that he ought to have more made him testy.

CHAPTER 23

Wolf *returned* from his first mouth-long stint in New York convinced that his decision to replace Jane Newman with Bob Perkins had been a smart one. Everyone, both inside and outside Chiat/Day, had wondered how Wolf would respond to Royal Caribbean's decision to put the account up for review. Perkins was generating even more positive feedback than Wolf had anticipated. The clients, each of which the two men visited in the weeks following the appointment, liked Perkins because he was gregarious and actively concerned with their well-being. He was an equally popular choice inside the agency.

Perkins had his first win two weeks into his tenure. The Chemical Manufacturers Association pitch had been Newman's project, but in the constantly revised history of the business, rewritten each time a new executive took charge, the win was perceived as Perkins's. Wolf and Perkins met with executives at Häagen-Dazs and were invited into a mid-September pitch. They talked to NBC about its pay-per-view 1992 Olympics programing, and made the finals for the $20 million Shearson Lehman Brothers account, a division of the American Express Company.

Wolf came back to Los Angeles physically exhausted, but energized. He hadn't felt this good since the first eighteen months he had spent rebuilding the Venice office. It was exciting to take over an office in chaos. He was getting to work earlier, to bed later, and having a great time.

To find time to spend with his wife and two daughters, he intended to keep to a daunting schedule. Twice each month, he would leave Los Angeles on the Sunday evening red-eye flight, which got him into New York in time to wash his face and head to the office. He would fly back at the end of the work day on Friday. With the time change, that bought him part of Friday with his family.

"The Widow Wolf," he joked, "is going to have a lot of frequent flyer miles."

For the first time in his nine-year-old life, Jane Newman's son had a monopoly on his mother's time and attention. He loved it. As her month's retreat drew to a close, he found his mother's Rolodex, dialed the number he wanted, and left a message on Chiat's answering machine.

"My mom's not coming back," he blurted out, without identifying himself. Then he hung up the telephone.

Kuperman and Clow were getting the Venice office under control, but Wolf was still in charge, and his arrival in September provided a blunt reminder. He held an annual operational meeting with each office president, to review income figures for the current year and projections for the next. It was his chance to challenge estimates, evaluate expected profit margins, and then order whatever budget squeeze he thought necessary, to make sure the agency stayed healthy.

On September 4, Kuperman appeared in 3 Mile Island before a tribunal of Wolf, Simon Bax and two other representatives of corporate finance. Kuperman was the supplicant here. There were no preliminaries, none of the usual chattiness that preceded most internal meetings. He sat down, consulted a yellow legal pad filled with notes and figures, and began to rattle off his vision of the present and future.

The 1990 figures and projections stood in depressing witness to the recession.

Eveready: "Flat."

Home Savings: "It'll stay where it is."

Minit-Lube: "Stays where it is."

Nissan national: "Flat." Regional spending might increase, but the client demanded proof of all decentralization costs before any reimbursement would be made. Kuperman wasn't very optimistic.

Taylor Made was already down to $3.3 million this year, from an anticipated $6 million, and next year would be "pretty much the same."

As soon as Kuperman finished, Wolf jumped in with his questions. Why was the creative budget up, if client spending was down?

Because Nissan regional writers and art directors in the field commanded $90,000–$95,000, not the $55,000–$65,000 they earned in Venice.

Why was travel up? If there were more people in the field, it ought to go down.

Because the new regional staff was expected to travel throughout the region, and because staff from Venice had to visit the outlying offices, to make sure they sustained the Chiat/Day culture.

Rent was up $1 million for fiscal 1991.

Kuperman sighed. That figure represented the rent for four regional Nissan offices in Atlanta, Dallas, Chicago, and San Francisco, as well as one and a half floors in the new Venice building.

Wolf teased Kuperman without smiling. "The margin keeps eroding. Eroding, Bob."

"Well, Jeez," said Kuperman. "I don't know if we'll ever see thirty-one percent again."

Simon Bax asked Kuperman what his new business targets were for the coming year.

Kuperman answered without hesitation: Two non-automotive accounts, each billing over $15 million. "We can't go out and win another $5 million piece of business," he said.

Wolf, clearly pleased with the answer, replied in a whiny falsetto. *"But what about the creatives?"* he pouted. *"Those are the fun accounts."*

Kuperman was brusque. "We have enough to keep them happy."

Wolf continued to needle Kuperman. He gestured disparagingly at the income figures and said, "Since when does *this* matter?"

"It matters now," said Kuperman.

"That's what I thought," said Wolf, approvingly.

Then he moved on to the real agenda of this meeting: finding fat in

Kuperman's budget. If clients weren't going to increase their spending, then the only way to improve the agency's profit picture was to continue to cut from inside. Besides, this was a good way to test Kuperman's commitment to his operational plan. Wolf liked to bait people, to see how hard they fought back. He was swift to move in when an executive expressed even the slightest doubt.

He wondered how many non-Nissan creatives the agency could afford to lose. Kuperman explained that Rabosky wanted to rotate people off of the Nissan account when they got burned out, for respite on another account, but that only made Wolf more determined. If the agency could afford to move teams off of Nissan, perhaps they didn't need so many people in the first place. He ran his finger down a personnel list and triumphantly counted up eight non-Nissan teams, as if that number proved the department was overstaffed.

But Kuperman was prepared. "Bob," he complained, allowing his voice to creep above its presidential register, "I've been through this. Do you think I'm an idiot? That I'd come into this room and not know we were going to get to this list?"

The financial people listened while Wolf and Kuperman argued. Wolf pounced on one name and complained that the creative only got one ad produced each year. Kuperman countered that he worked on two accounts that required a great deal of effort for very little yield. Kuperman said that the account services people complained that there were too few creatives. Wolf replied that the real complaint was that there were too few good ones. Kuperman said three of the five fired creatives had been replaced with better people, and Wolf became irate. In the interest of saving money, none of them should have been replaced.

"What are Rabosky and Potter on?" Wolf asked.

"New business and whatever else there is. Sparkletts, LaBatt's Blue," Kuperman said, referring to Toronto's LaBatt Breweries account, which was in need of creative help. "They do a lot of work for the other offices."

"They do it," said Wolf, "*because they've got nothing else to do*."

Kuperman had walked into Wolf's trap. They debated for a few more minutes about whether the department could stand a trim, and then Wolf divulged his plan.

"Say these numbers look fine," he said. "But if we said in a week, 'We need $250,000, $400,000,' where would you get it?"

"I wouldn't raid creative," said Kuperman. "I'd ask *why* first."

"Because maybe somebody else can't," said Wolf.

"I'm trying to run the office that pays all the bills," said Kuperman. "Why endanger that?"

"I'm not sure you would," said Wolf. "People aren't turning out enough stuff. I think we're overstaffed on non-Nissan creative. You don't need eight teams, that's like one hundred percent of a team on one account, and I don't think that's reasonable."

"Nobody's sitting on their asses here." Kuperman looked at his list. "I think it looks like they're real busy."

"Right," said Wolf. "It *looks* like they're real busy."

Bax asked Kuperman how much new business the current staff could absorb.

"Toshiba or Sparkletts with no new hires. But that doesn't mean we're fat."

"I disagree," said Wolf. "You're saying we could launch a major brand of water and a major computer . . ."

"*Or*," corrected Kuperman. "Not both."

"I'm not saying we're doing it now. I'm saying we may come back."

"It wouldn't surprise me."

"We'll let you know. Good budget."

Wolf left the meeting convinced that the Venice office could survive more cuts. If Kuperman had responded to his probing with real concern—if he had said they would lose business with a smaller staff—then he might have been inclined to hold off. But all he had heard was that everyone was busy, which meant that fewer people could be busier and the agency survive.

The issue of Clow's position in the Chiat/Day firmament no longer tormented him. It had been erased from his mind by his restored parity and by circumstance: the agency needed him. He worked on the Fantasy campaign as though he were a junior art director bucking for a promotion. The Nissan contingent was scheduled to see the rough cuts of "Car Company" and "Bob's Road" on Friday, September 7. On the Tuesday before the meeting Clow personally reviewed all 22,000 feet of "Car Company" footage, because he hated the feeling of, " 'Shit, I left one foot I liked someplace.' " By Thursday morning he had a cut, and all day to tinker with it in the darkened editing room on the second floor of the production building, watching, making split-second changes, watching again.

To ensure that the Sentra zipped past a properly neat piece of greenery, a crew had spent the better part of a morning hand-clipping the grass on a Smyrna, Tennessee, hillside, to the endless amusement of the Nissan employees. The scene never made it into the finished spot, losing out to a sequence that featured three Sentras zooming around a test track. But to Clow's eye there was a problem with that footage: the sky was too cool. It failed to communicate enthusiasm and excitement the way a deeper blue would. He would have to steal a better sky from another shot, an easy, if expensive, bit of nature thievery thanks to a computerized editing system called the Da Vinci. For $700 an hour, he could outline the piece of sky he wanted to enhance, outline another piece that was the right color, and instruct the computer to replace one hue with another.

A factory assembly-line sequence moved too slowly, so Clow instructed the editor to speed up the film, "to give us the sense of the engine being spit out of the factory." A close-up of a welder took on a steely blue tone, his complexion drained of blood by a few taps on the editing keyboard. Then Clow added fiery sparks behind the welder.

He provided his own sound effects for the still-silent footage: the sound of a jet for the opening shot of the office, and a hummed "Pomp and Circumstance" for the final shot of the car. When three Sentras roared into a banked turn on the test track, he squealed the appropriate, *"Sheeeee-uhmmmmm."* When they braked within inches of the actor's toes, he yelled, *"Scree-unk!"*

When Clow finally emerged, it was time for dinner. He was startled to see the sunset of a day he had missed.

"Look at this beautiful day," he said, peering out of the production office window while he munched on a slice of Johnnie's pizza. "Sunlight. And we're cooped up in this dark room." He stared west, at the departing sun, and when he spoke again it was as though he was recalling a long-forgotten dream.

"I'd love to take the dog to the beach today," he said, to the editor who sat on the window ledge. "She's an old, gimpy German shepherd, but she loves to go to the beach."

His reverie was interrupted by the arrival of Tom Patty, who had been out all week on jury duty but was not about to let the creatives show a rough cut to the client until he saw it. Clow escorted him into the On-Line Room and ran "Company Car" and "Bob's Road."

"It's good," said Patty.

"Pretty cool, huh?"

"Pretty neat."

"All these shots are really great," said Clow. "They just look shitty in the transfer."

"Nah," said Patty. "They look great."

They watched the commercials again, and this time Clow provided his assortment of sound effects. Patty's only criticism was that the opening freeway shot in "Bob's Road" didn't look crowded enough to make Bob's exit, on his own personal exit lane, seem triumphant.

"They're going to matte in more cars," explained Clow, "from another time of day." The Federal Trade Commission, which policed the industry and investigated consumer complaints, might frown on false claims about products, but the universe in which those products were advertised was a fiction, devised to enhance whatever commodity had paid for its creation.

Rinek and his staff (referred to by Clow, when safely out of earshot, as "John and the Johnettes") arrived at the agency at four thirty on Friday afternoon, and were escorted into the Fish by a nervous account executive whose instructions were to stall them for a half hour. Sittig was wandering the halls, nursing a hangover from the previous night's MTV award show. The two creatives responsible for "Bob's Road" were wringing their hands over the 373rd inappropriate voice they had heard for the voiceover. In a panic, they grabbed a young production assistant and made him record the script on the spot, while the editor frantically spliced in $12,000 worth of new footage, shot just the day before to replace unacceptable location footage of a Sentra being parallel parked. Clow and

O'Neill debated whether to show the two commercials in the On-Line Room, where the sound was better, or in the War Room, where the monitor was bigger.

Size won. Clow, O'Neill, and an uncharacteristically bedraggled Sittig watched "Car Company" on the War Room monitor, Sittig mouthing the words along with his character. Clow reminded them to expect resistance to the black photographer at the end. "It's a strong graphic," he said, "and then he's black, so the client wonders, 'Is it gratuitous? Will this look like a car for black people?' "

"I bet you we end up with the white guy with the mustache," said Sittig.

"I have to say, the black guy's a principal. The white guy's an extra," said the economy-minded O'Neill, "so he's cheaper."

"That shouldn't matter," said Clow. "The black guy has such an interesting face."

Back in the editing room, the editor and two assistants rushed to finish, while everyone else either paced or squirmed. It was now 5:15 P.M. The account executive appeared to ask how much longer the delay would be.

To get a preview of the client's reaction, Clow showed "Bob's Road" to the account man, whose job it was to anticipate, and mediate, that response.

"What do you think?" asked Clow.

"It's cool," said the executive.

"You're easy."

The account man smiled. "Oh, shit. That's right. *Does it show any car?*"

He was dispatched to collect his charges and bring them upstairs. Clow and a production assistant played a quick game of "Pig" while they waited. They shot anxious baskets with a miniature ball and a six-foot-tall hoop, and each time one of them missed, the other collected a letter in the word "pig." When that game ended too quickly, they played the longer version, "Horse," to help pass the interminable five-minute lull.

At ten minutes before six, twenty-one people elbowed their way into KEM-1, one of two editing rooms named for the brand of film-cutting table the agency used. Three monitors displayed frozen im-

ages from "Car Company"—the My Motor Company office, the test
track, and the display floor where the Sentra was unveiled—so that
the people from Nissan could see the quality of the film image before
they had to look at the grainier videotape rough cut.

The editor ran the sixty-second version.

"Pretty neat," said Brooke Mitzel, the national advertising manager for sports cars and trucks. "Pretty neat."

"There's a lot in there," said Madeline Eggan, her counterpart for
sedans. "Pretty amazing."

Clow proudly explained that the brief shot of the door opening to
reveal the factory took six hours to shoot.

"It's a great three seconds," said Eggan.

After a second viewing, John Rinek lead his team in polite applause—which was, in the client vernacular, a rousing show of enthusiasm. Sittig was thrilled. He had managed to make the Sentra
seem like a car worth having.

"It's not a tinny, tiny red box anymore," he said.

Rinek laughed. "This really has the feeling of bringing something
important to the world."

They watched the commercial a third time.

"Wow," said Rinek. "God, it's wonderful."

It was time to show the thirty-second version, which ended exactly
as the longer one had, with the black photographer hoisting his
camera and the flash bulb exploding.

"I'd lose that photographer at the end," said Rinek, immediately.

"He's great," said Clow.

Rinek ignored him. "And I'll tell you why." He liked the photographer in the longer version, "but you really hone in on him in the
thirty."

"He's too important," Clow agreed.

They watched again. Without further discussion, Rinek approved
the long commercial as it was, but he withheld approval of the thirty-
second version until the black actor came out and some slalom footage went back in. Clow had to agree that the Sentra looked wonderful
on the slalom course. They had put lead bags in the car to make it
ride lower, and as a result, the car looked "a little snootier" than it
did in real life.

*   *   *

"Bob's Road" waited for them in KEM-2, attached to the production assistant's voice. The agency wanted to use an old recording of the Crew Cuts' "Sh-Boom (Life Could Be a Dream)" for background music. They had researched the cost of buying the rights to it, and had been dismayed to learn that it was going to cost a minimum of $60,000, but Sittig had already planned his defense of the expenditure. Nissan had approved one version of a new Pathfinder idea, which was going to come in far below budget, and one of the producers had saved $80,000 by using some footage that had been shot for the Canadian campaign. All Sittig wanted to do was spend money that Nissan had already allocated for advertising.

"It's very additive to the commercial," Clow told the Nissan people, before they saw the spot. "Otherwise we wouldn't ask for it." He apologized in advance for the sparse freeway traffic in the opening sequence, and gestured to the editor to run the commercial. None of the Nissan people spoke up when it was over, so the editor showed it again. Still no comments. The room was utterly still. The members of the account staff who were still able to breathe managed only the occasional, shallow whisper of an inhalation.

Finally, Rinek spoke up. As far as he was concerned, the entire commercial was off strategy. "Bob's Road" was supposed to celebrate the sporty, SE-R model Sentra. The only shot that reinforced the car's style was one of the spoiler on the back. The rest looked like a "universal dream for any car," which was not at all what Rinek had in mind. Worse, the commercial seemed more intent on telling a joke than on showcasing the Sentra.

"The focal points feel like they're paying off the Bob gag," said Rinek.

"It's like, three-fourths joke and one-fourth car," said Mitzel.

"I'm not saying, 'More sheet metal,' " said Rinek, who knew that that kind of request was considered by the creatives to be evidence of subhuman intelligence.

"I guess some of the shots are a little tame," said Clow.

"The enjoyment of driving is not coming through," said Rinek. "In 'Car Company' you've got more of a feeling that this is a driver's car. This is a car for people who love to drive, and it's not coming through here."

Sittig warned him that they would lose their references to styling if they plugged in more aggressive driving shots, but Rinek said that he didn't see much about styling in the current version—so there wasn't much to lose.

Then Mitzel spoke up again. She didn't like the music. "I don't want hard-driving music, like for the 240, but . . ."

"What *kind* of different music, then?" asked Sittig, whose patience was beginning to fray.

"More energetic," persisted Mitzel. "Music that will rev you up, not make you feel like relaxing."

Rinek agreed. Even Clow agreed. This was one of those moments when it was important to be what he called a "creative adult," and figure out some way to work with the client, rather than let a disagreement escalate into a fight. Rinek had a point. Arguing, out of some misplaced notion of integrity, was only going to make him more obstinate. Clow would fight endlessly for something he believed in, but the music was not a life-and-death issue. It was important to know when to yield.

Encouraged by his support, Mitzel articulated her desire. "The heart," she said, "should be pounding with adrenaline."

Sittig and his aesthetic were suddenly alone in the room. He sang a blues riff to see if that was what the folks from Nissan had in mind, and when they smiled approvingly, he saw where the revised spot was headed.

"Maybe the reading," he said, in surrender, "should be more Clint Eastwood-like."

"I think you'd get more attention," said Rinek. "This is a little ho-hum."

The *Fantasy campaign* rough cuts had only to survive a single night of focus groups and scrutiny by Ron Hannum, Bob Thomas and Tom Mignanelli, which given earlier focus groups and meetings with the three executives, promised to be a smooth process. No one anticipated what one of the planners derisively called a "Mikey group," after a child in a long-running cereal commercial who hates everything that is put in front of him. The first of two focus groups in Los Angeles was a disaster. The participants didn't understand that "Car Company" was a dream. They didn't believe that a Sentra had any power. One woman was greatly impressed by the sixteen-valve engine, but admitted that she had no idea what that was. Two men got into an argument about whether the reference to good-looking door handles was a measure of Nissan's attention to detail or proof of the company's superficiality.

A revised, snappier version of "Bob's Road" was a body-language bonanza, with everyone in the first group leaning toward the screen and smiling, but the participants still managed to find things they didn't like. One man resented the slogan about rich guys, which made him feel poor. Several complained that there were not enough shots of the car. When the moderator asked who the driver of the Sentra SE-R in this commercial might be, a woman replied, "A fast-moving person—but not particularly bright."

The second group was no better. The people in the packed observation room, a dozen representatives of Nissan and Chiat/Day, took refuge in denial. One of the Nissan executives dismissed both groups for being too cerebral. They were the wrong audience for an emotional message. The commercials were not meant, he griped, to "reach up and smack them." The commercials were meant to smack *somebody*, but those somebodies were not in the room being videotaped. An agency planner blamed the telephone screeners.

By the end of the evening, the account staff was exhausted, staring at the prospect of a 7:30 A.M. meeting with Thomas and Hannum and wondering how to make the results sound like anything but a catastrophe.

Tom Patty, Nissan national management supervisor Pam Keehn and planner Ruth Amir arrived in Carson at six forty-five in the morning, an hour when everything—the San Diego Freeway and the dawn sky above it, the Nissan compound, the fluorescent lights in the seventh-floor conference room, the pallor of three apprehensive complexions—was a dull, lifeless gray, the trampled hue of defeat. They had forty-five minutes to transform the results of the previous night's focus groups into something positive.

Amir, who had been up most of the night, had an idea. The more enthusiastic the driver, the likelier he was to respond to the Fantasy campaign commercials. The people who didn't get it were on the fringes of Nissan's target audience to begin with, and the best way to reach them would be with the more rational commercials that comprised the regional campaigns, ones that stressed gas mileage and low price.

Patty agreed. "There's a cumulative effect," he said, as though rehearsing his lines for the meeting. "It's like arrows being shot into the body. Logical message from one direction, emotional from another." "Bob's Road" was emotional, the regional campaign was logical, and "Car Company," which had seemed deficient to him, now provided the perfect bridge between the two—a commercial that managed to explain a lot about the car without becoming too sensible.

"The closer you get to your purchase, the more you use rational elements to justify your emotional decision," said Patty, warming to the idea of a two-tier advertising approach. "So you need that information."

* * *

Rinek appeared at 7:15 A.M., followed almost immediately by Thomas and Hannum. First on the agenda was a regional spot that extolled Sentra's good mileage: A Sentra owner had to pull over to let his daughter go to the bathroom long before he had to stop for gasoline.

"Any sensitivity to the restroom?" asked Thomas.

"Yes, when people were just seeing the visuals," said Patty. "But as soon as they heard the copy, it was okay."

At that moment Clow and Sittig strolled in, both of them looking as though they'd just stepped out of the shower, pink-faced, hair still damp. Clow was carrying a carton of milk and a sweet roll.

"Wasn't this for seven thirty?" he asked affably.

The group debated the merits of a second regional spot, but the client's concerns were minimal. What everyone in the room really cared about were the two national commercials that had to establish Sentra's new image.

Sittig promised changes that would make the opening office sequence move more quickly, and then they all watched the sixty-second version of "Car Company."

Thomas reacted quickly. "My first impression is that it's outstanding," he said. He puffed out his substantial chest and smiled, mimicking the actor's pose. "Looks just like Sittig. Just like I imagined."

Hannum, the vigilant new executive, wanted to make sure they would shave time off the opening scenes.

"Yeah," said Clow. "It's gnat hairs, but it'll be a few seconds."

Upon reflection, Thomas decided he didn't like the voice.

"There's a few words he doesn't say well," admitted Clow. "We'll re-record."

"And it's not mixed," said Sittig.

"But he doesn't capture you at the beginning," said Thomas.

They watched the shorter version.

"I understand it's not mixed," said Thomas. "But the voice isn't *important.*"

"It's a kid," said Clow. "It's his dream."

"But he doesn't carry you. He limps through the spot. 'Even the door handles will be cool'? He doesn't sound excited."

239

"Excited's a good word," said Clow.

"I think excited's right," said Hannum.

Clow explained that there would be a sound effect when the three German engineers slapped their foreheads, as though they were saying, "Oy."

Thomas grimaced, ever so slightly. "You probably don't want a German engineer saying, 'Oy,' " he suggested.

"Bob's Road" had been recut so many times that the videotape now betrayed the multiple layers of film that had bumped their way through the editing machine. The tape image wobbled. Clow was careful to explain that the final film would be seamless, but Hannum fixated on every bump he saw—a blurry shot of the Sentra speeding past its own personal toll booth, and another shot that he said was "chattering."

Clow ignored him, because what Thomas was saying was infinitely more troubling. Thomas didn't like the final joke, where the mounted policeman got ready to ticket a parked Sentra until he recognized Bob inside. Thomas didn't like the cop's voice or, for that matter, his face. These were the kind of substantive criticisms that could unravel months of work, and required immediate attention.

The planner reassured him: The consumer was happy with the joke.

"But we can make it better," promised Rinek.

Thomas rose. It was eight fifteen, and he had another meeting scheduled. "Worthy spots, all," he said, and walked out the door.

Now Hannum was in charge. For the third time he pointed out the rough spots in the film. Patiently, Clow explained the physical process that caused the problem, and promised that it would disappear in the final version.

Hannum had another problem. The first decent shot of the car was of the steering wheel. Before that, the car was moving too fast, away from the viewer, for anyone to get a good look at it. Rinek explained that the point of the rear-view shot was to show off the spoiler, which communicated the SE-R's sportiness. That was the purpose of the shot and, according to the focus groups, it worked.

"And there are just a couple of times," said Hannum, still waiting for one of his objections to be acknowledged as a sign of respect, "where it's really *bumpy*."

Clow answered him very slowly. "Don't . . . worry . . . about . . . the . . . chatter."

"And to get to the big, big picture," said Amir, brightly, "this spot is just really easy to get into."

That ended the conversation about "Bob's Road." Hannum next wondered about the little girl who required a bathroom stop in the regional spot.

"So this little girl will be cute as a whip?" he asked.

Everyone agreed.

Hannum didn't want her dressed for church, but he asked, hopefully, "Will she wear a dress?"

"Right," said Clow, knowing when to give in. "One of the three girls in America who wears a dress, especially to drive cross-country."

For months, Bonnie Baruch had been on a personal crusade to contribute to the agency's coffers. Home Savings did not want her to take time away from the account to work on new business, so she devoted herself instead to making sure that Home spent every penny of its budget. The client had allocated $2 million to television advertising in New York and then decided not to spend it. As far as Baruch was concerned, the money belonged to Chiat/Day. All her account staff had to do was find a campaign Home Savings wanted to buy.

To her delight, one of the account supervisors had responded with an astonishingly simple and seductive idea. Home Savings used what it called "common sense" criteria to evaluate prospective home buyers—and regularly offered a higher percentage of a home buyer's annual income than the standard allowable mortgage payment of 28 percent. Home Savings loaned 32 to 36 percent, which meant a bigger loan for a house—or a bigger house. It wasn't a new offering, but it was a new twist. With real estate prices still out of most people's reach in California, the notion of more house on the same income was alluring. And if there was a question about how people would meet their higher monthly payments in the midst of a recession, it was not the province of the agency to supply the answer. The lasting financial consequences of the policy were an issue for the consumer, not the provider.

Baruch got permission from the client to develop a presentation. It was a foot in the door, both a professional and a personal victory. Baruch, who worried about the status of her department, was interested in the job of role model.

The account supervisor who came up with the buy-a-bigger-house idea for Home Savings couldn't believe his ears. Home's chairman and CEO Richard Deihl was saying, "Yeah, I want to kick our competitors' ass. Let's *double* the budget."

Then the account man woke up.

He had been nervous and excited for weeks, ever since his idea began snaking its way through the approval process. He wasn't anxious, really. He was ready to go. He imagined he was feeling the same thing that actors and musicians feel before they perform. His energy level was way up.

In a fevered attempt to prove his inspiration to be mathematically viable, he and the senior planner on the account had computed exactly how much larger a home a family could buy, based on the higher percentage Home Savings could loan. They came up with 45 percent, an almost unbelievably high increase, but the numbers supported it. For the creatives, it was a visual bonanza: a $290,000 house looked substantially larger than a $200,000 house, and their floor plans, shown side by side, made an eloquent argument in favor of Home Savings' mortgages.

From the client's point of view—or so Baruch intended to argue, when the staff met with Deihl and Home Savings president Charles Rinehart on September 19—the campaign solved two problems at once. Not only did it guarantee a response from potential buyers, it struck a profitable alliance between Home Savings and realtors. It was to the realtor's benefit to promote an association with Home Savings, since it enabled him to show the prospective buyer a more expensive property, and so earn a larger commission.

Unfortunately for Chiat/Day, the federal savings and loan regulators spent the morning and early afternoon of September 19 at Home Savings, on one of their regular visits. By the time Baruch had her chance to talk about getting 45 percent more house, Deihl's reaction was succinct: it sounded to him like "snake oil." He was not about to tarnish Home Savings' image with a campaign that sounded suspicious, no matter how many figures the agency had to back up its claim.

Baruch was not ready to yield. After a tense hour, the wary client acquiesced, and agreed to let Chiat/Day develop creative work. It was a minor accomplishment; the client had not yet committed the bulk of the $2 million, which would be spent on production and media. But it was progress, worthy of a joyous commute back to the beach, and a celebratory round of drinks at a restaurant around the corner from the agency.

Wolf refused to let temporary setbacks diminish his faith in the future. He had a plan, and if there were glitches along the way, the full shape of that plan remained intact. He kept himself going, on his bimonthly commute, by reminding himself that he had invented New York and resuscitated Venice. He would fix Chiat/Day and make it grow; it was all just a matter of time.

The discipline worked fine until late September, when the cab that was racing him from Kennedy Airport into Manhattan was involved in a multi-car crash that, Wolf was convinced, came perilously close to killing him. Suddenly he snapped, and all the difficulties of the recent weeks rushed in to surround him. He was fed up. No matter what he did, the New York office remained belligerently out of control, and as far as he was concerned it was all because of a bunch of rogue egos gone wild. What was the matter with these people? Jane Newman still treated him like a villain and refuse to talk about coming back to work. It wasn't that he hadn't tried. At Chiat's suggestion, he had called Newman to talk things over before he left Los Angeles, and happily reported that they had had a decent conversation—only to have Chiat reply that he had spoken to Newman, who was as resentful of Wolf as ever.

None of this seemed worth risking death on a crowded expressway. When Wolf got to New York, he confronted Chiat and said, "Life's too short. I can't deal with Jane." He wanted to call her and remind her that she was still under contract to the agency, and so expected to show up for work, but Chiat insisted on mediating the dispute. The three met at the New York office on Saturday, September 23, ostensibly to discuss how to bring Newman back in a way that made her feel comfortable. Instead, she asked for a financial settlement that would allow her to leave the agency permanently—and, for that matter, leave advertising, since the whole episode had, she believed, damaged her chance of finding similar employ elsewhere.

Wolf couldn't believe his ears, nor was he prepared for Chiat's conciliatory response. Chiat informed Newman that he would not settle, nor would he fire her. He wanted her back at the agency, working on new business, but he would not press her for a commitment. She could come back when she was ready to return.

If Chiat wanted to coddle Newman out of some misplaced guilt, Wolf had more urgent issues to face. Tom McElligott had become more of a presence in New York, spearheading the Royal Caribbean pitch, but now he and Michael Smith were getting in each other's way. The creatives McElligott had hired tended to ignore Smith. Smith's people had some interesting ideas for the pitch, but no one, so far, had any great executions.

In the midst of the confusion, the papers announced that Chiat/Day had lost the $2.5 million Arrow Shirts account. Wolf was furious. He'd written Arrow off in April, when the client stopped spending any money. When one of the account executives got a call from Arrow's new president, promising to gear up and start spending again, there had been a brief moment of euphoria—until the executive changed his mind and backed off. That was the account loss the press reported. It wasn't much of a loss, in terms of anticipated income, but it added to the public perception that New York was still floundering.

Wolf did not know what to do. He started smoking again, despite the fact that he found it a "filthy habit." The New York office lacked a center. There was no individual there to whom everyone looked for inspiration and stability. As he flew back to Los Angeles, he thought about Clow. Perhaps he was the one who could motivate the creatives to win back Royal Caribbean. When Wolf surveyed the available talent pool, he came to an unavoidable conclusion: Clow was the best creative mind the agency had. No. He was the best there was.

CHAPTER 25

At nine o'clock in the morning on Thursday, September 26, Wolf's secretary picked up his phone to hear Chiat snarl, *"Where the fuck is Bob? Goddamn it, where is he?"*

The secretary suggested that he try Wolf at home. Chiat already had. She suggested that he try Wolf's car phone. Wolf was scheduled to fly to Miami that day to meet with the people at Royal Caribbean, so he probably would not come in to the office.

Chiat hung up. The secretary got a series of equally brusque, mysterious calls that morning. When Ira Matathia called from Toronto, she said, "What's up?"

"Can't tell you," he said. Then he did, but only on the promise that she remain silent.

Rob White had spent a secret three-day weekend with his prospective partners, getting to know them and plotting out the new agency, but when he got back to Venice he agonized over his decision for a week. He couldn't bring himself to tell Kuperman, who, despite his gruff, demanding manner, seemed truly to value White's contribution. It was as though he leaned on White as hard as he did because he knew his planning director could stand the pressure; Kuperman, like Chiat, tended to mix respect and ragged expectation. White liked Kuperman. He had come to terms with the notion of leaving Chiat/Day, but having to tell Kuperman loomed as a major emotional obstacle.

The principals had agreed to announce the formation of the new agency during the week of September 23, a week that happened to include, for White, back-to-back new business meetings on Sparkletts and Toshiba. He would feel like a hypocrite sitting through those two meetings, only to tell Kuperman he was quitting. He removed some personal materials from his files, in case he was thrown out of the office immediately and told not to come back. Then, on Wednesday night, he called Kuperman's house and left a message with his wife: White had some things he wanted to talk over with Kuperman, and hoped they could meet at eight-thirty on Thursday morning.

Kuperman had commandeered Hardy as his own private conference room. He ushered White in, and as soon as they sat down White blurted out his confession.

"I'm really sorry to do this," he said, "but I'm resigning. I'm leaving to start a new agency."

"Where?" Kuperman asked. He was dumbfounded. He'd had no idea White was unhappy.

"Minneapolis," said White, braced for the next question.

"With?"

"Tom McElligott," said White. Tony Wright, director of account services at Chiat/Day's Toronto office, was also defecting, along with an art director from another agency, but those were incidental surprises. Kuperman was shocked that Rob White would leave—and reeling from the news that McElligott was walking out.

"Well," said Kuperman, shakily. "That's great."

Kuperman took odd solace in the news that White was going to be a partner. If he were merely changing jobs, Kuperman would have agonized over what he might have done wrong, or what efforts he could make to keep his planning director. But White was leaving so that he could own part of a business. Despite the fact that Kuperman never felt that entrepreneurial drive himself, he respected the desire in others. No one could compete with that. There was no benefit package in the world that was as good as being a principal, if that was what a man wanted to be.

They spent a subdued half hour talking about how best to handle the transition in the planning department—in part because Kuperman wanted White's input, but in part because he needed to buy himself a little time to think. If White was resigning on the West Coast, McElligott had to be breaking the news in New York. There was too much new business at stake right now to risk a collective depression. This had to be handled properly, or it would be devastating.

"I don't want you to tell anyone yet," he instructed White. "This is pretty big, and it's happening in all these different cities. I need to talk to Jay and Lee. Don't tell anybody. Keep it quiet."

White had intended to announce his resignation at a ten o'clock planning department meeting, because he didn't want his staff to hear the news from anyone else, but he would hardly cross Kuperman. He postponed that meeting until two and sat through the first half of the Sparkletts meeting like a zombie, paralyzed by anxiety. Kuperman got pulled out to take a call from Wolf, and when he returned White searched his eyes, looking for a clue as to what was going to happen, and when. Kuperman concluded the session without saying a word.

White, still worried about his staff, approached Kuperman. "I really want to talk to them by the end of the day, because it's going to be in the press tomorrow."

"Yeah, I understand," said Kuperman. "I'll let you know."

White was in the process of training two young, ambitious employees to be planners. They trailed after him like puppies, grateful to him for their very existence. One of them spent his lunchtime filing papers in White's office, and on Thursday he noticed that a group of files was missing. Frantically, he searched for White and gave him the disturbing news—at which point White escorted both his young charges into an empty conference room, disobeyed Kuperman's orders, and told them in strict confidence that he was leaving. His allegiance had always been to individuals rather than to the corporate entity that was Chiat/Day. He wasn't going to let these two kids feel that he had abandoned them.

By the afternoon, White still hadn't been given permission to make a public statement. He canceled the two o'clock planning meeting and disappeared into another meeting, to discuss, ironically, the departure of one of the Nissan planners. When he went back to his desk to take a phone call, one of the planners decided to check his electronic mail for messages.

What he got was a message from Jay Chiat, announcing the departure of Tom McElligott, Rob White and Tony Wright, who were joining together to form a new agency. Chiat wished them success in their new venture, and that was that.

An unsuspecting White found chaos when he walked back into the room. He was stunned. What had happened to telling his staff in person? Hastily he summoned together all the planners he could find. Then he began to roam around the warehouse, ducking into one room after another, looking for people who deserved to hear the news from him, trying to get things under control

Management at Chiat/Day branded McElligott a traitor, a man who had let the agency down and had used his new job as a springboard for his personal ambition. All of the hopes that had been invested in McElligott were gone. He was a pariah, his followers dupes, and his departure merely a signal that the hardy employees who remained were lucky to be among people they trusted. The agency found opportunity in adversity, as it always did: the message, in every conversation and at every meeting, was that McElligott would not be missed.

Convincing the business community and the press was another matter. Chiat was outraged that McElligott had walked out in the middle of the Royal Caribbean pitch, without consulting him about how best to announce the move. The agency had been taken by surprise. The outside world would likely interpret McElligott's decision, and the resulting chaos, as proof that Chiat/Day was a difficult, temperamental environment. If one of the best creative minds in the country couldn't find a place for himself there, then something was wrong.

Everyone took on a chunk of damage control. Wolf had to figure out how to credibly reverse his position on McElligott's importance to Royal Caribbean, having touted him all along as a savior.

Matathia canceled plans for a long weekend in New York and got on the first flight back to Toronto, to soothe the people at Canadian Air, a new account McElligott had helped to win.

Kuperman got M. T. Rainey on the phone in London and compiled a short list of possible replacements for White. Then he composed a calming fax and sent it off to Venice's clients.

Rabosky hastily assembled all the creatives who had been working on Royal Caribbean and instructed them to gather together all their work, no matter how crude—"Chicken scratches, scribbles, *whatever*. Whatever we have"—for an emergency meeting in the Fish to review their progress.

Clow rushed back to Venice from a Nissan meeting to look at the work. He was angry and hurt at the news about White's departure, but he was not about to let defections diminish the agency's chances with Royal Caribbean.

He sought out Kuperman as soon as he got back. "What does it take," he complained, "to be really committed?"

"Well," said Kuperman, "somebody calls and offers a job to work with Tom McElligott, starting an agency . . ."

"I've gotten a lot of calls like that, and I've never left," said Clow, petulantly.

Kuperman smiled. In Clow's simple view of the world, people who were valued by the agency should return the favor. He couldn't conceive of any reason to want to leave. Kuperman was more philosophical about it. The agency lost bad people, and sometimes it lost good people. What bothered him was that White was the first really good person to resign during his tenure as president. He resolved to review the status of valued employees, to make sure that none of them had been neglected.

Clow took over the Royal Caribbean pitch, which was costing the agency $250,000. He flew to New York to oversee the forty people who were working on the presentation. For three days he worked from eight in the morning until three the following morning, and then as soon as the October 4 pitch was over he got on a plane for Los Angeles.

The next morning he showed up for work as usual. He had been at his desk less than an hour when Chiat called to tell him that Royal

Caribbean had awarded the account to another New York agency, Rosenfeld, Sirowitz, Humphrey & Strauss. Reflexively, Clow came up with a rationale. "If it would have been a level table, I think we did the campaign for them."

He was resilient, but he told Chiat that he was worried about the people who worked on the pitch, who would be disappointed and fearful of losing their jobs. There might be more cuts, but for now they had to do something to prevent a stampede.

Chiat already had the answer. He was going to take the New York creatives to Clow's Art Directors Club Hall of Fame dinner on October 18.

"Jeez," said Clow, disparagingly. "They're going to love putting on tuxes and going to the Waldorf-Astoria. For $175 a head you could have put on one hell of a party.'

But the invitations were part of a grand scheme. Chiat also intended to buy tables for New York's existing clients, to remind them of what a valuable asset they had in Lee Clow.

Wolf didn't rebound from the loss as quickly as Clow did. He flew back on Thursday night as well, but he spent Friday at home, nursing his disappointment. What had become of his first year as CEO? The dream had seemed a logical enough extension of Chiat/Day's successes in the 1980s: Peppers was going to reel in one grand new business opportunity after another, which Wolf's hand-picked account executives would help to win, all the while keeping their existing clients happy. Instead, New York was in a full-blown slump. Wolf figured it would be months before the headlines died down and potential clients forgot that there had ever been a problem.

Peppers had become an expensive, expendable luxury. Wolf had hoped to make him the senior account executive on Royal Caribbean had Chiat/Day reclaimed the account. Now he had to figure out another way to justify Peppers's salary. The whole idea of prospecting had become something of an overblown fantasy. In New York the issue was survival.

Royal Caribbean could have put a stop to the downward momentum, but instead it turned a slide into an avalanche. For the moment, Wolf didn't see a way out, except to persevere and wait for the climate to improve, not a happy scenario for a man who had intended to reinvent Chiat/Day.

On Monday morning, he got to the office to find out that Michael Smith wanted to quit. Smith was aware that his resignation would look like a man deserting a sinking ship, so he offered to stay on until the agency could find a replacement. But he wanted Wolf to move as quickly as possible.

Wolf needed a new creative director, a new set of responsibilities to absorb the energies of his rainmaker, and something with which to placate Newman. What he didn't need was any more negative press. He had been planning a merger of two Chiat/Day subsidiaries, Anderson & Lembke and Perkins/Butler, into Chiat/Day Response, but he decided to postpone it. If he announced it now, the press would see it as a defensive, belt-tightening move.

He thought about Perkins's description of the climate in New York, and chuckled to himself. "Calm urgency," was what Perkins called it. Like jumbo shrimp, Wolf thought.

The economy nibbled at Kuperman's heels in October, not in any major way, but enough to spook him. Venice was supposed to be immune to problems, channeling all of its renewed energies toward winning Sparkletts or Toshiba, both of them substantial mid-range accounts. But niggling bits of bad news kept intruding.

Home Savings had purchased space for its new campaign in the October 15 *Los Angeles Times*, and scheduled a recording session for a radio spot. The day before the recording session, the client abruptly changed his mind. If Home Savings ever pursued the campaign, it would be in the spring of 1991, at the earliest. At the moment, it did not communicate the proper upstanding image. Baruch and the others who worked on the campaign were left to wander the agency halls and mourn the unexpected demise of their $2 million enterprise.

Kuperman's beloved Taylor Made had become the fiscal joke of the agency, the angle of its annual budget bearing a distressing resemblance to the ski slopes for which its French parent company designed skis. It was what Kuperman called a "guerrilla account," driven not by great work, but by the need to create and disseminate on the cheap. The creatives were reduced to bargain-basement concepts, such as $50,000 for a shot of the Taj Mahal at dawn, the peace broken by a golf ball plopping into the water.

The oversized card on the message desk read, "Cold Enough Is Not Enough," with a drawing of Rob White wearing earmuffs and a scarf. A little heart pin, inscribed "Chiat/Day," held the scarf close about his neck.

The conference table in the Fish was covered with party supplies, including two large cakes, one of which was shaped like the state of Minnesota and covered with three-dimensional decorations: an edible sled next to a plastic deer, a Nordic helmet with marzipan antlers, marzipan ears of corn, little jars of mayonnaise sporting bandages (for the Mayo Clinic) and a coffee cup with red wings on it, marking the home of Red Wing Pottery. There were frosting lakes and wheels of cheese, and a frosting Paul Bunyan, standing next to a frosting Babe, the blue ox.

Over a hundred people showed up for Rob White's farewell party on October 10, including one man who ceremoniously took a set of bagpipes out and began to play a mournful tune. White, who had chosen to wear his Chiat/Day Agency of the Decade T-shirt for the occasion, made his way around the room, shaking hands. When he got to the cakes he stopped, and stared reverentially at the decorations on the larger one.

"Nobody's going to cut this cake," he said. He asked his wife to find their camera and take a picture of it, while he cut the plain cake first.

There was a gift on the table, too, a box wrapped in ski-scene wrapping paper, with a logo that read: "SNOW COUNTRY." Inside there were twelve autographed golf balls and a hot water bottle.

He grinned. "Something to keep your balls warm, hm?"

"You like it?" asked Kuperman, gleefully.

"Something tells me you had a hand in it."

"You like it? Actually, it was my concept."

After a half hour of goodbyes, White stood on a chair and waited for the room to grow quiet.

"This is just amazing," he said. "Thanks to all of you for everything. This is the best agency . . . this side of Minnesota."

He pointed out that he'd worn his Agency of the Decade T-shirt on purpose, in recognition of what a great agency Chiat/Day was. "But it's not the Agency of the Century. I hope for that there will be competition." He might have said more, but his voice began to betray him, so he climbed down off the chair.

Kuperman got up and said that he knew he usually made a little speech at farewell parties, but this time he wasn't going to do it. He had already sent out a memo saying how happy he was for White, and how sad he was to lose his planning director. That was going to have to suffice. He was too disappointed to attempt the standard glib send-off.

"Sometimes you get up in meetings like this and say something," said Kuperman, "and people think, 'Oh, it's the same old stuff.' So maybe if you don't say anything it means more."

He waited a beat.

"Though at this place, everybody will probably think, 'Jeez, the guy didn't even say anything.' "

The only potential bit of good news, all month, caught the agency by surprise. Someone at The Nutrasweet Company leaked the news to the press that the company intended to put its $25 million Nutrasweet ingredient business, currently handled by Ogilvy & Mather, up for review. The announcement was premature—the company had not yet compiled a list of agencies to invite to pitch—but thanks to its work over the past seven months on a test brand assignment from Nutrasweet, Chiat/Day was in position to get noticed.

Sugar DeLight was Steve Rabosky's personal nightmare, a blend of sugar and artificial sweetener that was supposed to appeal to people who liked sugar's taste but wanted to cut calories. The product offended his vegetarian, health-food sensibilities, and worse, he saw no way to sell it. Consumers who used sugar were probably opposed to chemical sweeteners, and people who watched their calories knew that a teaspoon of sugar was only sixteen calories to being with. Sugar DeLight was eight calories per teaspoon, not a very substantial reduction. Rob White had agreed with him all along: Sugar DeLight existed not because anyone wanted it, but because technology made is possible, which was not much of a reason.

Still, they had labored for months on all sorts of campaigns, everything from an animated sugar bag that developed a waistline when filled with Sugar DeLight to expert ants who applauded the product's natural taste. Chiat/Day had worked on Sugar DeLight as though it were a major account, and not a hand-me-down from Ogilvy & Mather, whose initial work had disappointed the client. Rabosky had pushed his teams, even though he was willing to bet anyone that the product would be dead in a year. Now it seemed the effort might pay off. What had looked like a dead-end assignment on a marginal product had turned into a calling card for a major account.

Nutrasweet promised to be a difficult piece of business. The patent on aspartame, the sweetening ingredient in Nutrasweet, expired in 1992, which meant that the new agency would have to figure out how to enforce consumer loyalty to an invisible ingredient that no longer enjoyed a monopoly. There were already rumors about blended products with superior taste, and entrepreneurs eager to start a price war by setting up competing manufacturing plants. The agency that prevailed would have to show Nutrasweet how to make drinkers of both Diet Coke and Diet Pepsi, Nutrasweet's biggest accounts, believe that what they really loved was their artificial sweetener, not any particular brand of diet soda.

Trickier still, the war was to be waged around the world, requiring the winning agency to prove its international capabilities—something of a stretch for Chiat/Day, whose expansionist dreams so far extended to offices in London and Toronto, a not-yet-functional foothold in Europe, thanks to Brindfors, and the wobbly Mojo empire on the far side of the Pacific Rim, whose offices were floundering in a recession that had seen two of its biggest clients file for bankruptcy. Mojo had also been racked by management squabbles. Early in 1990, Chiat had replaced director of international operations Richard Whitington with Doug Watson, a creative. Watson was named new CEO, but that was not the last of the changes. Alan Morris (Mo) left, and Allan Johnston (Jo) stepped back from his management role to resume life as a creative. Mojo was hardly the sort of network with which to compete against major international agencies.

Still, this was a substantial, high-profile account, and theoretically Chiat/Day had an inside track. Nutrasweet received a barrage of phone calls from various agencies hoping to be included in the review, including a flurry of calls from Chiat/Day.

*   *   *

Nick Rosa, the vice-president and general manager of the Nutrasweet Beverage Group, was gratified to see who was coming calling. He and his selection committee drew up an impressive invitation list: the eight top agencies in the United States, in terms of revenues, and then, ninth on the list, Chiat/Day. In truth, they had little interest in hearing what Chiat/Day had to say, since the consensus was that the agency was too small to handle an international account. Still, the diplomatic thing would be to invite the agency to compete, since the executive who handled the Sugar DeLight account was such a big fan of Chiat/Day. There was no reason to insult him, and also insult an agency working on an admittedly problematic brand. Chiat/Day would find a way to eliminate itself long before the final round.

CHAPTER 26

Chiat arrived in Venice on Friday, October 12, in advance of the following week's Nissan dealer show, carrying a cumbersome piece of mental baggage. For ten months he had deferred to Wolf's judgment, the only logical behavior for a man who had entrusted his life's work to another. If Wolf was worthy of that honor, he was deserving of respect. Chiat had yielded, again and again, to what he believed to be Wolf's superior business acumen, as though the forcefulness of his support would help propel the younger man toward his goals.

But the agency was in disarray. There had been no new business pay-off as yet, losses were mounting, and valued members of Chiat's circle, like Newman, seemed unable to find a place for themselves. With every crisis Chiat's concern rose closer to the surface. What was Wolf doing with his baby?

Chiat and Wolf met with Clow in 3 Mile Island for a meeting about Chiat/Day/Mojo University, which had been postponed from Halloween to early November to Thanksgiving, a casualty of all the new business work. Wolf, always the one who tried to drive a meeting, came equipped with a list of discussion topics for the retreat—including the predicament that plagued his waking moments.

"We don't have enough money to reward our key people," he said. "We know we're *going* to be a global presence, but we have money problems. So what are we going to do for the next five years?"

Chiat cut him off. "I don't like the way that sounds. Bleak."

Wolf suggested getting a client to talk, or inviting one of the consultants who engineered new business pitches. The people who attended the workshop, he said, "need to recognize that we can't take $3 million accounts and grow. We have to go after the biggies who are least likely to take us on, because we have that home-run/strike-out image out there."

There was a perceptible change in Chiat's expression, and when he spoke his voice was low, and flat. "I don't agree with everything you just said," he said.

Wolf persisted. Perhaps they could get Bob Thomas, of their public relations subsidiary, to discuss how to manage the press.

At that, Chiat exploded. He still nursed hurt feelings over the way Wolf had dealt with Jane Newman. He had been appalled by his CEO's apparent willingness to criticize Newman in public, to trade her reputation for the chance to see himself in print. How could Wolf complain about the agency's image, when he contributed so handily to the notion of internal discord?

"You've been the most concerned about our chaotic image," he yelled at Wolf. "Yet every time you talk to a reporter, it's an explosion. You've probably contributed to the chaos more than anyone else."

The attack was so unexpected that not even Wolf could manage a response.

Clow attempted to mediate. Surely they all agreed on the need to reduce chaos. But motivation had to come from the people within the agency. It could not be imposed by a roster of outsiders.

"If our people don't get it," agreed Chiat, bitterly, "they shouldn't be at the agency in the first place."

In an effort to sell cars, the agency and the manufacturer conspired to create a car that was impossible to own. It had taken two full days, and the personal attentions of Mike Santoyo, to prepare a 1991 Sentra for its breathtaking unveiling in "Car Company." Santoyo was the general manager of The B.A.D. (Best Automobile Detail) Company, a firm that prepared cars for commercials, film and television work, and on a shot as important as this one, he was not above doing his own detailing work. Using a brush about the size of an eyeshadow brush, he stroked touch-up paint on the metal grill to camouflage its shiny surface and eliminate reflections from the overhead lights. He sprayed cleaner on the car's undercarriage and wiped away the slightest hint of dust. He upgraded the car's wheels, badges and the visible part of the interior, because the spot called for a top-of-the-line model, and Nissan had delivered the wrong one. He painted the side molding black, which looked better than the original gray.

There was a dimmer for the headlights, since their normal setting was too bright for film. The wheels had to be set to Nissan's specifications—the airstem at the six o'clock position, the Nissan logo straight across. By the time the car was ready for its close-up, it looked better than a real car, on a real street, ever could.

The same care was devoted to the print ads. The woman who ran the print production department was responsible for making sure that every Nissan that appeared in print, in newspapers, magazines or on billboards, was preternaturally lovely. Nothing, not even physical reality, was allowed to mar its appearance. Normally, a side-view mirror cast a harsh metallic reflection on the front door of a car, but the company that did the color separations for print ads could always add back some color to soften the distracting glare. The brightness of the hubcaps could be cooled down, so as not to detract from the body of the car. Even the trees in the background could be made to look more vivid, as though nature itself responded to the sight of a Nissan.

The advertised Nissan was one the customer could not own even if he marched into the dealership with an ad, pointed to the car, and said he wanted to buy that exact model. Advertising offered a product in an idealized form. It guaranteed a level of consumer dissatisfaction, which kept the buying public yearning for what they saw on television or in print.

So it was perhaps fitting that the nation's Nissan dealers would see the premiere of the new Fantasy campaign on a twenty-eight-foot screen with theatrical-quality sound at their Nissan New Car Show in Reno. To sell 165,000 new, more expensive Sentras, not to mention the other models in Nissan's line, the company had to sell its dealers on a far more potent image than the one that would be presented to the customer. The dealers had to go home from their two-day holiday certain in their faith, ready to convert skeptical customers.

There was, as Clow put it, "not a lot of outside to Reno," which made him fidgety. He endured a reception for Nissan's 2,200 guests on Monday night, October 15, but first thing on Tuesday morning he fled for a quick jaunt to Tahoe and a soul-cleansing drive down the Truckee River, away from the memory of a buffet packed with so much shrimp that it numbed whatever impulse made people want shrimp in the first place. He strode back into Bally's Casino at midday in a denim shirt, jeans and cowboy boots, a tanned, wind-blown millionaire who stood a head taller than most of the pale, stooped weekday denizens of the lobby gambling pit.

The slack-jawed men who sat in the rows of chairs beneath the Keno display bore a disconcerting resemblance to the brainwashed men in Clow's "1984" commercial. This was emphatically not a place he wanted to be. If he could have had his way, he would have spent the afternoon napping. Instead, he headed up to his room to change into tennis clothes. John Rinek wanted to play tennis on the courts that were wedged behind the hotel's lower-level arcade of shops. Clow had only beaten Rinek once or twice in his life, but he was always willing to try again. That afternoon, playing with a loaner racket whose grip was too small, he took the first set from Rinek. Clow immediately purchased two new rackets just like the one he was using, complete with the wrong grip.

At four o'clock, Nissan dealers and their spouses, Nissan execu-tives, and the Chiat/Day account staff all began migrating toward a caravan of buses that would carry them to Reno's convention center. It was a party crowd: older men in conservative business suits, younger dealers in snappy double-breasted suits, three dozen women dealers in understated business attire and dozens of dealers' wives in sequins, beads and silk dresses. Perfumes and men's colognes rolled in waves, as the soft slur of a voice from Georgia washed past a New Englander's harsh consonants.

Once four or five buses were full, two motorcycle policemen es-corted them to the freeway, stopping traffic along the way to let this carvan of commerce roll by. They discharged their passengers for drinks and turned back for another load.

The Chiat/Day contingent—Chiat, Clow, Tom Patty and a handful of account people, with Wolf and Kuperman off somewhere working the room—formed a tight, protective circle at the edge of the lobby. Would the dealers stand up and cheer? Would they jeer? As the crowd filed into the massive auditorium, guides tried to direct them to specific rows, but Chiat herded his group to the second row of the middle section, a good location for judging dealer response.

They were in Nissanland. White 1991 Nissans were raised above the crowd on huge metal lifts. A screen at the front of the room read: "Nissan in the 90s. Decade of the Dealers." Seven monitors, positioned around the hall, said: "NISSAN." The stage set behind the podium was of the Nissan headquarters in Carson, with projected clouds drifting by. The booming rock music was loud enough to make the floor vibrate. Three video cameras perched at the rear of the auditorium, to immortalize the event.

As the hall began to fill up, Clow glanced over his shoulder and muttered to Chiat, "We should have sat in the back so we could get out if they don't like it. They *always* know who the agency guys are."

Nissan's top management did not put the dealers in a receptive frame of mind. The same videotaped puppet who had prolonged Chiat's Leader of the Decade dinner, this time playing a sarcastic dealer, peppered the presentation with one-liners, but the gravity of the message was inescapable. One executive after another spoke of how important the dealer was to the purchase decision—and how Nissan's dealers had fallen short. In the future, according to Bob Thomas, "the hardware of the business will become less a differentiator than the software," which meant that everything but the car— advertising, marketing, dealer service before and after purchase— would matter more than the car itself. The problem, for Tom Mignanelli, was that the assembled dealers provided "substandard" service. If any of the dealers wanted to deny the accusation, Nissan's national sales manager was ready with the cold facts: the influential J. D. Powers & Associates automotive survey ranked Nissan twenty-eighth, out of a total of thirty-three automobile manufacturers, on its sales satisfaction index.

Clow sighed and whispered to Chiat, "Putting them in a good mood for the advertising."

By the time Ron Hannum got up to banter with the puppet and introduce the advertising, a chill had fallen on the hall. The dealers had come all this way and gotten dressed up for what they thought was going to be a celebration, an appreciation of their efforts and an inspiring look at the year to come. Instead, they had been told that their problems were, to a great extent, of their own devise. They were not in the mood to be entertained.

Hannum launched into his speech. He knew that dealers had complained about the lack of a consistent advertising strategy. Nissan was prepared to respond with the second year of the Fantasy campaign, a set of commercials that would benefit from the consumer's positive memories of the first season of Fantasy spots. To warm up the crowd, he showed the 1990 commercials for the Z and Turbo Z, the Maxima, and the 240SX, and reminded them of the image that the campaign communicated: ". . . smart, confident, good and upbeat," he said. "The spots communicate styling and performance."

The commercial got a smattering of applause, which made Clow's mouth relax just a bit. His leg began to pump nervously.

It was finally time to broadcast the sixty-second version of "Car Company" on all seven monitors. It got polite applause, which to Clow's mind, given the evening's tone, was all anyone could hope for.

"It was afraid they wouldn't applaud through the whole advertising section," he told Chiat.

"Bob's Road" got a much more energetic response. Clow's residual anxiety shot down to his fingertips, which began to tug at his mustache and beard. The first regional spot died without a sound. The gas mileage commercial, about the little girl who had to go to the bathroom, received a few chuckles. Sittig's Pathfinder spot met with a decent response. But no one cheered, not once, not for *anything* the agency had created.

Bob Thomas dismissed the dealers with a challenge, meant both to encourage and to flatter. He believed that the dealers in the room were capable of improvement. He wanted to be first in product, service and delivery in the J. D. Powers survey by 1995. It was just the sort of extravagant objective that made the recently meek feel powerful again; the dealers rose as one to make their way to their annual party, presumably sold on the idea that they could, and would, make a difference.

Clow shook his head and leaned toward Chiat.

"I would have believed it more," he said, "if he'd said number three."

*   *   *

The party was a 200,000 square foot extravaganza, the embodiment of Nissan's dream to conquer the United States of America. The floor was covered with a huge map of the U.S.A. There were regional food booths, full bars, musicians, and 1991 model Nissans, each of which was lovingly introduced to the dealers by a squadron of hired local talent.

Chiat was the first of the agency people to leave, since he had to catch the red-eye flight to New York, but Clow was close on his heels, eager to get home early enough to have a semblance of a normal evening with his wife. He ambled down the deserted airport hallway with the two regional creative directors, engaged in the usual round of reassurances, when he spied a little refreshment stand that sold Dove Bars. He bought ice cream bars for himself and his companions, then slumped into a chair by the departure gate, tired and happy. He figured that maybe his numbers were aligning, or whatever they were supposed to do when life started going well. He had snuck in the trip to Tahoe. He had stayed at the party just long enough to see Mignanelli, who said he was pleased with the Sentra commercials. He had found a Dove Bar. All in all, a good day.

CHAPTER 27

It was the dream of Bob Kuperman's life to be in the Art Directors Hall of Fame. As he walked into the Starlight Roof at the Waldorf-Astoria for the October 18 dinner celebrating Lee Clow's induction into that group, he realized with a twinge that it would never come true. The way he saw it, he had given up any hope of being invited to join when he left New York. He had been, by his own estimation, "in the limelight there," and if he had stayed he would have had a good chance. But he had chosen to move to Los Angeles and became an administrative creative director, and over time the people in New York had stopped paying attention.

Kuperman was thrilled for Clow, but he couldn't help thinking that he would have been more appreciative of the honor. "Typical Lee," he said, as he glanced over at Clow, who was, as he always was at parties, rooted to one spot on the floor. "*His* response is, 'Why do I have to go to this fucking dinner in New York?' "

Kuperman had misinterpreted Clow's paralysis. He wasn't uncomfortable, he was starry-eyed. The men he'd thought of as his heroes, the art directors whose books he'd studied as a young man, were walking up to him to shake his hand and say congratulations. All he had to do was stand still, clutching his drink, and advertising legends filed past him to acknowledge the fact that he was worthy to join their club.

He was an outsider in every sense. Most of the seventy-three members of the twenty-year-old Art Directors Hall of Fame had been honored late in life. More than half the members were already dead, and the survivors, as well as the two other art directors being honored, were old enough to be Clow's parents. Most had spent their professional lives in Manhattan, unlike Clow, whose only interest in the city was in staying as far away from it as possible. Reba Sochis, the evening's first honoree and only the second woman to be admitted to the Hall of Fame, was a graphic designer who had moved to Manhattan in 1934 and opened her own design studio in 1949. Her clients included Pappagallo, JP Stevens and Revlon. Frank Zachary, at seventy-six the oldest editor-in-chief in the country, had run *Town & Country* for eighteen years, capping a career as a magazine art director. Clow's award seemed the most remarkable, in part because the nominating committee of the club had reached beyond its universe to anoint him.

His fan club was also the most boisterous. The awards banquet was a symphony of urban civility—properly hushed conversations, the careful gnashing of cutlery, a descant of ice cubes lilting above it all—that played on long past the Chiat/Day contingent's tolerance for such ritual. When Chiat was called to the podium to introduce Clow, following dignified presentations of the other inductees' work, two tables of Chiat/Day staffers erupted in yells and whistles.

"I want to thank the Art Directors Club for having a men's room where no tipping is allowed," quipped Chiat. "I would have spent twelve dollars by now."

He had a story he wanted to tell. Seventeen years ago, Chiat had interviewed a copywriter and offered the man a job, only to to be told that he was being unfair. The writer's partner, Lee Clow, had been trying to to get into Chiat/Day for two years. He'd been interviewed three times, and still hadn't been hired. Three months later an art director position opened up, and Chiat hired Clow. The copywriter had since left to write for television. Clow had been the smart hire.

Chiat consulted the notes he had scribbled during the meal. What did he want people to know about Clow? That he was wearing "the finest tuxedo money can rent." That Eileen prayed, as her husband trotted down to the ocean with his surfboard, " 'God please don't hurt him too badly today for wanting to continue the dream.' " That Clow's idea of a good time, to Chiat's unending bewilderment, was a night at home with his wife and two dogs. He was describing a noble savage, a man who functioned on a more fundamental level than the other people in this room and had, by ignoring the trappings of daily business life, attained a higher plane.

In an indirect way, he was admitting the envy that Guy Day had remarked upon back in 1980, when Chiat had left Los Angeles to open the New York office. Day had always thought that Chiat found it hard to work next to Clow, the man who actually did the great work, while Chiat's real genius was his ability to elicit it from others. Chiat was one step removed from the creation, and to his day he marveled at and yearned for Clow's intimate relationship to the work. He would never have it, not for himself. Clow was the closest he was going to get.

The intensity of the moment made his throat tighten, and for a moment he could not speak—an uncharacteristic stumble for Chiat, who marshaled his feelings like troops, to be sent out, on command, to achieve effect. For a fleeting moment he lost control. He was unable to utter whatever glib praise he had planned to deliver. Then he recovered, and managed to find a way to say what he had to say without betraying himself.

"He has an uncanny, almost mystical knack to know what's happening," said Chiat, his voice a tone deeper than usual, "with a style, grace and elegance that makes *me* want to go home, have a beer, and watch television—preferably his."

At that, the room began to pulsate with sound, and two screens filled with images from Lee Clow's personal reel. An editor back in Venice had taken apart Clow's most famous commercials and reassembled them into what amounted to a commercial for Clow himself. There was the California Cooler beach crowd and the catatonic audience in "'1984." Randy Newman tooled down the street in a convertible, singing "I Love L.A." on behalf of Nike. There were clips from Nissan commercials and from a Pizza Hut campaign.

Chiat raised his voice over the applause and yelled, "Lee. Thank you for making the agency what it is. And me, what I am."

Clow made his way to the podium and shyly joked that the problem with being an art director was that it was hard to explain to his mother what he did for a living. He didn't take any photographs himself. He didn't shoot film or set type. All that he did, he said, was to find talented people with whom he could work.

"If you're smart enough to art-direct the right people," he said, with a shrug, "then you can have a dinner like this, too."

The levity was gone the following morning when the members of the North American Board dragged themselves into the New York office's fourteenth-floor main conference room for their quarterly meeting. The brashness of April was a distant memory, but July's panic had also subsided. There was a bunker mentality to the room: Chiat/Day's slump was the unwelcome guest at the table, one who could not be ignored.

There was another surprise figure in the room—Jay Chiat, who normally did not attend the North American meetings. He chose to sit on the large leather couch just behind the conference table, next to the buffet. It was impossible to help oneself to breakfast without acknowledging him.

Ira Matathia asked, "You sitting in on this meeting, Jay?"

"Haven't you heard?" Chiat replied, "I'm sitting in on every meeting. From now on."

At 9:05 he asked, "Any reason this meeting hasn't started?" and the others, obedient schoolchildren, took their seats.

There were lots of plans and promises and very little that qualified as good news. The fiscal year ended in less than two weeks, on October 31, so the window of opportunity was rather slim. Even the Venice office's numbers were down by $325,000. The new business pitches that were supposed to have cost the office about $260,000 were close to $300,000. Venice had donated $30,000 to Nissan's favorite charity, Athletes and Entertainers for Kids, to commemorate the carmaker's thirtieth year in the United States, a diplomatic coup, they all agreed, but still, $30,000 out of the till.

Existing clients reported that they were happier with the agency than they had been in years, but they were doing just what Chiat had predicted over a year ago—chipping away at their advertising budgets to compensate for diminished revenues. The office's margin was down to 28.4 percent from a projected 28.7 percent, not a huge drop, but a depressing indication that not even Venice was immune to a faltering economy.

The one thing that hadn't slipped, to Kuperman's proud delight, was morale. He believed that what kept the Venice office running was that management followed his lead and tried to listen to people. Encouraged by the response, he had drawn up extensive plans for what he called "rebuilding the Chiat/Day culture" in 1991—including a training program modeled after one that Doyle Dane Bernbach had used in the 1960s, more frequent meetings of the 320 Club, and thirty-, sixty-, and ninety-day meetings with new employees to make sure they understood what the agency was all about. He lectured the others just a bit: the important thing, until something broke, was to be vigilant about the one aspect of the environment they could control, the home turf.

Without referring to Wolf's more imperious stance, or Clow's lack of any conscious management style, Kuperman promoted himself to the group as the Chiat/Day executive of the 1990s. As office president, he had found a role that no one had yet played as successfully as they might. If Wolf was the strategist and Clow the creative spirit, Kuperman saw himself as the enlightened administrator, the inspirational link between the agency's lofty goals and the hundreds of people who had to carry them out. Over the past few months he had carved out yet another responsibility for himself, as a facilitator who could communicate with Wolf and Clow better than they could communicate with each other.

He didn't have to come out and say it. All he had to do was make his office report, which was still the best of the lot, despite the slippage. The object lesson for Perkins, Matathia and Rainey was obvious: Emulate me, and you too will prevail.

The other offices were too absorbed by economics to devote much effort to soothing the agency's soul. At the July board meeting, Matathia had predicted a break-even year for Toronto. Now it was clear that the office would end the year with a loss, due to a $150,000 cutback in Nissan's Canadian business and $200,000 in new business expenses for LaBatt's and Canadian Air. The office staff was "incredibly pumped," at the moment, in defiance of McElligott's departure; but Matathia needed to find two $10 million accounts and service them without adding any new staff members if he was to climb out of the hole.

Bob Perkins expected revenues for fiscal 1991 to be $11 million, down from $25 million in 1990 and $2 million lower than the July projections. New York had to be rebuilt. The question was how to do it.

Wolf saw an opportunity once and for all to retire the issue of big accounts versus small. Everyone was here, even Chiat, and they were facing a much graver question than whether to go after a single piece of business. There had to be a plan. Wolf announced that his goal was to refuse all small accounts—and even to consider resigning small accounts that had no growth potential.

Immediately Clow spoke up. How many times was he going to have to defend what he believed was a basic tenet at Chiat/Day? "Accounts that allow people to get some great ads through contribute a lot to the environment," he said rather shrilly.

Perkins agreed, in theory. The problem was that small accounts required as much attention as the larger ones. At least the big accounts paid for the additional hirings.

"I think there's another myth," said Wolf, "that little accounts become your showcase. The best advertising we're doing is on our big accounts, and the worst is on our small accounts."

"You can't generalize like that," said Clow.

"It's not a generalization. It's a fact."

Then Kuperman spoke up—and agreed with Wolf. He had expressed his philosophy about small accounts at the operations meeting in Venice, and had talked of setting a minimum dollar amount for new accounts, but now he was taking a public stand against them. The balance in the room shifted, ever so slightly, with both Kuperman and Perkins willing to follow Wolf's lead. No one was prepared to forbid Clow from looking at small clients, but from now he would have a much more difficult time finding the allies he needed to pursue that kind of account. Wolf, Perkins and Kuperman had boxed him in, and Chiat chose to say nothing.

Perkins had little hope of getting out of New York's slump in the coming three months, between the holidays and the perception that the office was "cold," but he intended to start fresh right after the new year. In the meantime, he was preoccupied with his pending $2 million loss. The only cut he could imagine was to further reduce the staff.

Clow cut him off. He was not going to let these people dismantle Chiat/Day brick by brick. There was a danger to watching the bottom line too closely. It bred conservatism in other areas. "You can't cut yourself to the profitability you want," he cautioned. "You've got to grow to it. You've got to figure out a way to grow offensively, or you won't be in any shape to go *after* the big accounts."

The subsidiaries, as presided over by Simon Bax, were a disintegrating network of unfulfilled profit fantasies, with the single exception of Bob Thomas & Associates. Jessica Dee and Keith Bright & Associates had been sold back to their original owners, and the merger between Perkins/Butler and Anderson & Lembke was on hold. The total subsidiary loss for fiscal 1990 would be between $1.4 and $1.6 million.

The only bright note was that Wolf had found a replacement for Bob Perkins at Perkins/Butler—Don Peppers, who would become president and chief executive officer, while Bill Butler remained chairman and chief creative officer. Peppers would spend all of his time on Perkins/Butler for the next six months, and then put some portion of his effort back into new business development.

"There's a lot of synergy between the foot in the door that Perkins/Butler can get and the win Chiat/Day can get," said Peppers, ever the rainmaker.

Perkins was pleased, because people would begin to think of "Chiat/Day generalized and Chiat/Day personalized"; that is, the agency and its direct mail arm.

Peppers said he was honored. He was also, for the moment, safe, which—in the middle of a recession, at a loss-plagued agency—was honor indeed.

By late afternoon the board had exhausted an agenda's worth of reports, projections and strategies. They had to talk about money—about what more they had to cut, and earn, to inch their way back to good health. Wolf assumed that he was looking at a new round of cuts, including the $300,000 to $400,000 in Venice that he had warned Kuperman about at their operational meeting, unless there was a big new business surprise.

"Kill the goose that laid the golden egg," muttered Kuperman, loud enough for everyone to hear.

Wolf ignored him. Even with these cuts, Chiat/Day's fiscal 1991 projections fell short. The problem was the agency's debt, the result of the 1988 recapitalization: $26 million still owed to banks, $11 million in junk bonds that had been issued at the time of the buy-back, on which the agency was paying 13 percent interest, and the $20 million junior debt, which was money still due the stockholders, at $3.92 per share.

Theoretically, the stockholders were supposed to get another pay-ment at the next recapitalization, which had been planned for 1992. At the moment, that was a cruel joke. Chiat/Day could meet its $13 million bank and junk bond debt payment in fiscal 1990, but there were no surplus funds. For fiscal 1991, the agency was $2.5 million shy of its $13 million obligation. To find $2.5 million in additional profits, the agency needed at least $5 million in income, which meant an additional $35 to $40 million in billings for the first six months of the fiscal year—and there still would be no money for the people in this room.

Wolf summarized the bleak picture: To get back to normal, they needed $90 million in new billings. Only then would there be enough money to make payments on the debt and lift the current financial restrictions. Chiat may have thought his intentions purer than those of the executives who had masterminded buyouts to inflate the value of a company—as long as business continued to improve, his plan had the potential to benefit every employee who demonstrated his loyalty. But the results were uncomfortably similar. The agency func-tioned in the shadow of its debt, a gloomy vestige of better days. The debt came first; employees, by necessity, second.

Kuperman wanted clarification. Once they reached the $90 million in new billings, was the raise and salary freeze off? Clow felt that ending the freeze was the agency's priority, before anyone should talk about ending the salary rollback for high-paid employees or paying off the junior debt. The people at the table, himself included, could continue their salary rollback for as long as necessary. The agency had to concern itself with keeping its young talent, the people who got lucrative offers on a weekly basis.

Kuperman wondered if they could start to play around with the 5 percent raise freeze—give some people more and some less. Wolf rejected the idea immediately. "The moment you break the universality of the thing you're in trouble," he said.

For the first time, aside from a few brief comments and some wisecracks, Chiat spoke up. "It wasn't all equal before," he reminded Wolf. "You've put yourself in a position where you're not managing well." Perhaps the answer was a $250,000 bonus pool, to reward deserving employees. If Wolf couldn't find that sum in the budget, Chiat was prepared to loan it to the agency.

More debt. It made no sense to Simon Bax, who offered to take out his checkbook and contribute to the establishment of a bonus pool, if the others were prepared to join him.

Impatiently, Wolf interrupted him. There was probably some way to find $200,000. He simply wasn't convinced that it was necessary. If the others were sure that it was, then he insisted on revising his figures to account for it. "It's got to come from someplace," he said, irritably. "We've been playing loose for a long time, but the fact is, we're short."

Kuperman refused to give up. They had to find some way to reward people like Bonnie Baruch, who had deferred her desire to work on new business to accommodate Home Savings and Foster Farms.

"But we've got to buy into the fact that we've got a problem," replied Wolf.

"Kuperman doesn't," said Chiat, with a teasing grin.

At that, Kuperman lost his temper and started to scream. If the board didn't do something the agency was going to lose people. That would mean losing business too. As relationships fell apart, clients would look for agencies where they felt they would be better tended.

Clow suggested expanding the equity pool—giving Employee Participation Units to more people—but that idea met with instant derision. Agency lifers believed that eventually their equity would translate into money, but the perception among most employees was that EPUs were little more than a management con, a worthless gift that spared the agency from actually having to spend money on its people. Rob White had not gotten a cent when he left Chiat/Day. That was how valuable equity was.

Chiat was fed up with the whole notion of reward. "We've *never* kept people," he protested. "Over twenty years. They get a better offer, they go. Every fucking year we had bonuses. And on January first a third were gone."

"The ad business is in the toilet," Wolf chimed in. "At least these people have got a job. You're going to lose some people. That's reality."

Clow, who would always be enamored of the lean, hungry agency where a few good people worked overtime, all for the love of advertising, wanted only to figure out how to keep the best ones. "The others," he said, "are just underfoot."

"Right," said Wolf, pleased that he and Clow had managed to agree on something. "That's how we find $500,000 in Los Angeles."

"Wait a minute," yelled Kuperman. "It was $300,000."

"It's like negotiating with the Mafia," said Wolf, with a smile. "Every time, the price goes up."

For the first time since July, the people who ran Chiat/Day— including Jane Newman—assembled with a single purpose, which was to win the Nutrasweet account. Newman, who had finally accepted Wolf's offer of a new position, showed up for an early morning meeting on Saturday, October 20, just four days before the credentials presentation, determined to mastermind a win and so atone for the account losses she had endured during her tenure as president. Chiat, Chow, Wolf, Kuperman and the other office presidents, management supervisor Bob Grossman (who had been tracking Nutrasweet since his days at Leo Burnett), and a couple of planners were as full of energy as they were terrified of yet another high-profile loss.

No one was allowed to admit that fear, of course. The rules of this game precluded expressing self-doubt, unless it was cloaked in humor. Jokes were an absolute barometer of the anxiety level in a room—and this morning there was comedy for every occasion. To solve the persistently troubling question of Chiat/Day's international capabilities, someone suggested having one person from each office attend the pitch.

Chiat managed a snide grin. "Should we have them dressed up in their native costumes?"

"Sure," said Kuperman. "We'll do a small world presentation." He began singing, "It's a small world, after all, it's a small world after all . . . ," while Chiat howled with laughter.

"We don't have a Mexico City office . . ." said Wolf.

". . . But we all have cleaning ladies," said Chiat.

Clow wanted to talk about "relevant and distinctive" advertising, as though that were enough of a lure to compensate for a lack of foreign offices, but Wolf wanted to talk about the strength of the agency's account planning department, and the consistency of its creative product, year after year.

"We're the best agency where we are. That's our strength," he said. "Our weakness is, we're not everywhere."

Chiat chided him. "There's got to be another weakness."

"We're a high-profile agency, and that can be a problem" said Kuperman. "Let's freewheel our weaknesses, and not be defensive."

"We're building an international empire, but very carefully," said Chiat.

Kuperman played the client. " 'You lose a lot of clients, don't you?' "

"We consider that a strength," Chiat shot back. "We're still here, aren't we?"

"We're attracted to entrepreneurial clients," tried Newman.

"They're as far from entrepreneurial as can be," said Chiat.

Newman tried again. "We're young?"

"We *used* to be young," said Matathia. "Now we're old."

Chiat suggested that someone wheel in a confessional box when they started to list their weaknesses.

Wolf wondered if they ought to borrow a technique that Hal Riney's agency used, which was anticipating and answering the client's questions before the client got a chance.

"Like, 'Are we arrogant?' "

The others hooted.

"Fuck no!" shouted Kuperman.

"No," barked Grossman. "Next question."

"I won't answer that question," said Chiat.

He was prepared to admit that Chiat/Day wasn't everywhere on the map, as long as they stressed that it was a high-profile agency in the cities where it did exist. And he wanted to mention the "battering" the agency had gotten in the newspapers, to show Chiat/Day's enduring strength.

"We're not too big and we're not too small," said Kuperman. "We're just the right size."

"And," said Chiat, "we'll blow your house down."

Chiat carried that bravado with him into the nine o'clock World Board meeting, which he chaired. He chastised the members of the North American Board for their gloomy attitude the day before, and insisted that things were not as bad as they seemed. Yes, the agency had spent about $4 million in mismanagement. That would be corrected: 1991 was a clean start. He wanted to begin the year with the assumption that they would get their profit margins back.

Having said that, he suggested that the agency's big problem at the moment was attitude. People were making decisions based on the pressure of paying off the junior debt. Even the relatively small debt the agency carried was influencing the way the agency functioned.

He challenged the board. They could decide to retire the debt. They could say thanks for the money they had already made in the 1988 buyout, enjoy their substantial salaries, and abandon the notion of another recapitalization. There was no chance of one before 1994 or 1995—and perhaps those days were gone forever.

He got the response he had expected and feared. The people in this room had learned how to spend their new wealth. They had grown into it, and were not so concerned about debt that they were willing to sacrifice future payments. They began to lob alternatives.

Clow prescribed "working our butts off" to make enough money to solve the problem.

Wolf suggested, "We should live within our limitations."

Accountant David Weiner believed that the problem was one of image, as much as economics. There was the cost of servicing the debt, and then there was the price top management paid with employees who resented the financial structure of the company. Employees complained to Weiner that short-term greed had replaced long-term investment as the motivating force behind Chiat/Day. That troubled him more than their temporary financial setback.

Chiat was angry. He had intended the buyouts as a benevolent gesture. Now Weiner was telling him that he had sullied the agency's soul.

"Where'd you get this?" he snapped. "Focus groups? What's your universe?"

"About thirty-five people in various parts of the agency," said Weiner.

"If you want to do focus groups," said Chiat curtly, "get professional help."

Corporate senior vice-president Sharon Stanley, a longtime employee who had started out as Chiat's assistant, shared Weiner's concern. "I know you don't want to hear it," she told Chiat, "but the perception is that top management is all the things David said. Not fair. People are upset."

"Can you get people to take this on like a religion?" Clow mused. "That's one of the hard things about being big."

Chiat had no answer. His gaze settled on Wolf. His successor might know his way around planning and profits, but he had failed in leadership. The agency did not look to him for direction, and it was time to say so.

He turned to Wolf. "Part of the problem," he said, firmly, "is that you haven't filled the gap. People perceive you as a tough manager running the place, and I've disappeared, which adds to the problem. They think it's a different place. The whole notion of handing this over to the next generation has bogged down, because too much of the next generation has left."

Wolf was speechless. The others, embarrassed, took refuge in financial nitpicking. Perhaps the sheer size of the payroll was what was making management feel pressured. Layoffs might have an unintended positive effect, if they made people feel freer about how they did business.

That was Chiat's point. He challenged them again. "Then let's retire the debt."

"That's easy for you to say," said Clow, resentfully. "You still have money." Then he suggested an answer that had never before been publicly discussed, though the others might have thought about it privately. Representatives of the Japanese advertising industry had toured several U.S. agencies recently, including Chiat/Day. It was well known that Tokyo-based Dentsu, the world's largest advertising agency, wanted to buy a stateside agency. What if Chiat/Day were to sell a 40 percent interest to Dentsu, as a way of building cash reserves?

Stanley gasped. If Clow was so demoralized—or so absorbed by his own personal needs—that he was prepared to surrender even a minority interest in Chiat/Day, then she had no hope at all for the future. It did not matter how high a price a piece of the agency might command. He might as well have suggested selling a member of the family into slavery.

"I'm not prepared to sell *any* of it," she said, firmly.

Wolf tried to detour back onto the subject of the agency's image. He had been thinking about acquiring a Japanese partner since the day he took over as CEO, but had been reluctant to talk about it, since it would be taken as proof of his purely pecuniary interests. He thought it was a great idea: Sell a minority interest for, say, $100 million, pay off the banks, and let people earn money on their equity again. The Japanese would probably be interested in increasing their share of the business, over time, which meant that people like Wolf and Clow would have ready buyers for their substantial holdings when they were ready to retire.

But the quickest way to sour such a deal was to make it look like a lifesaver for a desperate agency. Chiat/Day could not sell out of weakness. Wolf preferred to save the plan for a time when the agency operated from a position of strength—both to guarantee top dollar from the Japanese, and to ensure that the sale was regarded, both internally and in the business community, as a bond between equals. He did not want to talk about the Japanese today. Things were going to get better. What the agency really needed was a firm voice, announcing that the bad times were over, and better ones on the way.

"There's got to be some closure here," he said.

Chiat bristled. "You want autonomy?" he said, as though Wolf had wrested the agency from him by force. *"You do it."*

The implication was that Wolf was incapable of leading Chiat/Day out of its depression. That was all the impetus Clow needed. For the first time since January's management change, he gave in to his grief. He needed his father figure back.

"Look," he said, loudly. "Jay wanted to hand the leadership to the next generation so he could stop working so hard. So I'm president and creative director, and maybe I'm a great creative director, but I can't manage the company. And Bob runs the company, manages well, but he lacks the soul and passion Jay has.

"*So it hasn't worked.* The next generation hasn't taken over the leadership. The transfer hasn't worked. And until the recession's over, Jay's got to be the leader. He's the only one people will follow. *He's got to do it.* Then we'll have to see if we can manage to take over. But for now we need him to take charge."

He slumped back in his seat, spent by his confrontation with his own, and Wolf's, shortcomings. "I can say, 'C'mon, let's do great ads.' Bob can say, 'Hey, we can do this smarter.' We can give direction," said Clow. "But for now, Jay has to be the leader. He's the one we'll follow."

For once, Wolf did not contradict him. No one did. It was time to stop managing by halves, to stop squandering the agency's energy on factional disputes. Chiat was visibly pleased. Perhaps the one thrill that rivaled immortality was the delight that came from being considered indispensable.

CHAPTER 28

Clow had awakened on the morning of the World Board meeting with the solution to so many problems at once: The agency should name Dick Sittig creative director of the New York office. He could mobilize the weary New York creatives and would not flinch if firings were necessary. If the office started winning new accounts he would be a hero, a role more to his liking than group head under Rabosky. His departure would make Rabosky feel less like a lame-duck executive, which might, in turn, improve his performance. It was the perfect answer, and as soon as Clow brought it up the other members of the board embraced the idea.

Sittig leaped at the offer, only to have Nissan veto the move. What did him in was that Nissan now credited him with the very qualities the client had complained were lacking in him only months before: maturity, vision, an ability to rein in his imagination to fit neatly within the boundaries Nissan had drawn. Rinek had changed his mind since the Reno show, and now considered Sittig a fixture on the account. If Sittig needed career opportunities down the road, it was up to the agency to lay a foundation for the move, so that it wouldn't look like Chiat/Day was solving its problem at Nissan's expense.

"Look," said Clow, carefully, "*I'm* on your account, and then there's this guy, Sittig, who's going to move on."

"We know that," said Rinek, "but you've got to prepare for it."

*　　*　　*

Patty had changed his mind at the Reno show, too, and he expressed his newfound respect for Sittig by sharing with him the strategy that had won Patty a substantial raise a year ago: Ask for more money at exactly the moment when everyone has realized that you are capable of satisfying the agency's largest client. Financial restraints might be law for the rest of the agency, but no one was going to deny the architect of the Sentra launch a raise.

Sittig figured he had the money coming to him. He would have made more as creative director in New York than he was making as group head. It wasn't his fault that he couldn't accept the promotion. Asking for a raise seemed completely reasonable, despite the raise and salary freezes. All he wanted was the money the agency had been prepared to pay him in the first place, before Nissan intervened—acknowledgment that, whatever his title, he was as valuable as Rabosky was, if not more so.

He met separately with Kuperman and Wolf and made essentially the same speech to both men. He wanted them to understand that he wasn't complaining, exactly. He was being compensated as a senior copywriter—but his contribution was more important than that. What Chiat/Day needed, and had always had trouble developing, was dependable relationships with big clients. That kind of partnership required campaigns that lasted, an elusive creative commodity before Sittig appeared on the scene.

"The Fantasy campaign must be good enough, because Nissan won't let me go," he said. Then he took a swipe at the laconic Rabosky, who seemed to chafe at the performance aspect of a pitch as much as Sittig reveled in it. "In the future, who's going to make a pitch to twelve guys in good wool suits? I'm the guy."

Neither Kuperman nor Wolf argued with Sittig's conclusion. Kuperman wasn't happy about Sittig's timing, but he found himself amused by the younger man's nerve, which reminded him of his own brash tenure at Doyle Dane Bernbach. They would have to do something for Sittig—Rob White's departure was too fresh and painful a memory to risk letting another potential lifer get away—but Sittig was fast approaching the point where he would have to adjust his attitude about the agency.

To Kuperman's mind, an agency invested in young talent, and then talent returned the favor and invested in the agency. Kuperman had turned the corner. He contributed both professionally and financially, thanks to the salary rollback for top executives, to the health of Chiat/Day. There was going to come a time, and soon, when Sittig would have to stop expecting an ever-escalating set of rewards.

Wolf wanted Sittig to understand that whatever they decided to give him came with strings attached. The days of being a well-paid employee who took all the basic employee benefits offered him, such as vacations, were over. If Sittig were going to be treated like senior management in terms of compensation, he was going to have to learn that power demanded sacrifice. Wolf didn't see how Sittig could possibly take the month's skiing vacation he had planned. The New York office was already committed to pitch the Hardee's fast-food chain account, and there was no telling what other opportunities might present themselves. He expected Sittig to be on call.

Having informed him of his new responsibilities, they had to meet his demands. The only way an employee could receive a raise during a freeze was if he was given a promotion, so Sittig received a title he hadn't asked for, senior vice-president, to make sure that no one questioned his salary increase.

If anyone doubted the significance of Sittig's contribution, the October sales figures at Nissan were convincing testimony. "Car Company" aired for the first time on October 21, and "Bob's Road" followed a week later. Nissan's dealers made 100 percent of their sales goal of ten thousand Sentras in October, many of them sold to people who walked into the showroom quoting the "rich guys" line.

To make sure the commercials were working—that the message would continue to sink in after the news value of the redesigned Sentra had subsided—Chiat/Day and Nissan did two kinds of follow-up research. Clive Witcher, the director of account planning on the Nissan account, had little use for copy tests, which he considered an "artificial and useless" form of research, but on something as important as the Sentra launch there was no such thing as too much proof of effectiveness. A research company solicited people in shopping malls and screened the participants to make sure that they fell into the "enthused" category: men and woman, between the ages of twenty-one and fifty-five, who were willing to buy an import, wanted to buy a new rather than a used car, and would consider a car that cost less than $13,000. Two hundred acceptable subjects answered some questions about which car they might like to buy, and then saw five or six commercials. The test commercial—in this case, the sixty- or thirty-second version of "Car Company" or "Bob's Road"—was in the fourth slot, which was the most difficult to recall. If the subject ranked the Sentra more favorably after seeing the string of commercials, then the ads were working.

They took away exactly the message that Nissan, and Chiat/Day, had intended to communicate: That the new Sentra offered both sporty styling and affordability. Only 12 percent of the participants doubted the credibility of the commercials, which Witcher considered a "*very good score.*" Eighty percent said they liked the new Sentra better than the old model, and no one was bothered by the price increase.

The research that the agency usually relied on, Nissan's ongoing tracking study, provided more ambiguous results. The tracking study relied on daily telephone interviews with a national sample of screened respondents, one thousand per month, who answered questions on all of Nissan's models. Since it was a broader group— including people who had no interest in the Sentra—reaction to the Fantasy campaign launch was less dramatic here. Familiarity with the model, and people's opinion of it, were mostly unchanged. Purchase consideration was actually going down in the overall market.

But Witcher cared more what the enthused drivers had to say, and their responses were reassuring. In this category, purchase consideration was up, and it looked like people's opinion of the car was improving. These answers meant that the Sentra was on its way, as Witcher put it, "from a mass market also-ran to a desirable product for a specific audience."

Best of all, over half of the target-enthused market was aware of the commercials, which was an improvement over the first year of the Fantasy campaign. People had begun to recognize the campaign.

The single most exciting piece of evidence came not from the sales figures and follow-up research, but from a visit Nissan's Bob Thomas made to his local bank. He was wearing his Nissan sweatshirt. When he gave his name, the teller inquired: Was he the lucky

Bob from the Sentra commercial? The client had been made happy, firsthand. He and his car were famous. There could be no better response.

Despite the agency's respectable showing in Reno, and in spite of Patty's reminders that the goal for the Venice office was maintenance of its existing accounts, not growth, Kuperman started to unravel. He couldn't be satisfied with that. He wanted a win, and because he still did not have a strong pitch team in place, he felt the need to baby-sit all the new business work. He and Clow sprinted from one meeting to another—Sparkletts, Toshiba, Nutrasweet—all the while trying to keep current clients happy.

On Monday, November 6, the agency started working on the Toshiba portable computer pitch, which was scheduled for the last week of the month. On Tuesday, November 7, they had to pitch the Sparkletts bottled water account. On Wednesday, November 8, Kuperman and Clow were supposed to fly to Chicago for a briefing at Nutrasweet's Deerfield, Illinois, headquarters. As far as Kuperman was concerned, the agency still lacked a decent strategy for Toshiba and Sparkletts, and Nutrasweet was simply too long a shot to warrant even the slightest optimism. The discrepancy between energy expended and anticipated results made him impatient with everyone.

He despaired of finding a proper strategy for Toshiba, because the client wanted advertising to do two things at once: establish Toshiba as the preeminent manufacturer of portable computers, and in the process, convince customers that the desktop computer was a dinosaur, and the laptop, the full-service computer of the future. It was too much to ask of one advertising campaign.

Sparkletts' problem was equally frustrating: there was nothing the advertising could do, except to invent a new personality for the brand. There was no way to impugn the competition's water source, no way to imply that Sparkletts was a purer product. The ads could not claim superiority. All they could do was poke holes in the competition's image. It was advertising at its most amorphous; nothing to sell but style.

Worse, Clow and Wolf were both giving him trouble. Clow had begun to treat him as though he made made some Faustian pact to win a piece of new business and had lost his creative soul in the process. Kuperman, terrified that the client would go home feeling swamped, kept trying to edit down the creative presentation. Clow insisted that the more work the client saw at a pitch, the more he would be drawn into the relationship. Then Wolf got back from New York, looked over the Sparkletts work, and complained about the strategy. Kuperman had been trying to impose order for weeks, only to have Clow and Wolf threaten to dismantle his efforts.

Having nowhere else to go, Kuperman's manic energy imploded and shattered his hard-won control. He started to attack all available targets. He bullied his way through a Sparkletts rehearsal in the Boathouse, asking the planner to rehearse his comments twice and then commenting, "There. I don't think you're any stupider than I did five minutes ago." When Grossman joked that he was going to use some "blah-blah-blah's" in his section, Kuperman shot back, "It won't sound any worse than what you're saying now." He insulted every member of the team. It was old-style Chiat/Day management: motivation by sarcasm.

When he got home that night Kuperman was fed up with himself. He had reverted to his old ways, just at the point when the office needed to be able to depend on him. If he fell apart and forgot how to lead, how to dole out praise and criticism so that people were inspired to do better, how could he expect his subordinates to do their best work?

The next morning a contrite Kuperman sat at the head of the Treehouse conference table and addressed his department heads.

"For the last week and a half I haven't exactly been an inspirational leader," he said. "I've been riding people, yelling, uptight, and for that I apologize. Part of it is, I really want to win this piece of business—*any* piece of business, Sparkletts, Toshiba, whatever. I think everyone here wants to. But I haven't been leading in the way I expect you people to. I've been giving people hard times. So accept my apologies."

He thanked those who had worked on Sparkletts.

"I think we're going to get it," he said. "And if we don't, we'll just go on."

*   *   *

When Wolf was a teenager he had had a summer job driving a truck for a car dealership. One day the slickest salesman on the showroom floor got a call from an irate customer, who had expected his new car to be delivered the day before.

"So the salesman says, 'I wouldn't send it out until I liquid-glazed it. It's only forty or fifty bucks extra,' " recalled Wolf. "So the customer says, 'Great. Definitely. Do it.' " So the salesman yells, 'Wolf—*wash it.*' "

He told the story to the demoralized Sparkletts team, by way of illuminating their dilemma. They could not sell process, even though the client liked to talk about his filtering process, because filters made people suspicious. What was wrong with the water in the first place, that it had to be cleaned up? They could not sell source, because that was what everyone else was selling.

He understood that all they had to sell was image—but unlike Kuperman, who was halfheartedly pushing a just-folks approach, Wolf wanted it to sound like a big deal. He exhorted them to look beyond the campaign to its larger significance. Wolf had been thinking about the 1990s a lot of late, ever since his admittedly hungry ten-year-old daughter had refused to eat at a McDonald's because the chain used Styrofoam containers that could not be recycled. The boom of the 1980s was over. The next decade was going to be about simpler values—caring for the environment, buying value instead of flash, prizing leisure time over the eighty-hour, big-money work week. Sparkletts could get in on the trend at the start. Chiat/Day had something to sell that was much more than an advertising strategy. It was a prescient move, in anticipation of a social trend.

"Talk about the back-to-basics attitude in this country," he advised. "Away from the pretentiousness of the eighties, all that phony-baloney stuff. You have to use what's going on in the world here."

He relished having a captive audience, since people rarely solicited his views on anything but money. "People who can afford a BMW are buying a Lexus because they're not going to pay more for a fancy hood ornament. And people aren't going to buy fancy French waters. The changing value system of the time is on their side, back to values and trusted brands."

Without realizing what he was doing, he began to address the client directly, as though he were in the pitch right then. "Now's the time to focus on what you do have," he said. "We can turn the source thing on its heels. The time is right, and your brand is right. It used to be the best at any price. Now it's the best at the best price."

As he saw it, the challenge was simple: "Take them from a down-to-earth folksy company with great service to a down-to-earth folksy company with great-tasting pure water."

Kuperman worried that Clow, who had not attended the strategy sessions, would be a loose cannon at the pitch. The executives from Sparkletts were a very buttoned-down group. Clow was in a work frenzy, as though his metabolism were compensating for the year's slow start. If he went off on one of his tangents, he might spook the client.

Wolf said it was up to the group to rein him in. He was not recommending a free-for-all. What he was after, he said, was "orchestrated spontaneity."

When that got a laugh, he trotted out a line he had used before, and would use again.

"Sincerity," he advised. "Once you learn to fake that, you've got this business down."

The point of the November 6 tree meeting was to present Clow with a surprise gift from the Venice office, commemorating his membership in the Art Directors Hall of Fame. Kuperman climbed up into the ficus pot, leaned against the tree, and quickly ran through his agenda items. When he was finished, someone lugged in a big framed photo of Eileen Clow and two mid-sized dogs and gave it to Clow, to wild applause.

He shuffled forward, clearly moved by the gesture. "The dogs weren't lucky enough to be there the whole time, but Eileen was," he said. His words came in an emotional rush, as though he were hurrying to finish his thoughts before he began to cry. "She's not here, but I'm going to say this anyhow. Advertising's a hard business. We've been married for twenty-two years and she's been with me all this time, and it's been really important to me to have her there."

At that, Eileen Clow stepped out of the crowd, wearing a faded black T-shirt and jeans like her husband's, and embraced him.

"Okay, that's it," shouted Kuperman. "Let's get back to work and win some business."

The next morning, just hours before the review team from Sparkletts arrived for the pitch, Kuperman pulled his car into the agency lot. The agency was about to make a risky presentation, having rejected Sparkletts' stated preference for campaigns that glorified the company's water source and filtering process. Chiat/Day had decided to sell style—but if the client wasn't prepared to make a leap of faith, the best creative in the world would fail to convince him.

Kuperman hesitated. He had a stuffed Energizer Bunny in the back of his car. He leaned in and rubbed the Bunny's tail, but he told no one what he had done. If they won Sparkletts, it would be good luck. If they lost, better that it was his own, private weirdness.

After the pitch, he felt confident, almost cocky, but he said nothing. Better to wait and see than to be publicly proven wrong.

Clow and Kuperman were pacing each other toward the same goal, but they were not yet partners. That bond was forged in the elevator at Nutrasweet's headquarters. There were two representatives from each participating agency, all on their way to the November 8 briefing, each one a vivid visual reminder of just how far from the mainstream Chiat/Day sat.

Clow craned his neck. There were duos from Backer Spielvogel Bates, D'Arcy Masius Benton & Bowles, DDB Needham, Leo Burnett U.S.A, Ogilvy & Mather, J. Walter Thompson, Young & Rubicam and Foote, Cone & Belding—"all the heavy breathers from every packaged goods agency in Chicago and the Midwest," he thought to himself—and then there was Chiat/Day, the outsider, the agency that had sneered at packaged goods often and loudly enough to earn that lucrative category's unending distrust. The imbalance had an odd effect: it reminded both Kuperman and Clow that their real enemy lurked outside the agency, not among the people who worked at Chiat/Day. Tradition, which implied to them a certain smug indifference, was the true threat to the agency's integrity. It was as though an elevator's worth of men in serious suits created a force field, repelling the two men from Chiat/Day and pushing them closer together. The factions within Chiat/Day had been quarreling among themselves for too long. All it took was a look at the rest of the advertising universe to remind them that they were allies.

They filed out of the elevator and into a large conference room, where they sat, silent, waiting for the client and for the team from incumbent Ogilvy & Mather. By the time the last ad man sat down, the tension in the room was making everyone rather uncomfortable.

Kuperman couldn't stand it.

"Okay," he said. "Let's talk merger."

He got little more than chuckles. The Nutrasweet contingent arrived and proceeded to brief the agencies. After a formal presentation to a respectfully subdued room, the team opened the meeting for questions—as long as they were submitted on index cards. Clow couldn't believe his ears. When the client relented and decided, hesitantly, to allow the agency representatives to speak, Clow jumped right in. He figured that the only way to make an impression was to ask the blunt questions that the others would be too timid to ask.

He asked the most provocative questions he could think of. Why wouldn't Coca-Cola start manufacturing its own brand of aspartame, and cut Nutrasweet out of that business entirely? Why did Nutrasweet think there was any way to leverage its two biggest clients, Coke and Pepsi-Cola, when those two companies had been at the mercy of Nutrasweet for years, and bitterly resented its monopoly?

Kuperman followed Clow's example. Why not take the $50 million advertising budget and put it into pricing instead, so that Nutrasweet could be what he called the "best cost producer"? Why not forget about marketing and spend the money where it would do some good? He was hardly recommending the strategy, but he knew the company must have considered it. If Chiat/Day couldn't mimic the upstanding, institutional dependability of its competition, at least he and Clow could show that they arrived at the smart ideas faster than the others did.

After the meeting, they tried hard to convince each other that they represented anything more than a novelty act to Nutrasweet. They did what they always did when faced with a long shot: they sold themselves on what they had to offer, and minimized the appeal of things they didn't have, like an office in Paris, or, for that matter, Chicago.

"Shit," said Clow. "If you want people who can come over and service you, you can hire the guys who work at the Hyatt Hotel. They may not know anything about doing advertising, but they're right across the street."

He encouraged Kuperman to be confident. "If we get aced out for being too brazen or too succinct," he said happily, "then we're being eliminated for all the right reasons."

Clow and Kuperman had no idea just how close they had come to missing the Nutrasweet meeting altogether. The consensus at Nutrasweet was that Chiat/Day had made a predictably poor showing at the credentials presentation, and had worked too hard to pretend that it had an international network in place when everyone knew that it didn't.

As Nutrasweet's Nick Rosa saw it, there were a few agencies bunched at the top of the list, a few in the middle, a few at the end—and then, trailing even that group, there was Chiat/Day, with no worldwide network, no massive research department. It was what he called a "ninety-nine to one shot." The members of the committee agreed that the merciful thing to do would be to eliminate Chiat/Day. But all the other agencies had supporters on the committee, so none of them were going to be cut. It would be terribly humiliating for Chiat/Day to be the single casualty at this stage of the process.

An executive was dispatched to call Chiat and tell him that Chiat/Day was a long shot at best, in the hope that the agency would decide not to go ahead with its pitch. The call did not have its intended effect. Instead, Chiat/Day took the lukewarm response as a call to arms.

The client anticipated that the agency would come back with a flashy campaign, but not a solid, enduring one. "Let's be guarded," Rosa advised the others on the committee. "Let's not be swept off our feet by a fabulous campaign."

Economic concerns dictated the cancellation of Christmas bonuses, in favor of a week off between Christmas and New Year's. Chiat/Day/Mojo University, at this point a distraction to everyone but Chiat and Clow, was postponed until some time in 1991. The employee Christmas gift, as mandated by Chiat, was a cardboard box festooned with cartoon figures and copy blocks about the lack of minorities in advertising. There was one white sock and one black sock in each box, a symbolic reference to the $150,000 the agency had devoted ("that's YOUR Christmas gift plus some more $$") to establishing minority scholarships and internships with pay.

Those were the responsible reactions to a trying year, but as the holiday season approached, Chiat and Clow confessed their frustration to each other. The agency had to do something, however small, to reward its employees and motivate them for the coming year. It was the quintessential Chiat/Day challenge. They had to come up with a gift that did not cost a lot of money, but was so wonderful that no one stopped to think about how much it had cost. The style, not the scrimp, was the point.

Sittig had told Clow that Brindfors had bought its employees bicycles, in a tight year. Clow told Chiat.

They decided on bicycles.

They wanted 751 bicycles, for under $100 apiece, and they assigned Chiat's assistant Carol Madonna the task of finding them. She balked at the idea. "I'll do it," she told them, "but we're not giving bonuses, there's a raise freeze, the sock box said there was no gift, and then this bicycle shows up. Ninety-eight percent of the people here would be happier with the $100 bill."

Chiat and Clow insisted. She might be right, but this was about gesture, not reason. She found out that Huffy made a bike for the right price, so Chiat/Day placed an order for 751 Huffy fenderless beach cruiser bikes, some black, some red, to be delivered to the Venice, New York and Toronto offices.

Kuperman *was in a* Nutrasweet planning meeting with Wolf, Clow and a half dozen staffers when the War Room phone rang and one of the account executives jumped to answer it.

Her face flushed a bright red and she gasped, "Are you serious?" She turned to the others, beckoned Kuperman to the phone, and chortled, "We've got Sparkletts!"

Kuperman grabbed the phone, muttered something, listened for a moment, and hung up. "Nothing," he reported. "It's nothing yet."

A second call came moments later. This time Kuperman fought a smile. Before anyone could interrogate him, one of the secretaries rushed in and handed him a phone slip. Without a word, he rushed out the door.

When he came back, he refused to meet anyone's gaze. He sat down and slipped a note to Wolf. Three of the Sparkletts executives, including vice-president of marketing and strategic planning Dave Neufer, who had overseen the review, wanted a meeting at four fifteen this afternoon to discuss staffing on the account. It was a good sign, but not enough to start celebrating. Besides, the only way to survive a new business push was to compartmentalize each day. The goal, this morning, was to figure out what Nutrasweet's strategy ought to be. Anything short of a formal announcement that Chiat/Day had won Sparkletts was a distraction.

There was a split within the agency over the basic direction Nutrasweet ought to take. Wolf was insisting that the client had to solidify its position before the aspartame patent ran out, while Clow and the creatives were focusing on competitive issues they could address in advertising, such as taste.

"Let's use a Cold War analogy," said Wolf. "If you want to start a dialogue, you have to make your alleged enemies believe you control their destiny. Walk softly but carry a big stick. Nutrasweet's big stick is consumer belief in the product. So we've got to go out and make people believe that they've got to have Nutrasweet."

"The problem is that people like Diet Coke because it's Diet Coke, not because it's Nutrasweet," said Kuperman.

"Reclaim taste," suggested Clow.

"You could lose to a blend," said Kuperman.

"That's not the issue," insisted Wolf. "That's after the fact. We've got to figure out what to do before the fact."

Clow wondered if they ought to do a campaign about how great Nutrasweet was—one that showed what the world was like before Nutrasweet, or how bad things would taste without it.

Kuperman didn't like the idea. Nutrasweet had proved its superior taste once, when it debuted ten years ago. He preferred a "generally suspicious" approach. "Like, 'If it's not there, what is?' "

Wolf held up a can of Diet Coke and affected an announcer's voice: "What's in here? A world of taste and twenty-five years of experience."

Clow yawned, loudly.

"Slogan police, slogan police," shouted Wolf. He smiled at Clow. "Make it a character."

"The Pillsbury Doughboy," shouted Clow.

Wolf answered in a falsetto. " 'I'm Nicky Nutrasweet.' "

Kuperman was as close as he'd come all year to a win. The men from Sparkletts complained about the quality of the creative work, but Kuperman had an answer ready. The agency approached a pitch as though it were a work session, part of the Chiat/Day process. If the client didn't like what he saw, he could rest assured that the real thing would be much better. The Sparkletts executives seemed happy with that. They were predisposed to choose Chiat/Day. To their surprise, they had liked the agency more than they had expected to, given its reputation for arrogance.

Kuperman could hardly contain himself. If everything was all right, then why had Sparkletts asked for a meeting? To give him the good news in person?

Not quite yet. There was one other problem. Sparkletts had worked with a small agency in past, and was used to getting some of the work on a discount, if not for free. Would Chiat/Day accept a 12 percent commission if that clinched the win?

Kuperman was devastated. He figured that the agency needed 13.5 percent to make money on the account. A bargain rate was often the only thing that distinguished two otherwise similar agencies, but Chiat/Day's stance had always been that full price paid for premium service—that no other agency could duplicate what Chiat/Day offered, at any price.

The economic climate made it more difficult to maintain that position. Clients were hurting, and they expected their agencies to share their suffering. Still, Kuperman knew what his answer had to be. He explained that as much as he wanted to win—and he wanted the men from Sparkletts to appreciate just how badly he wanted to win—he could not allow the agency to take on another account like Dep, one that sapped people's energies and did not make money. He was sorry, but he could not alter the fee structure.

Kuperman got another call four days later, on November 19, and when he heard Dave Neufer's tone of voice his heart sank. He had heard it before—it was the grave voice of bad news, just what he did not want to hear only hours before Chiat was scheduled to deliver his State of the Agency address.

But to Kuperman's surprise, Neufer said that he really wanted to choose Chiat/Day for the account, and the only remaining issue was compensation. Couldn't they close the gap between what Sparkletts wanted to pay and what the agency wanted to earn, and agree on 12.5 percent?

Kuperman weighed the psychological value of a win. "Let me think about it," he said, "and I'll get back to you."

As soon as he hung up, he went looking for Chiat and Wolf.

"Look, here's the deal," he said. "We can have the account if we want to meet them in the middle. What do you say?"

Chiat didn't even wait to hear where the middle was. *"Take it!"* he said.

"Well, that's my feeling," said Kuperman. "Let's take it because we need it."

Neufer called again before Kuperman could get back to the phone. He picked up the phone gingerly, expecting to hear that the client had changed his mind.

On the contrary, Neufer was calling to apologize for not having sounded more excited when he called the first time. He had been preoccupied with other business matters, and he wanted Kuperman to know that he was happier about the decision than he had seemed.

"I thought you were calling to tell me we didn't get the business."

"No. Everyone's excited, and we'd really love to have you guys."

"Well," said Kuperman, "we've talked it over and we'll do it."

He hung up and said, aloud, "We've got the account," and then the telephone rang again. It was Neufer.

"Oh shit," said Kuperman.

But this time the client only wanted to invite Kuperman to have a drink and celebrate. The deal was done. Kuperman had his first new business win as Venice office president—a fact he chose to keep secret until the end of the day, so that Chiat could have the pleasure of announcing the news to the assembled staff.

The purpose of the State of the Agency address was to bring everyone up to date on how the agency was doing, to squelch rumors and serve up a nice mixture of fact, history, and optimism. Chiat/Day might be in trouble, but it had been in trouble before, and had always found a way out. Anyone—Wolf, Clow, Kuperman—could have delivered that message, and in fact the speech was based on an outline from Wolf that was, in turn, based on conversations with Clow and Kuperman. The point was to put Jay Chiat behind the podium and let him speak to the masses. Over the past year he had shown up in Venice for board meetings and in the middle of crises, or touched down halfway through a longer journey, always a fleeting visitor. The State of the Agency address was meant to mark a place in time: Chiat had surveyed 1990 and developed a plan for 1991. He was back. Not his emissaries, but Jay Chiat himself.

At five o'clock he took his place at the front of the Carousel Ballroom at the Guest Quarters Hotel in Santa Monica, surveyed the sea of faces, most of whom he did not know, and consulted his notes. He played with the microphone for a moment, asking people in the back whether they could hear him, and then joked, "I guess we'll get into the psychological issue of whether you can hear me or whether you believe me."

He smiled. "Kuperman thought that I might not have anything positive to say tonight," he said. "So as I was walking up, he handed me a little note to announce to you that we were appointed the agency for Sparkletts."

He was interrupted by wild applause, which he made no effort to subdue. When it had died down, he went on. "That was a real win, because I would suspect that when we started out, it was about eighty/twenty against. They managed to get me out of the new business pitch. Probably raised the odds. And I understand that after a lot of negotiation he got the fee up to four percent or something. I'm delighted."

With that warm-up, he proceeded to review the past year. Chiat/Day had faced a doubled whammy—the jinx of being named Agency of the Decade by *Advertising Age,* which made prospective clients assume the agency was booked up, and an economic crash that had affected the entire industry, and made every client, old and new, skittish about spending money. Chiat liked to think that his anticipation of the recession had left Chiat/Day in somewhat better shape than much of the competition, that early cutbacks in hirings and expenditures had cushioned the fall. But he could not deny the gravity of the losses in New York, losses that for the first time in the agency's history had been difficult to replace. Three months after Chiat/Day lost Apple Computer and Nike in 1986, the agency replaced the revenues with new accounts. New York had not yet begun its turnaround, seven months after losing Reebok.

He refused to cast blame within the agency. Wolf may have sent Jane Newman into exile as punishment for the Royal Caribbean loss, but Chiat's public position was that the agency had acquitted itself admirably. Outside circumstance, not internal disarray, had done in New York.

"Royal Caribbean, the last piece and probably the biggest piece of business we've lost," he explained, "that was, I think, the result of a management change a couple of years ago. Systematically, that client changed their entire marketing staff. There were six people who we dealt with. They were all fired. We were the seventh to go.

"That one taught us a significant lesson—both in New York as well as in the other offices—that if you don't have the client relationships at the top level, then you're going to be in trouble eventually."

He enumerated other mistakes he felt the agency had made in 1990—unsatisfactory work from some of the subsidiaries, involvement in too many disparate projects that distracted management from the advertising work, bad timing on the Mojo acquisition ("I think they waited until they signed the papers, and then the Australian economy crashed")—all of them exacerbated by what Chiat felt was a predatory press corps.

"And then, finally, in 1990 there's been the saga of Tom McElligott," he said. "You've heard of him. I don't know where he went and who he took, but he's out there somewhere, and I think we'll get on without him. That's over."

He wanted to remind the loyalists who remained about the need for solidarity. Chiat knew that people in Venice were grumbling about their canceled Christmas bonuses, since Venice had managed to maintain its accounts all year, but their sacrifice was essential to strengthening the bond between the offices.

"The culture and history and mission of this agency is that we want to be the best agency in the world," he said. "Not the best L.A. office in the world, not the best Toronto office in the world, but we want to be sure that we do great work across the board. For every client. In every office. In order to do that, you just can't have mixed messages: 'You guys in New York really had a lousy year? Well, sorry about that, but everybody else is going to do well.' We can't function that way. . . . There's no way you can solidify an agency, make it march under one culture, and have different rules and different value systems."

He finished up with an inspirational flourish. "We're not about to cut ourselves out of this crisis," he promised. "What we're trying to do is *create* our way out of it. Great work and hard work is the only way we will work our way out. That means stay cool, stay loyal, service all your clients, that's very important.

"Great creative is what we're about. I want to see that pumped up, want to see the most outrageous yet responsible advertising we've ever done in this year. That's the only way we'll prove that this is not a two-decade flash in the pan. It's what built the agency. It's what differentiates us from everybody, and it's what kept us growing and will get us out of the mess in New York.

"So have fun, stay loose, try to have a good holiday," he concluded. "Just remember: We're still the pirates. We're not the Navy."

Chiat asked for questions and got only one, about the plans for the new building. He took the lack of curiosity as a positive sign.

"Things that good, huh?"

Clow followed up with a reel of the best work of 1990, and by the end of the hour most of the employees were suitably fired up, eager to rededicate themselves to the mission of setting a standard for excellence for the entire industry. If Amy Miyano resisted the wave of worshipful enthusiasm, it was because she had heard it all before. She knew, from friends in the New York office, that Chiat's speech there had included a reference to possible layoffs at the end of January. For all the brave talk, New York was still a mess. As for the business about being the pirates, she was tired of the line. She had hoped, given the gravity of the situation, that Chiat would tell them all something new.

Special events had a short shelf life. By the next morning Chiat's inspirational speech and the thrill of the Sparkletts win were dim memories. Kuperman had his victory, and Rabosky a substantial account whose campaign was not a hand-me-down from Sittig. But they also had a battery-powered Bunny who, to their frustration, had managed to confuse viewers about which brand he represented, a problem that quickly eclipsed whatever delight they may have felt.

The agency had spent much of the summer trying to explain away consumer confusion over whether the Bunny was selling Energizer batteries or Duracell, but as the lucrative fourth-quarter holiday season approached, promising 40 percent of the year's battery sales, the client got apprehensive. Bob Grossman, who was scheduled to visit Eveready's St. Louis headquarters at the end of November for an agency evaluation, found a distressing new item on the agenda. The client wanted to talk about the results of a tracking study that showed negative comments from 17 percent of the people who had seen the Energizer commercials. Some of that group also had positive things to say about the campaign, but there was a core of 5 percent of the respondents who did not like what the Bunny was doing. They missed the point of the parody entirely. Were these spots for Eveready batteries, or for some other product? It was too hard for them to tell. One of the research people at the client was worried, and she wanted to do more research to allay her fears. She wanted focus groups.

Kuperman emphatically thought it was a bad idea. "You're digging yourself a hole here," he warned Grossman. "Stop this thing right now. It's the *second most popular campaign in America.* You going to change the format? Have the Bunny stop interrupting? If there is a problem with the format, which I doubt, it's not fixable. We're not going to change it."

Grossman pressed him. It looked awfully defensive to refuse to do focus groups. It looked like the agency had reason to worry about the results.

"I'm not saying refuse," said Kuperman. "I'm saying, pin down exactly what you want to learn, or you'll end up off the campaign." He was hardly going to suggest a confrontation with a client. He had talked to the Sparkletts executives about their reasons for choosing the agency and gotten an unexpected response. The most important element was the recommendations they got from existing clients who felt well cared for—a nice contradiction to the notion that Chiat/Day was too full of itself to take its clients' needs seriously. He was not going to jeopardize the agency's improved image.

"It means more than all the impassioned closing speeches we can do," said Kuperman. "If they'd called and gotten negative responses, we'd be dead."

They were near death at Nutrasweet, though they did not know it, and facing a terminal case of confusion on Toshiba. The Toshiba pitch had been postponed until mid-December, but the extra time was of little help. Weeks went by without a functional strategy, and the creatives continued to comp up whatever ads they thought might work. But spirits were high. The thrill of being the outsider on the Nutrasweet business was reminiscent of the days when the agency really was the odd man out. Chiat/Day was the agency that launched Apple computers, after all. The memory was enough to convince everyone that the great idea was lurking just beyond the next fruitless strategy session.

The energy in Hardy, on November 21, was enough to make the drywall rattle: Wolf, Clow, Newman, Kuperman, Grossman and Coots, each one with his own inflamed reasons for wanting the Nutrasweet account, had this single afternoon to write the script for a November 29 meeting with the client—which would serve, in turn, as the foundation for the December 5 pitch. Newman, who had flown out to supervise the effort, began speaking immediately. She knew what Chiat needed to say: he had to acknowledge that Chiat/Day was the dark horse and turn it into an advantage.

"If you want a maintenance agency, go with Leo Burnett," she said, pacing back and forth in the tiny room, writing Chiat's lines for him. "But if you want to change your relationship to the consumer, we're your answer."

She looked at the others, as though daring them to contradict her. "High-profile advertising. We cut our teeth on problems. We're a young agency. We can do high-profile advertising that moves the needle. We have to crystallize our position," she said. Then she stopped. There was such a thing as going too far in any one direction. There had to be a way to reassure Nutrasweet that Chiat/Day could, in fact, service the account if the client liked its current image.

"Right," chuckled Wolf. "If you want maintenance, the agency can do that. Whatever you want."

Wolf's biggest worry was finding something fresh to say, something that the competition did not have. "We're up against the six, eight biggest agencies in the world," he said. "I don't think that consumer insight's a new story. A new story is 'You've got a two-year window to do advertising.' We want them to walk out saying, 'Oooh, that Bunny. Oooh, that Nissan advertising.' "

Clow thought the important point was that the agency knew how to communicate, and could be a better partner than the more conservative agencies it was up against. Newman liked the idea. They could point up Kuperman's and Clow's personal involvement on Nissan. Surely that was a unique level of commitment. Quietly, Grossman corrected her. Ted Bell, president of Grossman's alma mater, Leo

Burnett U.S.A., was active on the agency's Oldsmobile account. It was nothing special for a top executive to attend to a major piece of business.

"We have a way," said Wolf, his voice rising uncontrollably, "of believing our own bullshit. *What we do is not unique!* The Bunny is unique."

Clow was not about to tolerate Wolf saying that Chiat/Day was just like anyplace else. He started yelling. "What are we going to *do?* Show them a reel and put them on the plane? The glitz isn't enough."

"I know. But we need to drive this thing not on what we do but on what they need."

"We have to show the discipline and relationship," said Clow.

Kuperman broke in. The best approach was to be straight with the client. Nutrasweet needed a big idea. Chiat/Day could come up with one, and the point of the pitch was to show them how.

Everyone started to laugh. This was what it always came down to, despite all the talk of account planning, client relationships, retail experience or targeted media. Chiat/Day meant big ideas. That was what the agency had to sell—campaigns like the ones for Nissan, Eveready, and the NYNEX Yellow Pages.

"So what do we got?" asked Kuperman, ticking off the answers. "Three big ideas. Lee. And this place."

CHAPTER **30**

Chiat arrived in Venice for the November 28 dinner and meeting the following day with the Nutrasweet team, and immediately started behaving as though he alone could galvanize the agency and plot the big win. He cornered Kuperman, Clow and Grossman. He wanted to know what everyone was doing, on every aspect of the pitch. Nutrasweet had requested two reels, one of historical work and one of current work done by those who would work on the account. That meant Clow, Rabosky, Sittig and Potter. Chiat was not satisfied. The reels were weak on packaged goods, so he suggested adding an old Gaines dog food spot.

Kuperman protested. The creatives had not worked on that account.

"So what?" said Chiat. "They're going to know?"

"Let's not make the mistake of pretending we're something we're not," said Grossman. "They know we're not a big packaged goods company."

"Right," said Chiat. "But we've done some great packaged goods advertising."

He speculated on what the competition might put on its reels, and came up with a daunting list of major accounts: 7-Up, McDonald's, Marlboro cigarettes, Volkswagen, Bud Light. Kuperman tried to reassure him. "Our feeling," he said, "is that they can't put a reel together as good, of the people who will be working on the business."

"But if they're cheating. . . ." Chiat mused. He had another idea.

They could put Meow Mix on the reel, an account Kuperman had worked on at Della Femina, back in 1972.

"But if it's an idea from 1972, it's not very relevant," said Kuperman.

Chiat smiled goofily. "See how long a good idea lasts?"

He had a similar solution to the credit imbalance on the current reel, which featured about a half dozen spots from Clow and only two from each of the other creatives.

"Change the names," said Chiat.

"Cheat!" said Clow.

"I would," said Chiat.

Kuperman still resisted. Nutrasweet had asked for client references. Surely they would call clients and inquire about the people who were going to staff the account. What if the client didn't know who the people were?

Clow tried to calm him down. The references were probably just for the big case studies that the agency presented to show how well it served certain clients. No one was going to go back and verify every creative credit.

"Okay," said Kuperman. "We'll cheat."

When Wolf appeared, Chiat accommodatingly changed his focus to the agency's worldwide shortcomings. "We're going to get killed internationally," Chiat reminded Wolf and Kuperman. "Our only hope is to show great work."

"The only way we can win this is the two-year idea," said Kuperman, referring to a campaign that would establish the brand before the patent expired.

"The window . . ." said Wolf wistfully.

"Otherwise we're dots on the map," said Kuperman.

"Wait a couple of months," joked Chiat, "and we could pick up WPP," referring to the multinational advertising conglomerate, now racked by debt and account losses.

"Great," said Kuperman. "I'll ask them to postpone the meeting."

What kept people hopping was Chiat's ability to sound the death knell for the pitch one minute, and be obsessed with the importance of a dinner meeting with the prospective client the next. The agency had made a reservation at Chaya Venice, a fashionable Franco-

Japanese restaurant just a block away—a choice that Chiat found efficient but shortsighted. They had to turn their location into an asset. This wasn't Chicago, it was Los Angeles. They ought to be going to Spago, in West Hollywood.

"Let them think they'll see Madonna every time they come out here," he said.

The image of being stuck on the Santa Monica Freeway at rush hour with jet-lagged executives who would want to go to sleep early was not a pretty one. Wolf suggested Chinois instead, run by Spago's Wolfgang Puck but only blocks away. Chiat suggested Rebecca's or DC-3, two nearby restaurants favored by the art crowd, but he worried that they would be dead at six o'clock.

Coots pointed out that any restaurant would be dead at six o'clock. Perhaps they could hire people to eat at the restaurant of their choice.

They decided to stick with Chaya Venice. Chiat would take the men on a tour of the building, and after drinks in the Fish they would stroll over to the restaurant. He challenged Coots. What kind of table would they have?

A long, rectangular one, she expected.

He vetoed the idea. Someone had to go over to the restaurant and make sure they could have a round table. Long tables kept people at either end from ever having a chance to talk to each other. A round table facilitated conversation. He spoke with an urgency that demanded attention. From the international to the picayune, he saw the opportunity for fatal disaster everywhere.

In the midst of the manic planning, to try to keep things in perspective, Kuperman reminded Chiat of the time he was having trouble with an executive at Mitsubishi Electronics, and Chiat had suggested that he take the man out for a round of golf. The next day, they were having a conversation about a similarly difficult Nissan executive, and Kuperman remarked, "Maybe I'll take him out to play golf."

Chiat had exploded. *"Is that all you ever think of? Is that your answer to every problem?"*

When they had a quiet moment, Kuperman confessed what was really on his mind. He had been thinking about Chiat's role at the agency ever since Clow's comment, at the October board meeting, about their selling a minority interest in the agency to the Japanese. Kuperman saw how it might work, once the agency regained its feet, but it made Chiat's active participation even more essential. The idea of making Wolf and Clow function as a team was, Kuperman said, "a Frankenstein." There was an inspirational message that could only come from Chiat.

If Chiat no longer cared about the agency, then he could step back and it would find its own level. If the future mattered, as Chiat said it did, then Kuperman wanted him around to protect his emotional investment.

He said it with a passion that surprised even himself. He was becoming more and more preoccupied with sustaining Chiat/Day's personality—what had been policy for him at the beginning of the year was now a personal crusade. Chiat had to get involved again, at least until the enduring issue of his eventual replacement was resolved.

The day after the dinner and meeting, though, Kuperman felt trapped by his own contradictory feelings: he believed that Chiat had to lead the agency back to prominence, but he felt that Chiat's concern over the question of their international presence was misguided, and that it threatened to throw the entire pitch off course. His appraisal of the agency's performance was only, "I don't think we blew ourselves up."

For his part, Chiat was beginning to wonder if he had the right to expect that he could create a second generation in his own image. What were people taught, from the time they were children, but that there was a more powerful being on high who protected them? If religion didn't work, there was always the notion that the government had their best interests at heart. By the time most adults had discarded their belief in an omnipotent caretaker, they were in their thirties. Some people never did. They merely transferred their allegiance to the workplace, and looked for yet another father to tell them what to do.

He liked the part well enough; what power, to be able to tell a ballroom full of employees that things were going to be all right and see the relief wash over their faces. What he had realized since his State of the Agency address, though, was that he could not enforce his version of the future. He told Kuperman that he had finally come to terms in his own mind with Wolf—or, more specifically, with Wolf's inability to embrace the basic emotional tenets of Chiat/Day. Chiat continued to admire his new CEO as a superb tactician, but it had taken him nearly a year to accept that Wolf was never going to become a spiritual force merely by virtue of the top title.

"You know," he told Kuperman, "I used to think Bob wasn't getting it. Now I realize *I'm* the one who's not getting it. You can't change Bob."

What was missing, quite obviously, was the "intuitive trust" Chiat and Clow felt for each other. Although Chiat might have hoped that Wolf and Clow would achieve that level of rapport, it was clearly not to be. They trusted each other intellectually, but for the agency to work the way it had in the past, there had to be a deeper emotional harmony. That was the major sacrifice of the past year, the casualty of change. No longer was the agency run by men who considered themselves members of the same family. The men in charge of Chiat/Day had come there from different corners of advertising's terrain.

The best that Chiat could hope for was that the ideals of the agency would live on, as embodied by and promoted by Clow. In his self-deprecating way, he imagined that Wolf's management style might turn out to be an improvement. Chiat called himself a "scatological" manager, a meddler, and had always believed that people thrived in an unpredictable atmosphere. What had eluded him and Clow was balance, the discipline that made the place nuts enough to be fun, but always on the respectable side of craziness. Perhaps Wolf would be able to manage without chaos, and in so doing inject a needed element of predictability—the sort of reassuring rhythm that kept employees, and clients, from defecting.

Carol Madonna, wearing a Santa Claus hat, led her team of light-stringers along the row of trees on Main Street, trying valiantly to ignore the cranky outbursts of the Nutrasweet team, which had surrendered its Saturday morning to the still-elusive big idea. Today was December 1. The pitch was in four days, on Wednesday, December 5. The team was supposed to be working on a "taste you can trust" strategy, but Kuperman was the only one who embraced it. Newman, who had gone back to New York, had promised a "hot idea," but Clow complained that the fax she had sent delivered nothing more than a better understanding of the consumer. It was not yet an alternate strategy.

One of the planners had made the mistake of approaching Kuperman on Friday to talk about taste as an attribute, and reported to Clow that he had "really gotten beaten up for it." As the creatives pinned their work to the walls of the Fish, one ad director wondered aloud if they could ask the client to "take it on trust." The work was not yet good enough to overcome the agency's shortcomings.

Kuperman rolled in with a pugnacious look on his face, wearing an immaculate 1989 Creative Conference sweatshirt that bore the slogan, "The Next 20 Years," a not-so-subtle challenge to the creatives in the room. He had insisted that the teams try executions on his favorite idea, and bring back the gumballs Nutrasweet had used in its launch advertising, to celebrate the product's tenth anniversary. He had been pushing the idea for weeks, with Clow as his only ally. Today he wanted to see which creatives had lived up to his idea, and which ones had dared to take another path.

As they were getting started, the Christmas decorators made the mistake of laughing too loudly. Kuperman was up in a second, standing at the doorway of the Fish, screaming, "Hey, *Hey. Hey!*" in his best menacing tone.

Clow yelled from his seat, "Don't have any *fun* decorating those trees."

There was a series of animated executions designed to trade in on people's fears of the new artificial sweeteners. In the first, a man drank a beverage and his eyes bugged out, as the narrator said, "If it doesn't say Nutrasweet on it, you don't know what's in it."

"Is that a positive eyes bugging out, or a brains falling out?" asked Clow.

"The latter," said the copywriter.

In the next execution, a character poured a liquid over strawberries and the berries melted. Another man took a sip of a liquid and his innards began to poke out in all directions.

There was an "accept no substitutes" campaign that featured Luciano Pavarotti singing the national anthem, only to be replaced by Roseanne Barr; the two lip-synching singers from the group Milli Vanilli performing in their own voices; and a fat Elvis Presley impersonator. There were executions that exploited the Nutrasweet swirled logo—a joking reference to subliminal advertising, with a logo that spun hypnotically, a billboard with a moving swirl, and a series of find-the-swirl games. One team had an idea for a promotion: Find the one cola can without a swirl and win $1 million.

"Great," said Clow. "So somebody drinks it and throws away the can and they never find it."

"Who cares," said Grossman. "Save $1 million. Doesn't matter."

"Nah," said Clow. "I think somebody's got to win."

Kuperman shifted uncomfortably in his chair. The work failed to reflect the strategy. Bad enough that there was only one gumball execution from a freelance team. The rest of the executions were all over the place. It was the same problem he had encountered on the Sparkletts pitch. What seemed like a cornucopia of riches to Clow was going to look like disorder to the client.

"We can have a presentation so unruly," he warned, "that it touches on all these possibilities and has no focus."

Clow was blithe. "So we'll look at everything and then eliminate some."

"I think it's a waste of time."

Clow ignored him.

Rabosky added to the tension by presenting work of his own that had already been judged to be off-strategy. He was selling taste, but not the taste you could trust. He wanted to make fun of the weird taste of the competition's anticipated products, with exaggerated footage of grimacing babies and a man clutching his throat.

Wolf, Clow and Grossman laughed heartily at the ideas, which only made Kuperman more annoyed. He shoved his chair back from the table. Clow caught his gaze and admonished him. "I didn't know we had *any* strategy that could overrule an idea," he said.

With that, Kuperman walked out of the room.

Clow muttered something about "focusing the energy down" and dismissed the bewildered creatives. A moment later, Kuperman strode back into the room.

"We *have* a strategy," he said, " 'Taste you can trust.' But the creatives are all over the fucking place. 'Taste you can trust,' over and over. And a ten-year anniversary. Nobody's doing it." He gestured dismissively at the frozen image on the video monitor. "People like this? Then fine. Run this fucking stuff and forget it."

Rabosky grumbled that the ten-year anniversary idea wasn't a profitable one; the good ideas just were not coming. Kuperman countered that no one was paying enough attention to the idea. He didn't care if they dropped it and concentrated on the strategy, or dropped the other ideas and just pursued the anniversary, but something had to be done. The anniversary idea was a tricky one. It needed more attention.

Wolf reminded the others that the advertising had to make customers who reached for a six-pack of diet soda into Nutrasweet's allies—make them buy the ingredient, regardless of whether it was in Diet Coke or Diet Pepsi. Nutrasweet needed to be the low-cost producer to remain competitive, but if the advertising built the brand, there would be no need to be the low-cost provider.

"You may be able to sell for more," said Wolf, "and the difference between what you can sell for and what you *do* sell for is the value of the brand."

Kuperman liked that. "There's got to be something," he said, "that says, 'The cost of the product, plus the strength of the brand, equals the value.' "

Clow saw it as an evolutionary process—from the ingredient the consumer trusted, to the brand he trusted, to, someday, the company he trusted.

Without realizing it, Clow had just reversed himself and admitted that Rabosky's taste campaign was not enough. The advertising had to address trust. Suddenly, everyone was inside Kuperman's conceptual corral. He quickly closed the gate behind them. "That," he said, "is why taste isn't enough."

"Absolutely," said Clow, a bit surprised to see where the conversation had taken him.

Kuperman pressed his advantage. The problem with a lot of the work on the walls was that it was inappropriate to the company. It was a nice way to show the agency's range, but they had to be mindful of Nutrasweet's self-image.

"They see themselves as Norman Rockwell," he said.

"Hey, I'm not saying they've got to be wild and crazy," protested Clow. "But Norman Rockwell isn't going to get the job done."

They tried writing some new slogans, in the hope that they could inspire the creatives. Clow wrote the current candidate on the easel—"If it doesn't say Nutrasweet on it, you don't know what's in it"—and then added tag lines as Wolf, Kuperman, Grossman and Rabosky called them out.

" 'Remember how things used to taste before Nutrasweet?' "

"Do we have any with less than fifteen words?" asked Clow.

" 'Life wouldn't be as sweet without it.' "

" 'Ten years of making things taste great.' "

" 'The taste of the good life.' "

" 'Have your (fill in the blank) and eat it too,' " which was rejected because the company did not yet have a bakeable product.

" 'The taste you can trust.' "

" 'Thank you, Nutrasweet.' "

" 'You can't fool your mouth.' "

" 'There is no substitute.' "

" 'The taste that changed the world.' "

Clow reminded them that there was a global issue here—Nutrasweet actually enabled people in some countries to enjoy certain foods that would be too expensive if they had to be sweetened with sugar.

" 'Gumballs to Ethiopia!' " someone cried.

" 'Nutrasweet makes it better,' " said Wolf to approving murmurs.

"It's shorter than most of the other ones," allowed Clow. He considered the list. "We'll just keep going until we run out of time."

Wolf grinned. "Then we back-fill with a rationale, and put it in a tidy little presentation."

On Monday morning Wolf stumbled into the Treehouse, stared at the unfamiliar faces, and blurted out, "This doesn't look like a Nutrasweet meeting." It was, in fact, a Foster Farms meeting to discuss the issue of freshness, a prime selling point for the poultry company, but one that was mired in legalese. The government defined a frozen bird as one that was stored at zero degrees or less. Foster Farms' position was any bird whose temperature was under 32 degrees was frozen, which included what some of the competition euphemistically called "freshly thawed birds." Foster Farms took great pride in the fact that its birds' temperature never dipped below 32 degrees, but the company was having trouble communicating the distinction to consumers.

Wolf had no idea of the reason for the meeting, but he was quite clear on the client's generalized complaint about being ignored by top management. He recovered immediately and sauntered over to where Clow and Foster Farms general manager Tom Orr were seated. Wolf had the perfect rebound anecdote, about a golf game he had played with a member of the arch rival Zacky family, who had flattering things to say about Foster Farms. In less than five minutes, he acknowledged Orr as a man of substance, both in terms of chickens and golf, a sport Orr took quite seriously. When Wolf made his exit, it was not as though he was leaving to do something more important, but an indication that the time for socializing had ended. He did not want to intrude on the important business of the day.

Clow spent the morning talking chicken, and turkey; however much his mind might be on Nutrasweet, he had promised himself to Foster Farms. It was a particularly frustrating discipline, since one of the young copywriters had finally come up with a Nutrasweet tag line that everyone loved, "Making the world a better place to eat." Surely, if the Treehouse were to fall silent, he would be able to hear pencils and marking pens scurrying across sheets of tissue.

He had to miss the last Nutrasweet strategy session, but his absence became an advantage. The balance in Hardy shifted. Without Clow to challenge them, without his endless attempts to keep the doors of inspiration open, the others could get down to the business of selling the agency to Nutrasweet. Or, as someone had scrawled on the easel, in capital letters:

"BIG IDEAS," which were what Chiat/Day could provide, in terms of strategy, planning, and creative.

"HOME RUNS," which was what the agency's creative resulted in, as opposed to "strike-out campaigns" that were ignored.

"HIGH PROFILE," which was the kind of campaign Chiat/Day would devise.

"TURN AROUND," which was what the agency could do for Nutrasweet's underdeveloped brand image.

The pages of the presentation deck had been pinned to the walls.

Newman, who had shuttled back to Los Angeles for the last days' work, started to review them, pointing at one after another, her bangle bracelets jangling emphatically each time she tapped a page with her pencil. The agency was going to take Nutrasweet's most valuable asset, its track record, and exploit it, going step by step through its attributes—likability, acceptability, honesty, responsibility, integrity—until they arrived, breathless, at the top of the asset mountain, which was trust. Out of trust came a strategy, the tag line, and the creative executions—and, with any luck, a new account.

What Wolf liked about building up to "trust," he said, was that trust did so many things for the company. "It validates the Nutrasweet loyalist, provides needed assurance to the Nutrasweet skeptic, and undermines the competition, the potential wanna-be's," he said.

"Pretenders to the throne," said Newman.

"Pretenders to the gumball," said Kuperman.

Newman wanted to go even further. What about the underlying concern people had about chemical sweeteners, a distrust Nutrasweet had had to address ten years ago? Why not use it now to the company's advantage?

"The brilliant part of this strategy is that we're tapping into a latent fear, and two years from now we can really put the screws to the competition," Newman said. "We're clean. We're safe. We're in four thousand products. You're in how many? We've been around nine years. You, two months?"

Kuperman was reluctant. Reminding people of health issues might cause a Nutrasweet backlash. He suggested holding back on the fear strategy, for now. "Wait and see the climate," he said. "If it's not too bad, you can sing sweet songs of taste. If it's tougher, you can be more aggressive. Talk about trust—*then* say you can benefit from this fear of new food products. You've got the hammer. What you do with it depends on the size of the nail you've got to hit."

For an hour they revised and argued, Newman flying around the room, pulling down pages and scribbling revisions along the edges, moving chunks of the presentation up, or back, as the group decided, building a path from Nutrasweet's current taste strategy up to the new, expanded strategy of "the taste you've come to trust."

When they were finished, they stared up at what they had created, approvingly.

"It's relevant now, and it's a bridge to the future," said Wolf.

"It's relevant to their customers," said Kuperman, referring to the cola companies, "not just to the consumer."

"But it enhances the host brand . . . ," said Wolf.

". . . In a way that's advantageous to Nutrasweet," said Kuperman, completing this thought.

Wolf savored the idea. "The velvet hammerlock. It's an advantage to the host product if they keep it—and a challenge if they give it up."

It was, in a strange way, too logical for Chiat/Day. Trust seemed too predictable a conclusion, not the revelation they wanted it to be. What it was missing, Kuperman realized, was Clow. The emotional outbursts that would have made this meeting take longer than it did were as essential as they were distracting. They could think without Clow, but they couldn't communicate what they thought without him. He was the only one who could infuse a strategy with life.

Kuperman wanted Clow to get at the pitch and talk, in his "urgent, executional way," about how advertising would bring the issue of trust "smack up into people's faces real quick. He's got to say, 'This may be a great idea but nobody thinks about it.'

"You have an unleveraged brand equity, and you've got to do something with it," said Kuperman, "because you've been playing in a sandbox alone, and in two years there are going to be fifty other companies who want to be in that sandbox." He got to his feet and started pounding on the wall for emphasis. "You've got to tell them, 'You want to play? Better bring a fucking big shovel!' "

They repinned and rewrote some more. Kuperman's only caution was that they articulate all the aspects of the strategy before Clow got up to speak, because there was no way of guaranteeing that he would remember all the points he was supposed to make. They could draw a chart for him, or give him notes, but once an idea got hold of Clow there was no telling where it might take him. His job was to inspire. The others would take care of the information.

Clow and Miyano were in the creative art studio, busily constructing customized leave-behind boxes for the Nutrasweet pitch. The copy on the box read: "Nutrasweet is on everyone's lips. We want Nutrasweet to be on everyone's mind." Inside was a black notebook that featured a photo on its cover—a person's face, the mouth covered by a black rectangle, the forehead sporting a Nutrasweet swirl logo. Clow was madly cutting out little black rectangles when he glanced up and smiled.

"Anybody ever notice," he said, loudly enough for a dozen people to turn around, "how the rest of top management disappears and I'm still here working?" He turned back to the notebooks and wondered, aloud, if a paper sleeve around the outside would look better than the box did.

"You can't do custom in a day," complained Miyano.

"It's possible," said Clow. "Possible." He grabbed a piece of paper and fashioned a makeshift sleeve, wrapped it around the notebook, and told Miyano he wanted sleeves instead. Patiently, she repeated that it couldn't be done on time—so Clow dispatched another art director to figure out how it could be done. A half hour later, he and Miyano were fooling around with the border on the existing Nutrasweet logo, which Clow disliked because it was too thick. With a straight edge and a razor blade, she shaved one sixteenth of an inch off of it for him. He grimaced. What he was trying to do, he explained to her, was get "people to concentrate on the name and not on the border." She shaved another one sixteenth of an inch, and grudgingly, he accepted the result.

The issue of succession did not apply to the pitch team, not at this point in what Chiat was beginning to believe was the roughest year in the agency's history. The Nutrasweet pitch was not the moment to initiate Rabosky or Grossman, neither of whom was an impassioned speaker. Clow and Kuperman would be the ones who would be promoted to the client as his guardians at Chiat/Day.

"It's not as important to show them the day-to-day guys," Newman said bluntly, "as it is to have the best presenters, Kuperman and Lee."

Everyone who was working on the pitch gathered for a rehearsal in the Treehouse on Monday evening at six. The new deck was pinned up on the walls, and the team talked confidently about pounding the competition with a big shovel—the loyal consumer—while their nerves quietly gave way. One by one, Clow, Wolf, Grossman and Jeffrey Blish, the Home Savings planner who had been promoted to replace Rob White, broke the agency's no smoking rule and lit up cigarettes. Kuperman fingered a cigar.

Clow did not want to stay for the run-through, because he had work to do on the executions that were still being prepared in the art studio, but Wolf issued a single directive before he left. All the executions had to address one of two interpretations of "taste you can trust"— either rekindling the love affair with a ten-year-old product, or getting people scared about the unknown dangers of new, competing sweeteners.

Once Clow was gone, the others got back to fine-tuning the presentation. Kuperman offered Wolf a line: "You want the Maginot Line? Hire Leo Burnett. Want the Viet Cong? That's us."

Someone jokingly suggested that Kuperman bring a bunch of souvenir shovels with him, to reinforce his oft-repeated line about beating up the intruders in Nutrasweet's sandbox.

"But what if I forget to say it?" said Kuperman, laughing. " 'What are all these shovels doing here?' "

Blish was quick with the answer. " 'It's for all the shit we just left in the room.' "

At the dinner break in the Fish, Grossman looked at the production people who were feverishly preparing the boards for the presentation. "Six months from now we're going to see some really bad advertising on TV," he muttered, "because nine agencies have spent a month working on Nutrasweet."

By 11:00 P.M. they were finished, though they all knew that Chiat, who would meet them in Chicago, reserved the right to rip the presentation apart at the last minute. Clow wandered back out to the Fish and stared at the rows of paper on the walls.

"I think we actually have a terrific understanding of their business," he said, as Wolf and Kuperman stood by, silently reading the pages. "Whether it'll come through in this presentation, I have no idea."

Before they left, Laurie Coots issued travel instructions. Everyone had to check all of his luggage through, so that they could divide up the computer equipment they needed and haul it on board as carry-on luggage. She had also devised a buddy system, pairing people who had an automatic upgrade card, like Wolf and Kuperman, with those who didn't, like Clow. The frequent flyers could get first-class up-grades for their companions. On this pitch, everyone was going to travel in style.

The only thing they forgot to do was rub the Bunny's tail. It had worked for Kuperman on Sparkletts, which was enough to convince everyone that it would work on all new business from now on. As soon as they got to Chicago they called Venice and asked to have the Bunny shipped, overnight delivery.

And if one superstition was good, two were better. On the morning of the pitch, Kuperman ceremoniously loaned a necktie to Clow—the tie he had worn to the final Sparkletts meeting.

On Wednesday, December 5, everyone in the Venice office kept consulting their wristwatches. It was 11:00 A.M. in Los Angeles and 1:00 P.M. in Chicago; the pitch was halfway over. It was 1:30 and 3:30; the team from the agency must be on the way to the airport for the flight home. Finally, at 2:00 P.M., Clow called from the airport. He felt the presentation had gone well, but this was the first time the client had gone through a review. There would probably be some sort of intermediate step, maybe a second meeting, before a decision was made.

Kuperman could not manage to be as optimistic, despite extremely positive feedback from the executive who handled the Sugar DeLight account, who had reported that the agency had gotten a "glowing" report. The presentation had gone fairly well. Newman was terrific, as was Clow, even if he was a bit unfocused, and Kuperman's assessment of his own performance was that he had been convincing, al-though he had given in to emotion and lost his train of thought at one point.

But during the question-and-answer session he had the sinking feeling that the group had started to come apart. The Nutrasweet review committee had thrown a surprise question at the agency: Should the company ignore the issue of whether Diet Coke and Diet Pepsi continued to use Nutrasweet, and focus instead on expanding its 1 percent share of the tabletop sugar substitute market to 5 per-cent? On reflection, Kuperman thought the answer was easy—the company had to stick with the sodas. But the Chiat/Day team had not been prepared for the question, and so gave what he called the agency's "typical seven-person answer." Newman tried to respond but hadn't understood the question. Chiat cut her off, and he, in turn, was interrupted by Wolf, Kuperman and Clow.

Kuperman was abashed, and decided right then to institute a new pitch rule. He didn't care who answered a client question, or how badly they botched it. One person, and only one, could follow up. The rest had to keep their mouths shut.

Even more troubling, he found himself wishing that Chiat had not come to the pitch. He had eliminated himself from the managerial structure a year ago, and when he returned people became confused about what role they were to play. As Kuperman saw it, Chiat became Wolf, who became Kuperman, who became Grossman, which meant that Grossman had nothing to do.

When Chiat made his closing remarks, he started talking about how he and Wolf did not have to be there, how they were "bookends," as though he had read Kuperman's mind. He mused about not being needed, and ended his comments with an offhanded, "See you." For all the talk about how he had to come back, he seemed a displaced person, a figurehead. The ranks had closed, however imperfectly, behind him. He was more valuable as a reference point, as the embodiment of a vision, than he was necessary to the action.

Nick Rosa was taken aback by Chiat/Day's presentation, but not for the reasons Kuperman imagined. Rosa had expected Chiat/Day to show up with off-the-wall creative work that would confirm Nutrasweet's intention to dismiss the agency. He was shocked to see the gumball anniversary executions. He thought to himself, "Isn't it great that these guys didn't feel the need to go out and create something new?" It demonstrated a sensibility and maturity that he had not anticipated from Chiat/Day. Rather than showing off, the agency had done what was best for the company. Rosa liked the attitude, and he liked the work better than a lot of the new work the competition had shown.

He was happy with the strategy, too, and wildly impressed by Jane Newman. He didn't care what had happened when she was president of the New York office. She struck Rosa as an original thinker, in much the same way that Clow seemed a creative genius. He liked the others, too—and was pleased, not dismayed, when they fell all over themselves trying to answer the question about whether colas should be a priority. Rosa prided himself on his ability to foster debate inside Nutrasweet. He liked to hear people thrash out a problem together. The agencies that had a pat answer for everything worried him.

By the end of the week of pitches, the Nutrasweet review committee found itself at a surprising pass: the two top contenders were DDB Needham, which had been a frontrunner since the beginning, and Chiat/Day, which emphatically had not. Nutrasweet had never conducted an advertising review before. With two such different candidates, the committee began to worry about making a mistake. If only a clear favorite had emerged.

On Tuesday, *December 11,* a week after the Nutrasweet pitch and three days before the Toshiba presentation, Kuperman got a cryptic phone call from Chiat, who wanted him and Clow to drop everything and get on a plane for Chicago. They were not to book the flight themselves. The tickets would arrive from New York in time for a Wednesday morning flight. They were to tell no one where they were going, despite the fact that a day and a half's absence right before a pitch qualified as extremely odd behavior. Chiat, Wolf and Newman would meet them at the hotel. They were having dinner with two of the men from Nutrasweet on Wednesday night, and would meet with them—not at Nutrasweet headquarters but in an anonymous hotel room—on Thursday morning.

The next morning the tickets arrived in an envelope marked, "To be opened by addressee only," and Kuperman and Clow, joking privately about their abysmal "yellow number seven security clearance" and exclaiming loudly about a phony conversation with a phantom out-of-town client over a dog food account, headed for Los Angeles International Airport.

They were 90 percent sure that they had gotten the Nutrasweet account, and on the plane ride they tried to convince themselves another 10 percent's worth. Surely a client would not invite the principal of the agency, Chiat himself, to come to Chicago just to hear in person that he was not going to get the business. They wouldn't waste his time that way.

When they arrived at O'Hare, they hopped into a cab, and the Iranian driver asked where his fares wanted to go.

"Where are we going?" Kuperman asked Clow.

"I don't know. The Embassy Suites or something."

"Let's look at the itinerary." Kuperman opened his ticket envelope, but there was no itinerary. Only the tickets, in the interest of security.

Still, the Embassy Suites was where they had stayed for the pitch, so it was the likely candidate. They headed north, the cabbie unsure of where the town of Deerfield was, Clow and Kuperman promising that if he just got them close, they would recognize the hotel from the road and point it out. When they arrived, around four o'clock, no one else from Chiat/Day was there, but it was too soon to entertain the possibility of error. They sat down for a cup of coffee, and after a little while the New York contingent showed up.

Kuperman griped to Chiat that they could have used the hotel's address.

"Yeah?" said Chiat. "So you can call somebody back in L.A. and tell them?"

"No," said Kuperman. "So we could tell the cabdriver where the hell to take us."

That evening, the two Nutrasweet executives took the Chiat/Day people out to dinner. There was only one preset condition for the meal: they were not to discuss business. When they immediately began to talk business, having nothing else that they knew of in common, one of the Nutrasweet men nervously reminded them of the rule. The table instantly fell into an awkward silence.

Kuperman couldn't stand it. "So," he said, "how about those Chicago Bears?" He knew nothing about football, but he figured the topic was good for a few minutes of conversation.

The point of the meal was to get to know each other better, which seemed another concrete bit of evidence that Chiat/Day had won the Nutrasweet account. But as the evening wore on, Kuperman began to wonder. He knew that Nick Rosa, the senior executive on the review team, was out of the country, which might explain why no one was making a formal commitment; perhaps Rosa insisted on doing that himself. Still, the contradictory statements he was hearing made him nervous. One of the executives talked about working together on a project next year, only to add the qualifier, *"When* we decide on this thing," implying the jury was still out.

The next day's meeting, which was supposed to end at noon, went on until three, while they thrashed out issues of compensation and staffing, and addressed questions about a long-range campaign and the agency's strategy. The Nutrasweet executives did bring up a particular sore spot—Chiat/Day's tendency to lose clients more quickly than was the industry norm—but they were careful to couch it in the most gracious of terms. They did not want to make the same mistakes that previous clients had made, they said. What had Chiat/Day learned that might help prolong this association?

Chiat, Clow, Wolf and Kuperman arrived in Venice at dusk, on the night of December 13, looking awfully cocky for men who had just had a preliminary conversation about a dog food account. Kuperman asked Laurie Coots to save a copy of the recent issue of *Adweek*, announcing the Sparkletts win. If they won both Nutrasweet and Toshiba, he was going to put together a composite page that listed one "awarded to Chiat/Day" after another.

Chiat started to feel much better than he had during the Nutrasweet pitch itself. He might have to carve out a new territory for himself, to make the others feel at ease, but it seemed that his presence at the pitch had made a difference. He rolled into Venice in a sweatshirt and jeans, loitered happily in the creative department, and told everyone he encountered that New York's slump was about over. The pitch there for Shearson Lehman Brothers had gone well, and New York had a meeting next week with the people from Hardee's fast-food chain.

"Everything's clicking," Chiat told Rabosky and Sittig, who were in the Treehouse working on the Toshiba creative presentation. "It feels good. Everything feels good right now."

The Toshiba rehearsal was scheduled for seven o'clock in the Boathouse, but first there was a dinner break in the Fish, the perfect opportunity to review the latest scuttlebutt. Rumor, like superstition, took on an outsized significance as the pitch approached and the number of practical opportunities for blinding insight dwindled.

"The mole says it's us and Ketchum," reported Kuperman. Kuperman had swiped the Taylor Made golf account from Ketchum last year, and Ketchum's creative director was a disenchanted ex-Chiat/Day employee, reportedly eager to show up his old shop.

"Ketchum got a call today that Toshiba really likes their stuff," said Richard O'Neill.

"Della Femina dropped out," said Clow.

"And Dailey already presented," said Rabosky.

"They're out of it," said O'Neill.

"Ketchum really blew it out," said Kuperman, who needed a little something to worry about, as sustenance. "A month of nights and weekends, while we were doing three pitches."

"This isn't good news," said Chiat. "It would be better if they self-destructed."

"But they didn't," said Clow, "so we'll have to do good."

Everyone but Chiat headed out to the Boathouse. He lingered at one end of the Fish's angular conference table for a moment, while production people prepared executions at the other end. For all his public chat about how well things were starting to go, he was, as usual, unsatisfied. Sparkletts was a good win, and Nutrasweet, if it came through, was a stunner. Now Chiat wanted Toshiba. He wanted Venice to end the year with three wins and no losses.

He strode out to the Boathouse and confronted a burned-out, confused pitch team being smothered by details. The younger generation, with all its research, was too smart and not romantic enough by half. They were still worried about how to say that portables were the next generation of computers, and Toshiba was synonymous with portables, and they were swimming in facts that supported both contentions.

Chiat stopped them cold. Taking a defensive posture, trying to prove two points in one commercial, was suicide. What they needed and did not know how to find was the grand statement. "The really big idea is creating a *new* category," he told them, "that already exists but nobody owns. You need something to show that this," and he slowed his voice for emphasis. "is . . . a . . . really . . . big . . . idea."

"You have to *create* the fact that portables are the next generation," he said. "That's what advertising does."

He proceeded to the Treehouse to review the creative work. He rode everyone, even Clow, who got barely a paragraph into his presentation before Chiat broke in. "Say you're really excited," he said. "You think it's brilliant advertising. You can hardly *contain* yourself, you're so excited."

Clow scribbled some notes and grinned, delighted to have his mentor back in place. "Okay," he said. "We're going to show you some *brilliant* fucking advertising."

Rabosky tried to show the work, but Chiat glanced at what was pinned on the walls and stopped him. He didn't like the sequence of the creative presentation. The long print ad Rabosky wanted to show first was not the kind of execution to make a client pay attention. Chiat preferred a "computer of tomorrow" effort that Kuperman had rejected because it sounded like "a regular old ad," hardly what the client would expect from Chiat/Day. Or they could begin with the "Evolution" campaign, which featured a parade of bipeds, from monkeys lugging desktops on up to today's executive, who naturally carried a Toshiba. The drawing of the monkeys and men, in simple silhouette, was a perfect new logo for the company.

"Do that first, if branding is part of the assignment," urged Chiat. "You've found this incredible visual tool that communicates immediacy. Here's how it works on outdoor, here's how it works on boxes. Here's how it works on *condoms.*"

The only problem was that the creatives were reluctant to push a campaign that was tied to a logo, because they all knew that the logo eventually would feel like a trap to them, an element that imposed limits on the imagination.

Chiat was exasperated. Then start with the dinosaurs, he suggested, referring to a campaign that featured stock movie footage of battling dinosaurs, meant to represent IBM and Apple. Show the Evolution campaign next, and finish up with executions about the desktop's funeral.

Kuperman put his head down on the desk and moaned. "I'm pretending to be one of these guys," he said, "and I don't know where the fuck you're taking me."

"The point is," said Chiat, "you've got to show the desktop is dying. . ."

". . . But it isn't a continuum," protested Clow.

Kuperman insisted he wasn't talking about a continuum. He just wanted to see a structure to the presentation.

Clow was used to thrashing this out with Chiat, which was an explosive enough process. He didn't need Kuperman nipping at his heels, selling orderliness as though it were a virtue.

"I'm not going to go around the room," Clow said, "saying 'And then we'll run, and then we'll run, and then we'll run.' "

"I know," said Kuperman. "But you've got to tell people where you're going."

Clow tried to accommodate him, straining to come up with a rationale for the presentation as it now stood, but no one in the room was buying. The room fell silent, save for the sound of Chiat nervously swinging his legs back and forth, kicking his shoes against the floor on each pass.

Suddenly Kuperman sat straight up. He saw it: they could start with the desktop executions and talk about being stranded on the desk, unable to move. That led, naturally enough, into a look at what he called the "archaic," period, when desktops ruled, with the dinosaur commercials. That, in turn, led to the Evolution campaign, out of the Dark Ages and into the portable present day.

Clow was taken aback. Kuperman had seen something he hadn't seen in the creative presentation—the one segment of a pitch that was supposed to belong to Clow, and Clow alone. Kuperman, the lapsed creative, had shone him up in front of Chiat. Whatever relief he felt at the solution was overshadowed, for the moment, by the uncomfortable feeling that his place in the agency family had been usurped.

"That's it," he said, his voice tinged both with congratulation and envy. "Good thinking, Kuperman. Good thinking."

Chiat understood, in an instant, what had happened. He leaned over toward Clow. "You loosened the cap for him to take off, Lee," he said, with a surprising gentleness. "It's okay."

Clow got up and busied himself rearranging the work. "Anybody want to help me repin?"

*   *   *

At seven o'clock in the morning on December 14, the day of the Toshiba pitch, Clow called Kuperman's house, but he was out walking his dog. As soon as he got back and got the message, he called Clow, who had already left for the office.

"What color jacket was he wearing?" demanded Kuperman of Clow's wife, Eileen.

"Blue suit," she said, wondering why it mattered. Kuperman hung up before she could inquire. Given the extent of Clow's wardrobe, it had to be the same blue suit he had worn to the Nutrasweet pitch. But he couldn't loan Clow the same tie again. That was too heavy-handed a gesture. Kuperman selected another tie from his collection for Clow to wear and headed to the office.

At 9:30 A.M., a half hour before the Toshiba executives were to arrive, the pitch team congregated in the Boathouse. Coots ceremoniously carried in the Energizer Bunny, so that everyone involved could rub the tail that had, so far, won the agency one account and the tantalizing promise of another.

Chiat/Day was in a pleasant, if unfamiliar, position on the Toshiba pitch. Its strength was not the work, not the strategy, but the relationship Clow had established with Tom Martin, vice-president of marketing for Toshiba's Computer Systems Division. Martin was a slender, pale man whose stooped shoulders betrayed a certain tense urgency. He always seemed to be having two conversations at once—the audible one, and an internal dialogue—and because he loved nothing better than a good debate, he relished every chance to talk with Clow. He was outspoken about his preferences, joking that in addition to being anti-desktop, he was anti-Bunny, and did not want to see any cute executions. Once Martin and Clow took off on one of their philosophical flights, they could be gone for days. It was just the kind of relationship that could bond a client to an agency.

So no one knew what to think when Tom Martin fairly slunk into the Boathouse on the morning of the pitch and slumped into a chair. The body language was not promising: he folded his arms across his chest as though daring a good idea to get through to him. He plunked his portable computer on the conference table, and when someone asked if he was going to open it, he shot back, "I'll open it if I hear something exciting," and then didn't. Early in the presentation, various speakers made lame references to the closed computer, joking about how they hadn't yet impressed Martin, but he did not respond. Chiat broke into the presentation several times to highlight the big idea the client might otherwise have missed. Martin's expression did not change. Kuperman, in a panic, passed notes to some of the other agency people, wondering if they had any idea what was going on.

The account people and planners went through their paces. They talked about how to make Toshiba one of the top three computer manufacturers by the year 2000—how Toshiba could claim the innovative, user-oriented segment of the market as Apple moved into a more traditional position, alongside IBM. The agency was prepared to position Toshiba as the company that was "dedicated to making personal computers more useful," which was a way to redefine the personal computer category and assert Toshiba's instant supremacy in it.

After an hour, Martin and the two other men on the review committee had failed to utter a single syllable—no criticism, no questions, no praise, nothing. Kuperman could stand it no longer. When the group took a break before migrating to the Treehouse for the creative work session, he took Martin aside and asked him if there was something wrong. He tried not to smile with relief when Martin confessed to a migraine headache. The medication contained a sedative that made him feel like a zombie. Freed of the terrifying specter of an agency gaffe, Kuperman was as solicitous as could be. An ill-conceived pitch was a terminal problem, but Martin's pounding brain was only a temporary obstacle.

Still, the creative presentation was hardly a lively one. The men from Toshiba chuckled at the dinosaur Ripomatics. They laughed at the execution that featured a Neanderthal man carrying a desktop computer down a Manhattan street. But they didn't have anything to say—a disconcerting reluctance, given the seeming camaraderie that had been established over the past few weeks.

Clow finally asked for their reactions. Martin stood and announced. "*We* want to talk now," and strode around the Treehouse, analyzing the various creative efforts. Bill Johnson, the Computer Systems Division vice-president and general manager, who described himself as "the most anti-establishment forty-eight-year-old in American business," worried that some of the work was too far out. It reminded him of the Lemmings commercial for Apple, in which a blindfolded herd of conformist businessmen walked to their deaths off the edge of a cliff, all because they lacked the vision to see beyond what IBM had to offer.

Chiat stepped in to correct history. That commercial had not been a failure. It had tested well, got a good response, and was strategically on target. Clow pointed out that Apple had asked for far-out advertising. If Toshiba wanted something less avant-garde, Chiat/Day could do that, too.

Once the Toshiba executives seemed reassured, Clow slipped out to the bathroom—unfortunate timing, since Martin chose that moment to divulge what was really on his slowly clearing mind. What came out of his mouth was a condensed litany of every complaint that had ever been hurled at Chiat/Day.

Martin was worried that the agency wouldn't listen to the people at Toshiba. "We're the client," he said, "and finally it's our word. At some point we'll say, 'This is what we want and that's that,' and what will Chiat/Day do? And are you going to sit up here in L.A. and come down once or twice to Irvine to present the holy grail?" He went on as the agency people stood in shock. Throughout the process, they had seen Martin as an ally—not a pushover, certainly, but an intelligent, demanding man who seemed to like Chiat/Day and be excited at the prospect of working with Clow. Now he sounded like he had brought the traditional line about everything that was wrong with the agency.

They were cornered, and they had about five minutes to redeem themselves, so they backed into all the deferential double-talk they ridiculed when a staid competitor said it. Kuperman talked about how advertising was essentially a service business, and everyone at Chiat/Day understood that. Hank Antosz sprinted down the hall to retrieve Clow, who returned to make an impassioned speech about the "mutual bond" Chiat/Day and Toshiba would have. He told a funny story about how things had changed since Chiat/Day had won, and lost, the Honda account. Back then the creatives had come up with an ad the client didn't like. The agency produced it anyhow. The client still didn't like it, and fired the agency.

"We've learned," said Clow. "We're adults."

*   *   *

As soon as the Toshiba executives left, Chiat and Kuperman conferred and agreed. Someone had planted the idea that Chiat/Day wouldn't listen. Someone from a competing agency had taken Martin to dinner and sold his own stalwart agency against a disparaging characterization of an arrogant, self-absorbed Chiat/Day. As infuriating a tactic as it was, they were just a bit flattered that the competition considered Chiat/Day such a formidable foe.

That afternoon, Kuperman got a call from a secretary at Nutrasweet asking that a reel of the agency's work be sent to the company's headquarters. He was ecstatic. Clearly, Nutrasweet intended to show the winning agency's reel on Monday. He called the secretary back to say that the reel would be sent out on Saturday.

That was fine, she said. A couple of other agencies couldn't get their reels out until Saturday, either.

Kuperman's mood plummeted. Then he got another call. Nutrasweet was going to fax a rough agreement to the Venice office, to be reviewed over the weekend. Again, his hopes soared. Nutrasweet could do whatever it wanted with the reels, but surely they didn't fax agreements to all the agencies as a consolation prize.

When the agreement arrived, it didn't have Chiat/Day's name on it anywhere. It was nothing more than a general agreement that anyone could have received. Intellectually, he understood that Nutrasweet must be prepared to award the account to Chiat/Day; no company would waste this kind of time negotiating with multiple finalists. Emotionally, though, this was the longest week of his life. Every time he thought he was standing right next to the biggest of the new accounts he had pursued, someone lengthened the expanse between them.

The 1990 Christmas party was called for eight o'clock in the evening. At eight o'clock plus five minutes the cavernous Arena nightclub in Hollywood was virtually empty except for the bartenders, the food servers, and Lee and Eileen Clow, who stood side by side on the deserted dance floor and wondered what the point was of starting a party at a given hour if no one ever showed up until two hours later. The invitations called for "elegantly twisted" attire, which gave Clow permission to ditch the tuxedo in favor of a black sweater and slacks. He chatted with his wife in cozy isolation, as though they were standing in the kitchen of their own home, while around them the finishing touches were being applied to the party.

Kuperman showed up in a business suit that got him a lot of teasing. Twisted? He looked like he had come straight from the office. Wolf, keeping to his own internal vision, wore a tuxedo, while Chiat's nod to the sartorial instructions was to plant an incongruous bow tie atop his dark shirt and blazer. As always, they gravitated toward each other. They knotted together for a conversation about which competitor had Tom Martin's ear, broke up to chat with employees, and then regrouped to whisper about Nutrasweet, which by the end of the evening was a sloppily kept secret.

The possibility of winning three pitches in a row, what Clow was referring to as the "iron man triathlon," made them all giddy before they ever got near the bar. Chiat sidled up to Kuperman and said, "Before I get drunk, I just want you to know what a great job you did this year."

It wasn't until Monday, December 17—after Chiat/Day had sent its reel and Wolf and Kuperman had spent their weekend discussing the faxed agreement by phone with a Nutrasweet executive—that the client's review committee sat down for a formal vote. Nick Rosa, who had been out of the country, was gratified to see that he had near-unanimous support for Chiat/Day. He placed a call to Chiat from the airport in Atlanta, where he had flown for a meeting at Coca-Cola's headquarters, and told him that he had the account.

"Oh boy," said Chiat, in what Rosa found a disarmingly low-key manner. "That's great. You just made my day."

As soon as he got off the phone, Chiat called Clow. "Okay," he said. "We can tell people. We got it. Nick called me from the airport. Great job—tell everyone it was a great job."

Chiat told Clow that Shearson looked good.

Clow told Chiat that Toshiba looked good.

Then Chiat went off to a meeting with the people from the Hardee's fast-food chain, armed with a one-hour presentation that Wolf had put together over the weekend.

*　　*　　*

One woman surveyed the long table of chips, salsa, soda and beer that had been set up on Main Street for the tree meeting and observed. "Must be good news. There's good food."

Kuperman, who liked to choreograph good news for the best effect, insisted that the reason for the meeting was only to make some announcements and bring people up to date on new business. He wanted them to know that the Toshiba pitch had gone well, which was what mattered most.

"It would help if we get it . . ." he began, but Clow broke in.

"Then," he yelled, "we'll have *another* party, right?"

Ceremoniously, Kuperman took out a piece of paper and began to read the list of agencies who had competed for the Nutrasweet business.

"It's quite a list," he said, beaming. "Unfortunately for them, the winner was Chiat/Day/Mojo. A real great win for the agency. The list of agencies that were involved in this thing, as you see, were just really great agencies who had international capabilities and all the other things that one could imagine, including a big, full-service Chicago office and the rest of it. But I think in the end what won was the smart thinking, smart work, the dedication and the passion that we have as an agency. That is what got us the business."

That was his public face. At home he complained to his wife that the effort had taken its toll. "It's really draining," he said. "You get to be happy for about ten minutes. Then you've got to *do* it."

The next morning he started off his management meeting by acknowledging that fact: "I just want to remind everybody that while getting new business is difficult, keeping it is the goal."

"And more difficult," added Tom Patty.

There was no time for prolonged self-congratulation. Patty had seen the downside of the new business surge, and intended to put Kuperman on notice. There was no advantage to winning new accounts if the effort pulled in people who should be working on Nissan. Sittig, Clow, and the two regional creative directors had drifted away over the past few weeks and he wanted it to stop. The arithmetic was simple. Nissan was as good as about ten of these new accounts, and risking the agency's largest client for the chase was suicide. Clow and he had been joking about Clow's various commitments, and the way they tallied the percentages, about 520 percent of Clow's time was accounted for.

"That's a lie," said Kuperman. "It's 135 percent, and maybe with Toshiba it'll get to 175 percent. But hey. We can handle it."

They had no choice but to handle it. For all the celebrating in Venice, New York was still crippled. Sittig had been pulled in to mastermind New York's Shearson creative work, and had canceled his ski trip to work on the Hardee's pitch. Chiat and Wolf made it clear that they wanted the top people—Clow, Kuperman, Newman, Sittig, Rabosky—available as a roving new business team, ready to work overtime to win accounts at any one of the offices. Until the entire agency looked healthy again, Patty would have to work a little magic, and make what time the creatives did have look like all the time in the world to the client.

By the end of the day, Sparkletts had been added to the list of enervating obligations. The first meeting with the new client had dragged on for hours. Kuperman staggered into the warehouse at five o'clock, muttering, "I'd rather get them than have them." A few minutes later Clow wandered in, looking tired, and dopily referred to himself as "Mr. Vendor, just trying to be sensitive to the needs of my clients."

"I'm glad," said Kuperman, dryly, "to see this new side of you."

The only one who seemed immune to exhaustion was Chiat. He was revitalized, convinced that the agency was on a winning streak. If that was true, then it was logical to assume that he, too, was on the ascent. He looked around for a project worthy of his renewed energies, and saw the perfect opening. Michael Smith was gone, and Dick Sittig was handcuffed to Nissan for the next six months. Jay Chiat appointed himself interim creative director of the New York office and took a desk on the fifteenth floor, with the working copywriters and art directors. Someone had to step in until Sittig was available. The New York creative department had been decimated by the year's losses, so there was no likely candidate already at the agency. It made no sense to hire a creative director for what was guaranteed to be a dead-end job. Besides, Chiat would like to see any other agency in town show up at a pitch with its founder in tow to present the creative work.

CHAPTER 32

Clow was thrilled to see the bicycle boxes—each with an employee's name scrawled on it and a card from Chiat—standing in pairs at the entrances to a couple of cubicles. He rushed out to the parking lot to help Carol Madonna unload the rest of the cartons from the truck, and then crisscrossed the warehouse, again and again, dragging sets of boxes to the appropriate doorways.

There was a demonstration model of a black Huffy Good Vibrations already set up in front of the Fish, so that people could see how the assembled bicycle was supposed to look, but the most eager cyclists swiped it, one after another, for a spin around the warehouse. The others quickly paired up and began putting their bicycles together, and as they finished they jumped on for a test ride. By lunchtime Main Street was clogged with kids doing cycle sprints.

Chiat and Clow had grasped the need for a gift, back when they needed to distract people from their canceled Christmas bonus. What better time to indulge people just a little bit than after a year of progressively tighter finances. The bicycles were an economical reminder that better days were surely just around the corner.

Then everything had started to change. Venice won Sparkletts and Nutrasweet, and had a chance at Toshiba. Even New York had had its first piece of good news, winning the $20 million Shearson account. Circumstance had accommodatingly changed the message of the gift. Bicycles were not what Chiat/Day could manage to eke out of a strangled budget. Bicycles were cool.

The bikes effectively closed down the agency a day early. People hung around the office until the early afternoon but got little work done. They were arranging transport home, since the gift did not include door-to-door delivery and everyone had been cautioned to get the boxes and bicycles out of the hallways as quickly as possible, lest they become an unwelcome part of the office art collection. People with pickup trucks and convertibles found themselves the objects of instant affection, and the parking lot was the scene of great wheedling and negotiation. The Huffys had done their work on several levels. They had cheered everyone up, made them feel hip (surely no other agency in town was handing out beach wheels), and brought them together better than a tree meeting ever had.

It was as if Chiat had willed the year's end. After a period of great struggle, Chiat/Day had emerged triumphant—and, most important, had prevailed without altering its course. That was what the bicycles symbolized, after all, an irreverence so enduring that it had become a distinct aesthetic, and not just a reaction against the norm. Chiat/ Day had institutionalized its point of view. This year, it had bumped its head rather hard on what everyone feared was the ceiling Chiat had always spoken of so darkly, the place beyond which the agency could not grow without losing its edge. But by Friday, December 21, the pain had subsided. The diagnosis, with hindsight, was that the agency had collided with a rough edge, a fiscal ledge that had caught them unawares—but that there was still plenty of room for upward growth.

If a handful of executives understood that the victorious image was as unrealistic as the suicidal one had been, they were in no hurry to communicate that fact. Chiat/Day's losing streak might be over, but the continuing recession was affecting everyone. Chiat believed that there wasn't a client anywhere in the industry who hadn't cut his advertising budget at least 20 percent. People might go home for Christmas assuming that they would come back to the end of salary and raise freezes, but Kuperman had done his arithmetic and knew, to a pinched penny, that they would not. Existing clients were reducing their spending. The new business wins merely compensated the office for money lost, rather than adding to its coffers. There would have to be more new business without a lot of new staffing for the agency to start spending money the way it used to.

Still, there was no reason to send everyone off for a nine-day holiday on such a depressing note, particularly when some of them weren't really going anywhere. Toshiba had managed to squelch whatever plans the pitch team members had by announcing a new assignment that required they work over the agency's holiday break.

Delayed gratification held little appeal for Kuperman, whose sense of proportion demanded all three wins before the Christmas break, in calendar 1990. He instructed the people who already had plane tickets to take whatever trip they had planned. The rest of the team would work on Friday and Monday, and hope that would be enough.

By four thirty in the afternoon only Kuperman, Clow and a handful of stragglers remained. Clow cornered Sittig to talk about the Hardee's pitch ("Let's make it the promotion burger," he said, having tried the same idea out on Kuperman. "It's the place where you *always* have a chance to have more than a burger"). Then he settled into his cubicle to watch a reel of computer commercials. The nine-day vacation was for people who needed a treat. Clow would be back after the weekend, as always, in need of nothing more than a challenge that charmed him.

On the other side of Main Street, Kuperman shuffled through a stack of magazines, clipping competing computer ads. He considered his new bicycle. One of the lifers in print production had bought him a present at lunchtime, a vanity license plate that read, "KUPE," and he had already fastened it at the base of the seat. On a whim, he grabbed his unlit cigar and pulled the bicycle out to Main Street. The ride past Huey, Dewey, and Louie toward the Fish was an easy one, because Main Street was wide and deserted. He curved to the left, toward the reception desk, and immediately faced a decision. He could roll right out the door, down the ramp to the sidewalk, and be on the street with the cyclists and strollers who inhabited the neighborhood, the only risk being the occasional hot-rodder who roared down Hampton Drive and might consider a well-dressed middle-aged man on a bicycle to be too inviting a target to pass up. Or he could bank the bicycle into a sharp left turn and head up the narrow aisle on the far side of the warehouse. It was a route fraught with danger—several of the people working on Toshiba were still in their cubicles on that row, and someone could walk out of the restrooms or mailroom and cause a crash—but it was the way back to his own cubicle. Besides, risk in a familiar location never seemed quite as frightening as risk outside the agency walls. What was Chiat/Day about, if not taking chances?

As soon as he turned, the walls seemed to close in on either side. The bicycle began to wobble. Kuperman grasped the handlebars with one hand and raised his other arm high for balance, brandishing his cigar above his head as though he were some rodeo cowboy with a lasso.

"Watch out," he hollered. *"Watch out. WATCH OUT!"*

Everyone did. Somehow he managed to emerge unscathed at the other end of the corridor, which inspired him to take a lazy victory loop behind Clow's potted ficus before he headed home to his own office. So what if he was going to spend his vacation arguing about yet another set of executions. For all his grousing, Kuperman didn't mind. Like Clow, he would just as soon be here as not. He was sold on the place.

Chiat's wish—a three-for-three new business sweep—came true in January 1991 when Toshiba awarded its computer business to Chiat/Day. It was the start of a dizzyingly successful year for the agency—particularly the New York office, whose recovery was as dramatic as its recent descent. Chiat/Day New York won back a chunk of the Reebok account in May, and in the fall swiped the $60 million American Express Card account from Ogilvy & Mather, which was still smarting from its Nutrasweet loss. In December the office picked up The Boston Company, a private banking firm with $5 million to spend on advertising. New York's president, Bob Perkins, departed for a job with Pizza Hut, but Wolf's continued presence—as well as the arrival of Dick Sittig as the new creative director—kept the office in balance.

Chiat/Day's Toronto office also beat the agency's expectations. In 1991 it picked up Toshiba, American Express and Microsoft, a computer software company, all in one heady rush in the spring, and then was named Agency of the Year by *Strategy*, a weekly trade magazine.

In November 1991, the agency moved into two floors of its new Venice headquarters. For the time being the third floor was empty. Chiat/Day was healthy enough to gamble on its ability to fill the entire space before too long.

But then, in a frightening echo of 1990, New York began to come apart again. Shearson Lehman Brothers, a division of American Express, and the Chemical Manufacturers Association left the agency in

August of 1992. In late October, American Express called Chiat at an agency board meeting in Hawaii to inform him that the company's account was going back to Ogilvy & Mather. The trade press had been critical of Chiat/Day's "Icon" campaign, in which the American Express card appeared as everything from an airplane's tail to a bridge over a golf course water hazard. Still, the agency had new work it was proud of. The client's decision was as surprising as Royal Caribbean's call for a review.

Suddenly it was time to start scrambling again, to lay off staff and to push for new business with the people who remained. New York had the $20 million NYNEX account and a handful of smaller clients—Viacom's Nickelodeon and MTV divisions, New York Life, and the distiller William Grant & Sons, Inc.—but Reebok represented well over half of the office's billings. New York was hanging by a shoelace, dependent on a single corporation for its continued good health.

Chiat had called Kuperman just days before the American Express announcement. Chiat was unsettled by the client's grousing, but he was more troubled by his own role in damage control. He seemed to spend much of his time putting out fires. This was not the future he had envisioned for himself when he installed his new management team in 1990. How could he address the question of where the agency was headed when he spent so much time mired in problem-solving?

Worse, he failed to save the account. After the firing, Chiat spent a wretched week wondering what had gone wrong and how the agency had managed to misjudge American Express so badly. The loss was a tidy little bundle of his enduring worries: a big impressive client gone after less than a year for reasons that no one at Chiat/Day could quite fathom; a public embarrassment.

But a week later, on October 29, he got the kind of phone call that could make people forget about their day-to-day frustrations. Nissan wanted to see Chiat, Kuperman and Patty right away, and no, nothing was wrong.

On Monday the trio drove to Carson to meet with Tom Mignanelli—who invited the Venice office to take over the $75 million Infiniti account. No pitch, no months of anxious preparation (though Clow would joke that Chiat/Day's successful launch of Nissan's new 1993

Altima was the equivalent of a pitch). Mignanelli simply offered them the account, which would be Venice's second largest.

Infiniti had been handled by the Los Angeles office of Hill, Holliday, Connors, Cosmopulos Inc., the Boston-based agency that had taken Reebok from Chiat/Day back in the spring of 1991. But Hill, Holliday's efforts on behalf of Infiniti had been even more roundly trounced than Chiat/Day's work for American Express. It was Chiat/Day's turn to try.

The decision—which the client described as an efficiency move— led Hill, Holliday to close its West Coast office and put 115 employees on the street. At Chiat/Day it was cause for stunned celebration. People were being fired in New York in the wake of the American Express loss, but the Venice office made plans to hire as many as eighty new staffers to service Infiniti.

Construction began on the still-vacant third floor of the agency's new headquarters, to make room for the account staffs for Nissan and Infiniti—an autonomous subagency within the larger Chiat/Day. The agency would finally occupy the entire building in the spring of 1993.

On January 1, 1990, Chiat/Day was on the brink of an experiment in international expansion and diversification. That experiment came to a formal close on November 18, 1992, with the sale of the company's Mojo division in Australia to Foote, Cone & Belding Communications, an agency with annual worldwide billings of over $5 billion. Foote, Cone believed that Australia's recession had ended and the time come for aggressive growth; the agency was eager to get a foothold in the market. Chiat, disappointed by Mojo's inability to pick up the Nissan account, tired of supporting an "opportunistic" alliance that wasn't working out, was ready to let Mojo's $180 million in billings go.

He couldn't do much for Mojo, not with the constraints of his own agency's debt. Foote, Cone came in and started talking about a bonus pool and management rewards; maybe they could jump-start the operation. Chiat had bought Mojo as part of a larger deal for $77 million, and immediately sold off some of its operations for $35 million. He sold what was left to Foote, Cone for an undisclosed sum, estimated to be less than half of the original $77 million price tag.

The press talked about how Chiat/Day had failed to become an international presence, but for his part Chiat seemed more relieved than disappointed. He had been overextended. Kuperman had been saying for some time that the only way to transplant Chiat/Day was to transplant the culture, but there weren't enough dedicated lifers to go around. Owning Mojo, an agency that didn't fit in, was a exercise in futility. The two groups never merged, not in terms of work style or philosophy. There was something comforting about the decision to stop trying.

Wolf was happy about the Mojo deal. "Mojo was the last vestige of an eighties view of the world," he said. "Throughout the 1980s there was a sense that anything and everything was possible. Start-ups, acquisitions, below-the-line companies. All of those are gone. This is a strategic decision to leverage the brand. A recognition of the value of the Chiat/Day brand." Wolf believed that Chiat/Day was better off without the ancillary companies or the far-flung offices. He was even talking about changing the name of the agency's successful public relations subsidiary, Bob Thomas & Associates, to Chiat/Day Public Relations, to make it seem an integral part of the agency.

That was what this decade was going to be about. Chiat/Day was not meant to be a corporate octopus. It was time to pay attention to being a great $750 million advertising agency.

The energy the agency had spent on expansion was turned inward instead, with equal intensity. As usual, Chiat was the one to shake people up. He talked about the need to reinvent Chiat/Day from the inside out—and in the fall of 1992 he formed an internal task force called Chrysalis, to debate how the agency ought to look and function at the turn of the century.

He suggested that Chiat/Day needed a structural overhaul as well. Perhaps the agency ought to abandon the traditional hierarchy and establish a partnership instead, like a law office. Abolishing the management pyramid would free people from political concerns about how to get ahead. It had never been done before, but that only made Chiat more interested in the concept.

Ideas zoomed through the halls. With Mojo gone, Chiat and Wolf had essentially the same job; Wolf, a step closer to succession, wanted to show what he could do as CEO. He believed that he and

Clow could lead the agency now that the mess of outsized dreams had been cleared away—and if Clow stepped back in five years, or eight years, Wolf would be ready to run the place himself. Even a partnership needed someone who was just a bit more senior than the rest. Kuperman, meanwhile, championed the partnership plan. He wanted to see a team run the agency; he scurried around, admittedly more impatient than ever, looking for ways to improve the environment.

For a time Clow maintained a cubicle in the warehouse and one in the far front corner of the new building, near Chiat and Kuperman, but he quickly abandoned the corporate executive charade and moved all his worldly goods back into the warehouse. He griped about having to be the "filter" who kept bad work from going out the door, but Kuperman filed those complaints along with Chiat's and ignored them. Clow was happy hanging out with the creatives, and the agency was best off when he did just that. Other people took Lee's cue and moved from the new building back into the warehouse, or the reverse, because they felt more comfortable. In February 1993, Chiat/Day announced that Dick Sittig would return to Los Angeles in the newly created position of associate creative director, helping Rabosky on Energizer and a few other accounts—and working independently, according to Wolf, on "new business around the empire, wherever we need him." His replacement in New York was Toronto's creative director, Marty Cook. The agency never seemed to hold still.

Chiat watched it all with a mixture of frustration and hope. He liked Wolf's energy. He was proud of Kuperman's "new ambition," a deepening of his commitment to the agency. He was relieved to see Clow where he belonged. If he got tired of his own plight—and longed at times to take on the role of mentor, to start acting like the chairman of the board—there was nothing he could do but hassle people and wait. It was too soon to tell what would happen, or who would prevail. At least the ride promised to be interesting.

"I have no problem with unpredictability, with chaos," he said, "as long as it's controlled."

Ten days after the American Express loss—the very day that Chiat/Day got the good news from Infiniti—chief operating officer Adelaide Horton kept an appointment with two representatives of the Morgan Guaranty Trust Company of New York, the investment bank that had supplied the agency with its first line of credit in July of 1990. The two bankers wore their funeral faces, and were taken aback by Horton, who fairly bubbled with delight.

We won Infiniti, she told them triumphantly. A $75 million piece of business.

It was too much change for the financial mind to absorb. Advertising was the most ephemeral of businesses. Tens of millions of dollars rode, as often as not, on whim and politics. Great work was at the mercy of the remote control and the recycling bin. Long life was a sixty-second commercial for a client the agency managed to hang on to for more than three years.

The impermanence, the rush that a self-confessed adrenaline junkie like Adelaide Horton found so thrilling, rattled the linear mind.

One of the bankers blurted out, "How can you people *live* like this?"

I N D E X